Studies in Childhood and Youth

Series Editors
Afua Twum-Danso Imoh
University of Sheffield
Sheffield, UK

Nigel Thomas
University of Central Lancashire
Preston, UK

Spyros Spyrou
European University Cyprus
Nicosia, Cyprus

Penny Curtis
University of Sheffield
Sheffield, UK

This well-established series embraces global and multi-disciplinary scholarship on childhood and youth as social, historical, cultural and material phenomena. With the rapid expansion of childhood and youth studies in recent decades, the series encourages diverse and emerging theoretical and methodological approaches. We welcome proposals which explore the diversities and complexities of children's and young people's lives and which address gaps in the current literature relating to childhoods and youth in space, place and time.

Studies in Childhood and Youth will be of interest to students and scholars in a range of areas, including Childhood Studies, Youth Studies, Sociology, Anthropology, Geography, Politics, Psychology, Education, Health, Social Work and Social Policy.

More information about this series at
http://www.palgrave.com/gp/series/14474

Aldrie Henry-Lee

Endangered and Transformative Childhood in Caribbean Small Island Developing States

palgrave
macmillan

Aldrie Henry-Lee
University of the West Indies, Mona Campus
Sir Arthur Lewis Institute of Social and Economic Studies (SALISES)
Kingston, Jamaica

Studies in Childhood and Youth
ISBN 978-3-030-25567-1   ISBN 978-3-030-25568-8   (eBook)
https://doi.org/10.1007/978-3-030-25568-8

This Palgrave Macmillan imprint is published by the registered company Springer Nature Switzerland AG.
The registered company address is: Gewerbestrasse 11, 6330 Cham, Switzerland

Dedicated to my family

Foreword

Studies of childhood are fascinating and important, as that phase of life remains a mystery despite attempts to decipher, explain and understand how children steer or are steered along their paths into adulthood and the factors that influence this journey. Aldrie Henry-Lee shares with us, in this valuable publication, the dangers which children in Caribbean Small Island Developing States (SIDS) face as they grow, develop and survive within this environment in which the very nature of childhood is threatened, and also proposes ways in which these dangers could be averted through a transformative childhood. Henry-Lee has used the various United Nations (UN) proclamations on the status of children as the foundation of her discourse on policy, legislation, practice and experiences of childhood in the Caribbean, focusing mainly on four countries: Barbados, Haiti, Jamaica and St. Lucia. Barbados and Haiti are at opposite ends of the ratings on the Human Development Index (HDI), with Jamaica and St. Lucia falling in between the two. The 30th anniversary of the Convention on the Rights of the Child in 2019 warrants an assessment of progress in the Caribbean, particularly in light of the need to focus on the UN Sustainable Development Goals (SDGs), which have been designed to bring an end to poverty, fight inequality and injustice, and tackle climate change by 2030. The data assembled and presented force the conclusion that Caribbean childhoods are endangered, and the author proposes a model of transformation devised to reduce or eliminate much of the danger posed by the social, political and cultural factors currently in play.

Chapter 1 of the book provides a context for examining the various policies relating to children and their lives. Global concern with the status of children is recorded in an historical review of policy statements emanating from the international community since 1919, when the Save the Children Fund was established. Several other initiatives led to the founding of the United Nations Children's Fund (UNICEF) in 1946 and later to the 1989 Convention on the Rights of the Child. This Convention addresses issues such as the definition of who is a "child," ensuring inclusiveness of children with disabilities, immigrant and refugee children, those who are in conflict with the law and those who are parents, and justifying this in the face of cultural and social norms which contradict the criteria. Identification of mechanisms which need to be established for the provision, protection and participation of children from different countries and cultures of the world and making suggestions and recommendations for implementing such mechanisms were critical components of the Convention. Ratification of the Convention by several Caribbean countries was endorsed by the involvement of the Caribbean Community (CARICOM) and provided a stimulus for national policy initiatives which would reflect the importance, relevance and value of the Convention in improving the lives of Caribbean children. Response and uptake by regional and national agencies and development of policy and practice in response to the Convention are set out as they evolved in the Caribbean.

The author's concern is focused on childhoods in Small Island Developing States (SIDS), a categorization which identifies the unique features of certain geographical entities and which creates special vulnerabilities for their populations. Chapter 2 explores the economic, political, social and cultural advantages and the disadvantages of physical hazards as well as limitations posed by size on SIDS's access to trade agreements and other benefits and their susceptibility to corruption. Children in these environments are more vulnerable than those in developed countries because of the historical, environmental and socio-cultural factors that shape their childhoods. The threat posed by the many facets and implications of climate change and how this accentuates the disadvantages of being a SIDS are examined. The extent to which these vulnerabilities can affect the processes of child development is explored through a review of several theories of childhood, all of which emphasize the impact of adults in children's development and the importance of a stable environment within which the child is nurtured. The author uses Bronfenbrenner's Ecological Systems Theory (1979) and the Social Risk Management Model of Holtzmann et al. (2003) to propose what she terms an "Endangerment Theory": the central tenet of which is the possibility of extinction of "quality" childhood because of the interactions of factors among and within the micro-, meso- and macro-environments of children—factors such as family structure, health, education, social services and international trade. While accepting that resilience on the part of some children can allow them to overcome endangerment, such children are in the minority. Using data to identify the vulnerabilities which arise from international, regional and local contexts and their effect on children in the target countries, Henry-Lee develops a profile of "endangered" childhood in these Caribbean islands.

Climate change and its potential for endangerment of childhood in SIDS is the focus of the next chapter, in which policy issues relating to this phenomenon are discussed. Agreements and decisions taken as part of the Kyoto Protocol highlight the discipline and responsibility which developed countries need to embrace in order to ensure that developing countries can adapt to and counter the negative impact of climate change. Particularly vulnerable in the face of the potential effects are women and children, whose shelter, food and mere survival are threatened. Data on the natural disasters to which Caribbean SIDS have been exposed support the view of UNICEF that the major casualties of such disasters are children.

The chapters which follow use data from a range of sources, including primary data, to underline the vital importance of countries investing in children who constitute their human capital and the danger posed by systems which are lacking and/or inequitable in terms of the services provided in protection, health and education. The violence to which children are exposed in their home, school and community settings calls for action to meet the demand of Article 19 of the United Nations Convention on the Rights of the Child (1989)—that countries should

take all appropriate legislative, administrative, social and educational measures to protect the child from all forms of physical or mental violence,
injury or abuse, neglect or negligent treatment, maltreatment or exploitation, including sexual abuse, while in the care of parent(s), legal guardian(s)
or any other person who has the care of the child. (p. 118)

After reviewing the data from the focus countries, the author quotes
Bailey et al. (2014) thus:

Although the Convention of the Rights of the Child was ratified in these
countries, strict adherence to international laws was still lacking and as
such Caribbean governments needed to bring their policies in accordance
with the accepted standards for the treatment of children. (p. 138)

Sexual abuse, bullying and cyberbullying, as well as suicide, are part of
the range of concerns and threats to the well-being of children and the
experience of favourable childhoods, explored by the author.

Debates surrounding Articles 12, 13 and 14 of the Rights of Children
to freedom of thought, opinion and expression are presented and discussed. The importance of empowering children to be participants in the
decisions affecting their lives has been disregarded by those who consider
children's lack of experience and maturity as drawbacks to their contribution and participation. That this has been a contentious issue is evidenced
by the several models which capture the ways in which child participation has been and ought to be viewed and implemented. These include
Hart's (1992) "Tokenism to Citizenship" as well as models developed by
Treseder (1997), Organization for Economic Cooperation and
Development (OECD) (2001), Sheir (2001) and Sheir et al. (2012),
Martin (2010), the Department for International Development (DFID)
(2010) and Davies (2011). Henry-Lee reports on advances made in several countries worldwide in children's participation and shares data on
the strategies employed in the target Caribbean countries. She notes that,
although there has been some progress, the change from Caribbean children being "informed" to being "consulted," and to "participating," is
slow and could be summarized as a movement from their "complete
voicelessness" to their "limited voiceness." She cites Girvan (1993) and

Moncrieffe (2015), who recommend age-appropriate ways in which countries can encourage child participation.

The author's designation of Children on the Periphery includes

those living in poverty; those whose birth is not registered; children whose mothers are incarcerated; those with disabilities; children who are affected by and infected with HIV/AIDS; child labourers, teenage parents, missing children and those who are affected by migration. (p. 195)

She also adds, in her narrative, children who are victims of, and who commit, crimes, as well as those, especially women and girls, who are victims of human trafficking. These children, who survive on the periphery of society, have little or no access to those basic services that would allow them to develop the skills to participate as citizens in a fully functioning society. The data on these children are chilling and make a mockery of these countries' ratification of a Convention which seeks inclusion and participation of children in decision-making at various levels of society.

Chapter 8 interrogates the concepts of coping, resilience and transformation, and the author shares eight case studies of young people whose life experiences demonstrate these characteristics. The chapter gives readers a measure of hope and also raises questions as to the triggers which allowed them to adapt within their endangered childhood and exhibit the resilience that allowed them to transform their lives.

It is this transformation that Henry-Lee seeks to bring about among the endangered children of Caribbean SIDS. The final chapter of the book is titled "Re-engineering Childhood in Caribbean SIDS." The author summarizes the status of the four target countries in relation to the Articles of the Convention. While she notes that Haiti lags far behind the other three countries, she still bemoans the fact that, though reasonable, their status leaves much to be desired. Deficiencies in education and health services and exposure to and experience of violence and abuse—exacerbated in those condemned to a peripheral life, by virtue of their poverty, disability and other factors—lead to a large proportion of Caribbean children suffering social exclusion and endangered childhoods.

Henry-Lee's Theory of Transformative Childhood aims to reduce the vulnerability of children living in SIDS to endangered childhoods. It targets the child as well as significant adults such as those in the family, school and community in the child's environment. It also points to the role of legislation, policies and programmes which can bring about change in the lives of children. The "mindset" of all in the society towards positive childhoods is critical, as it is when the entire population values its children that society will undergo the cultural transformation needed to ensure that children's childhoods are beneficial, progressive and empowering.

This book provides a wealth of important information for a wide audience: the theoretical reviews and the research data, along with analyses of these data, will be valued by sociologists, researchers and students, as well as by agencies that advocate for and work on behalf of children. Teachers in training, religious leaders, community leaders and social workers should also be exposed to the material in this publication, as they are significant adults in the childhoods of our youngest citizens and have the potential to be agents of transformation in their lives. Professor Henry-Lee is to be congratulated on providing a most valuable resource which will stimulate thought and discussion and trigger ongoing research on Caribbean SIDS and the childhoods experienced there.

Kingston, West Indies   Elsa Leo-Rhynie
May 2019

References

Bailey, C., Robinson, T., & Coore-Desai, C. (2014). Corporal punishment in the Caribbean: Attitudes and practices. *Social and Economic Studies, 63*(3), 207–233.

Bronfenbrenner, U. (1979). *The ecology of human development*. Harvard College.

Davies, T. (2011). Rethinking responses to children and young people's online lives. Retrieved December 15, 2018, from http://www.lse.ac.uk/media@lse/research/EUKidsOnline/Conference%202011/Davies.pdf.

DFID-CSO Youth Working Group. (2010). Youth participation in development: A tool for development. Agencies and Policy Makers. Retrieved May 2, 2019, from https://youtheconomicopportunities.org/sites/default/files/uploads/resource/6962_Youth_Participation_in_Development.pdf.

Girvan, N. (Ed.). (1993). *Working together for development: DTM Girvan on cooperatives and community development 1939–1968*. Kingston: Institute of Jamaica.

Hart, R. (1992). Children's participation from tokenism to citizenship. Essay for UNICEF. Innocenti Essay No. 4.

Holzmann, R., Sherboune-Benz, L., & Tesliuc, E. (2003). The World Bank's approach to social protection in a globalizing world. Retrieved November 21, 2018, from http://siteresources.worldbank.org/SOCIALPROTECTION/Publications/20847129/SRMWBApproachtoSP.pdf.

Martin, P. (2010). E-participation at the local level: The path to collaborative democracy. Retrieved May 5, 2019, from https://www.ippr.org/files/images/media/files/publication/2011/05/e_participation_in_local_government_1258.pdf.

Moncrieffe, J. (2015). *Caribbean child research conference: Summary of policy and strategy recommendations*. Kingston: Sir Arthur Lewis Institute of Social and Economic Studies.

Organization for Economic Cooperation and Development (OECD). (2001). Citizens as partners—Information, consultation and public participation in the policy making. Retrieved April 27, 2019, from https://www.internationalbudget.org/wp-content/uploads/Citizens-as-Partners-OECD-Handbook.pdf.

Shier, H. (2001). Pathways to participation: Openings, opportunities and obligations. *Children and Society, 15*(2), 107–117.

Shier, H., Méndez, M. H., Centeno, M., Arróliga, I., & González, M. (2014). How children and young people influence policy-makers: Lessons from Nicaragua. *Children and Society, 28*(1), 1–14.

Treseder, P. (1997). *Empowering children and young people: Promoting involvement in decision-making*. Retrieved from Amazon.co.uk.

Acknowledgements

I wish to thank my family, especially my Mom, who is my biggest fan. I thank my mentor, Professor Neville Duncan, who has always supported my career and advancement. There are many other persons too numerous to mention who helped me to complete this book. Research support was received from Claudia Barned, Staciann Williams, Krystal, Yhanore and Nicole. Ms. Carol Lawes, who reviewed the book for logic, grammar and referencing; my first son, who kept asking *when will this book* be completed; the staff at my institute who supported my writing spells, to all of you, I express my gratitude. To the respondents who willingly provided the data for the book, it would not have been possible without you. To Professor Emeritus Elsa Leo Rhynie, I express my profound gratitude for agreeing to write the foreword. Finally, to Amelia Derkatsch, the reviewers and all the staff at Palgrave Macmillan who were involved in the publishing of this book, a big thanks for accepting my book. To all the readers, I hope that you will find the book informative and, even more, the findings will encourage you to be an advocate for increased adherence to children's rights.

About the Book

All nations are committed to the UN 2030 Agenda with its seventeen Sustainable Development Goals (SDGs). In 2019, the Convention on the Rights of the Child (CRC) celebrates thirty years of its adoption. What has been the progress in the implementation of these two important global commitments in the Caribbean? It is already evident that achieving these goals by 2030 will be problematic for Small Island Developing States (SIDS) given their social, economic and environmental vulnerabilities. To achieve sustainable development, this group of countries must depend heavily on their human resources in order to break the cycle of dependency and poverty. With 30 per cent of the population aged under eighteen years, if investment in children is inadequate, then the returns from that investment will be insufficient to attain sustainable development.

Caribbean countries (Caribbean SIDS) have not yet recognized the full potential of the children in their countries. There is unsatisfactory policy attention on children, and it is only since the adoption of the Convention on the Rights of the Child that gradually children are receiving increased it. However, there are several policy gaps and programmatic deficiencies. Children face several vulnerabilities every day, with some groups of children (e.g. children with disabilities and child labourers) needing immediate attention. There is a lack of urgency to the plight of children in SIDS and inadequate recognition that they are the foundation for sustainable development. Thirty years after the CRC and with twelve years more to "catch up" and reach the targets set by the UN 2030 Agenda, it is an opportune moment to analyse the progress made for children in SIDS.

This unique book contributes to the debate on "children in the policy space" and provides a situational analysis of children in the Caribbean region, with a special focus on Jamaica, St. Lucia, Haiti and Barbados. These countries were chosen because they represent various levels of human development as indicated by the Human Development Index (HDI) yet share similar historical contestations of slavery, colonialization and globalization. Many previous books focus on one country and generalize about the Caribbean. This book discusses the experiences of childhood in four SIDS and presents the different nuances of childhood that exist there. The author, through the examination of the data, concludes that children in Caribbean SIDS experience an endangered childhood. The book ends with recommendations for transformative childhoods in Caribbean SIDS.

Contents

List of Figures

List of Tables

1

Our Commitments to the Children of the World

In 2019, we commemorate the 30th anniversary of the adoption of the Convention on the Rights of the Child (CRC). In 2015, the United Nations (UN) committed to seventeen Sustainable Development Goals (SDGs) to replace the eight Millennium Development Goals (MDGs). In 2030, we will be called upon to account for our progress in the fulfilment of these SDGs. What has been the progress for children in the implementation of these two important global commitments in the Small Island Developing States (SIDS)? It is already evident that the rights of large proportions of children are being violated every day (Goodman and Cook 2019; Korang-Okrah et al. 2019). It is also clear that achieving these goals by 2030 will be problematic for SIDS given their social, economic and environmental vulnerabilities (Mycoo 2018; United Nations Development Programme 2017):

> Every child has the right to a fair chance in life. But around the world, millions of children are trapped in an intergenerational cycle of disadvantage that endangers their futures—and the future of their societies.[1]

© The Author(s) 2020
A. Henry-Lee, *Endangered and Transformative Childhood in Caribbean Small Island Developing States*, Studies in Childhood and Youth,
https://doi.org/10.1007/978-3-030-25568-8_1

A large proportion of children whose futures are endangered live in SIDS. To achieve sustainable development, SIDS must depend heavily on the enhancement of their human resources in order to break the cycle of dependency, poverty and inequality. If investment in children is inadequate, then the returns from that investment will be insufficient to attain sustainable development. While the adoption of the CRC has resulted in increased attention on children, they face several vulnerabilities every day, with some groups needing immediate attention. Thirty years after the CRC and with twelve years more to "catch up" and reach the targets set by the UN 2030 Agenda, it is an opportune moment to analyse the progress made for children in SIDS.

Using primary and secondary data, the book examines childhood in four Caribbean SIDS—Barbados, Haiti, Jamaica and St. Lucia. Primary data were collected in Jamaica from

- 103 high school children,
- 10 senior citizens,
- 10 recently released mothers and
- elite interviews with children's advocates in St. Lucia and Jamaica

Although the samples are unrepresentative, they present informative indications of the issues that the children experience in Caribbean SIDS. Data from the 2016 national Jamaica Survey of Living Conditions (JSLC) were also analysed to examine the disparities among children living in poverty and those who do not. The research topics presented by child researchers at the annual Caribbean Child Research Conference held in 2006–2017 were examined to determine the main issues that concerned children in Jamaica. Similar studies were not completed for the other countries under discussion due to cost constraints, and the discussion on childhood in Barbados and Haiti depends heavily on secondary data.

One of the limitations of using secondary data is that very recent data are not always available for all the Caribbean countries under discussion. The analysis of this data seeks to provide sociological answers to the following main research questions:

1. What are the definitions, perceptions and experiences of "children" and "childhood" in Caribbean SIDS?
2. What theories best explain the nature of childhood in Caribbean SIDS?
3. How can we transform childhood in Caribbean SIDS?

The countries in focus were specifically selected because they represent various levels of human development with Barbados at the top of the scale and Haiti, at the bottom. Their societies have also been shaped by distinct cultural characteristics even though they share some common historical experiences.

The book consists of nine chapters. Chapter 1 provides an outline of the main international regional and local commitments to children. Chapter 2 reviews the SIDS debate and some of the main theories of childhood, ending with a presentation of the main elements of a theory of endangerment of childhood in Caribbean SIDS. Chapters 3, 4, 5, 6 and 7 provide a more in-depth analysis of childhood and the status of children in these four Caribbean SIDS by analysing both secondary data from international, regional and local databases, and primary data from quantitative and qualitative studies carried out by the researcher. Chapter 8 provides examples of children who have broken the cycle of endangerment while Chap. 9 summarizes the main findings and presents the author's *theory of transformation* of childhood in SIDS. This first chapter sets the contexts in which Child Policy Agendas have been implemented in the four countries in focus. We begin with an examination of the emergence of a Global Child Agenda.

The Growth of the International Child Agenda

None of the International Conventions and Agreements pertaining to children originated in the Caribbean. International focus on children began in the developed countries, mainly at sessions of the United Nations. From as early as 1919, international attention focused on children with the establishment of the Save the Children Fund. By 1924, the League of Nations adopted the Declaration on the Rights of the Child (also known as the World Child Welfare Charter). The United Nations Children's Fund (UNICEF) was founded in 1946, and in 1959, the United Nations adopted the Declaration on the Rights of the Child.

The year 1970 was declared the International Year of Education and there was international focus on the provision of education and the improvement of existing facilities in developing countries. Education was seen as the tool to stimulate significant economic and social change (UNICEF 2014). The 1974 international conference focused on the inter-relationship between development and population concerns,[2] and the year was declared World Population Year. The conference highlighted the need to ensure that population policies and issues formed an integral part of socio-economic development policies.[3]

In 1975, women were recognized in a year declared International Women's Year. The international conference on women held in Mexico in 1975 discussed a broad range of issues that affected women globally.[4] The conference organizers called for the strengthening of laws globally to ensure that men and women had equal representation and human rights.[5] They also underscored the need to implement a global system of checks and balances, to ensure that both legal and social protection systems for women were enforced.[6]

The year 1979 was established as the International Year of the Child in the context of increasing numbers of undernourished children in developing countries and the limited access to basic education and basic amenities for a good quality life (UNICEF 2014). Children and youth received increased international attention in the 1980s and 1985 was designated International Youth Year by the United Nations during which calls were made for the strengthening of youth participation and development. The 1985 international conference emphasized the role of the youth of the world in shaping public policy. Youth were encouraged to value human life and to seek sustainable peace (Ansell 2004).

In 1989, the most important child-focused Convention was adopted by the United Nations. This was the Convention on the Rights of the Child (CRC), which called for all members of the United Nations to secure increased provision for, and protection and participation of children. The UN adopted an international definition of "children" which comprised that social group of individuals under the age of eighteen. A clear set of parental responsibilities and societal obligations to protect all children from physical and psychological harm was delineated (UNICEF 2014).

The CRC was not wholly accepted by all and there were some criticisms, such as:

- It failed to find a balance between overprotection and too much freedom. For example, although children were expected to take on more and more responsibilities as they got older, it was often the parents who were held financially responsible for the misdemeanours of children who were under eighteen years of age. The child, therefore, could be seen as more of a burden than as a responsible individual (Humanium 2015).
- Rights don't exist without their counterparts: responsibilities. These international rights regarding children mainly suggested only moral obligations, such as respect towards parents, and were therefore often seen as irrelevant (Humanium 2015).
- The International Convention on the Rights of the Child states in its first Article that "'child' means every human being below the age of eighteen years 'unless under the law applicable to the child, maturity is attained earlier.'" This age limit, however, was just as ineffective, as it still allowed for children to be treated as adults too early. It would be more protective to impose a lower age limit below which one could not be considered an adult under any circumstance. For example, it would be reasonable to imagine a minimum age limit which protected all those under the age of 16 (Humanium 2015).
- Children's rights were sometimes criticized as being unrealistic as they did not take into account economic, social and political differences which existed between countries. In practice, it is difficult to apply the same rights to all children in the world since they do not live in the same conditions. It would be irrelevant, for example, to apply a right to leisure time in countries where the right to life or the right to water could not even be enforced (Humanium 2015).

Notwithstanding, these criticisms, the CRC has gained global acceptance.

The 1990s saw the momentum of the concentration on children increase and there were several international events which focused on children. In 1990, the UNICEF World Summit for Children was held, and developed an action plan to tackle many of the problems facing children all over the world.[7] The conference discussed strategies to ensure that nations accepted children as being very important to sustainable development and cautioned that neglect of this group would have very dangerous developmental consequences. The World Summit advocated that governments, non-governmental organizations and the private sector of developing and developed countries become more involved in securing the health and well-being of children.[8]

The year 1994 was recognized as the International Year of the Family. Members of the United Nations demanded a greater focus on the family as an important institution in the society at the local and regional levels (UNICEF 2014). They discussed strategies to encourage governmental and non-governmental agencies to fund and support domestic campaigns that advocated on behalf of families (UNICEF 2014).

In 1996, the Education for All International Conference, held in Jomtien, Thailand, focused on getting universal primary education for all member states of the UN. The conference deliberated on strategies to engage more young girls in the education system from a very early age (Hendricks 2007). Girls from the Middle East and Asia received special attention, including advocating for programmes to ensure that children remained engaged in the educational process during summer. This was based on the recognition that when children returned from these holidays, they had to re-learn most of what they had been taught before (Hendricks 2007).

There were three world youth forums held in the 1990s—in Vienna, Austria, in 1991 and 1996 and in Braga, Portugal, in 1998. All three forums underscored the need to strengthen the link between youth and development planning (Ansell 2004). For example, the 1996 forum emphasized the importance of greater participation of young men and women in social work, political activism and poverty alleviation. Training of youth in diplomacy and non-violence were also seen as priorities (Ansell 2004).

The eradication of poverty was also emphasized in 1996 and the year was declared the International Year for the Eradication of Poverty. Members of the United Nations highlighted the need to reduce extreme levels of poverty in both the developing and developed worlds, and to examine its root causes. A Poverty Eradication Advisory panel was established and tasked with ensuring that all member states were fully committed to the goal.[9]

In 1998, the World Youth Forum focussed on the need for the creation of youth networks to ensure that issues facing the youth were addressed in public policy.[10] Attendees discussed the high levels of youth unemployment globally and noted the need to engage the private and public sectors in combatting this phenomenon.[11] The forum called for young women and men to be empowered to participate in the process on terms equal to those of other groups of citizens.[12]

By this time, the International Child Agenda had expanded significantly, and there was increased policy focus on children internationally and locally. Some other important events thrust children to the centre of international policy discussions. By 2000, the UN Millennium Development Goals (MDGs) set targets for fulfilment by 2015, with three of the goals being directly related to children—reduction in infant and maternal mortality, and increased access to primary education. In 2001, the World Youth Forum in Dakar, Senegal, developed the Dakar Youth Empowerment Strategy. The Global Movement for children was also launched in 2001, and in 2002, a United Nations Special session formulated a Global Action Plan for children. In that year also, the United Nations adopted the Convention on the Rights of Persons with Disabilities.

The Millennium Development Goals (MDGS) have however raised many questions and received much criticism, such as:

- Why had these particular goals and targets been chosen rather than others (Kanbur 2004 in Khoo 2005, 47)?
- How were the different goals and targets to be prioritised since difficult allocative decisions would have to be taken (ibid.)?
- Goal number eight on global partnership was seen not as an end but as a means for achieving the other goals (ibid.).

- The MDGs being donor-led paid little attention to local contexts, effectively penalizing and stigmatizing the poorest countries where achieving the goal was a greater challenge (Easterly 2009 in Melamed and Scott 2011, 2)
- The MDGs missed out on critical dimensions of development such as climate change, the quality of education, human rights, economic growth, good governance and security (Vandemoortele and Delamonica 2010 in Melamed and Scott 2011, 2).
- The MDGs neglected the poorest and most vulnerable since they were based on average progress at a national or global level (Holmes and Jones 2010 in Melamed and Scott 2011, 2).
- The MDGs failed to take into account the initial conditions of the various regions and counties, that is, the difference in effort countries would need to make in order to make the same relative degree of progress (United Nations 2012, 8).
- The MDG Agenda was not explicit as to the perceived structural causes of poverty and social exclusion or in regard to strategies and policy actions necessary to address the structural causes to facilitate achievement (ibid.).

The MDGS, however, galvanized global efforts to pursue sustainable development.

In 2002, the United Nations' Special Session on Children, the Global Plan of Action for Children reaffirmed the UN's commitment. Members discussed strategies such as the formation of a broad coalition of academics, NGOs, civil society and many others to increase child protection. A progress report on the fulfilment of child-related Millennium Development Goals concluded that the issues of malnutrition and the sexual abuse of children needed increased policy attention. A special session prepared an outcome document titled "World Fit for Children" (UNICEF 2014).

The 2010 conference marking the International Year of Youth drew attention to the need to develop in youth an innate respect for fundamental freedoms and for the dignity of others, through a programme of community engagement. The attendees recognized the challenges and struggles that faced youth and encouraged the young participants to devote their enthusiasm and creativity to economic and social development (UNICEF 2014).

When 2014 was declared the International Year of Small Island Developing States, these countries received more special attention. Previously, there had been two other sessions on small states, in 2002 in Johannesburg and in 2005 in Mauritius. In 2010, the UN called for a review of the progress made in the implementation of the Mauritius Strategy, and in 2014, the international conference of small states held in Samoa reaffirmed that to achieve sustainable development, SIDS would need to promote sustained, inclusive and equitable economic growth, create greater opportunities for all, reduce inequalities, raise basic standards of living and foster equitable social development.[13]

In September 2015, the United Nations committed to the Sustainable Development Goals (SDGs) to replace the Millennium Development Goals (MDGs). There are seventeen Sustainable Development Goals (SDGs) which aim to end poverty, fight inequality and injustice, and tackle climate change by 2030.

However, like the MDGs, the SDGs received critical scrutiny:

- The goal on poverty requires further specification to address the provision of basic income and social protection to eliminate extreme poverty, as well as effective and equitable processes of wealth creation and distribution, employment and insurance in the present and the future (Deacon and St. Claire in International Council for Science 2015, 18).
- Additional dimensions should be considered for SDG 4 (Inclusive and Equitable Education) to address the problem that most educational policies and programmes do not yet reflect the purposes and goals of sustainable development. The emphasis on sustainable development must be strengthened in at least two of the targets, while a new target is recommended on life-long learning (Sterling in International Council for Science 2015, 30).
- The targets regarding gender equality and the empowering of women and girls need to have outcome statements, they need to be time-specific, and there needs to be inclusion of a number of key economic and social targets on employment, pay, education, and mental and

physical health (Nyasimi and Peake in International Council for Science 2015, 30).

Whatever the critique of the SDGs highlights, these current goals shape the way the world focuses on children and social development. The conclusion is that children receive international attention based on decisions made by the members of the United Nations. While the increased policy attention is laudable, the historical analysis shows that this begins in the developed countries. While the developing countries are members of the United Nations, they are not the economic powers of the world and none of these international commitments and conventions has been initiated in the developing world.

The Regional Context and Response

The Caribbean countries continue to take their policy cues from the developed countries. In response to the World Summit on Children and the adoption of the Convention on the Rights of the Child, the Caribbean Community (CARICOM) and Latin America have held several ministerial meetings on children and social policy some of which are listed below:

(a) *Mexico (1992)*—Declaration of Tlatelolco[14]
(b) *Columbia (1994)*—Nariño Accord[15]
(c) *Chile (1996)*—Santiago Accord[16]
(d) *Peru (1998)*—Lima Accord[17]
(e) *Jamaica (2000)*—Kingston Consensus[18]

Some of the CARICCOM Meetings held were:

(a) *Belize 1996 (Ministers resp. for children)*—Belize Commitment to Action for the Rights of the Child
(b) *Jamaica 1997 (Ministers resp. for children)*—Kingston Accord
(c) *Jamaica 1997 (Heads of Govt.)*—Above two proposals ratified

The Belize Commitment to Action 1996[19] identified three priority areas for Caribbean action:

1. *Budgeting for an Enabling Environment*—ensuring social investment in accordance with the 20/20 formula (which encourages States and donor countries to spend 20 per cent of budget on basic social services) and fiscal/economic measures to aim at poverty reduction.
2. *Legal Reform and Law Enforcement*—harmonizing national laws with human rights conventions and strengthening the capacity to enforce laws; establishing office of ombudsman or equivalent for children and appropriate sentencing and rehab for child offenders.
3. *Family Development and Empowerment*—requiring governments along with NGOs and communities to address the needs of children and families.

A Children's Resolution was also included reflecting the position of fifty-two children who attended the Children's Forum which formed part of the Caribbean Conference on the Rights of the Child. It set out 14 responsibilities of governments, parents, teachers and children in relation to issues such as education, crime, and abuse.

The main commitments from the Tlatelolco Declaration, Mexico, 1992,[20] were to

- change National Action Programmes into tools for social policies and into the basic strategic components needed in order to fight poverty and reduce social and cultural inequalities;
- ensure joint participation by government sectors and civil society;
- ensure complementary participation by local organizations in the National Programme;
- complete the design and execution of the information systems in order to put national programmes into practice, since the information systems are the tools needed for monitoring and evaluating those national programmes; and
- try to attain a higher level of international cooperation; and form networks for the exchange and coordination of information resources, as

well as human and technical resources, so as to ensure that the programmes are fulfilled (Bruno n.d.).

The Nariño Accord 1994[21] stated that it

identifies common goals for education, including developing alternative
models for initial education, reducing repetition, improving the quality of
primary education, introducing changes to the curriculum, training teachers, ensuring that school hours are sensitive to the needs of the country and
facilitate effective learning, identifying strategies to reduce attrition, and
developing options for vocational education and technical training.
(Pare 2004)

At subsequent ministerial meetings on children and social policy, this
agreement was referred to as a historic event, since it was the first commitment to state that children and adolescents were to be given priority
in the Hemisphere's Social Agenda" (Bruno n.d.). Commitments were
also made to

- link economic and social policies, through an integrated approach that
  makes it possible to overcome those structural factors arising from
  poverty; and
- promote the institution of family as the nucleus at which those programmes corresponding to public social policies are aimed, and where
  these same programmes are strengthened (ibid.)

The Santiago Accord, Chile, 1996,[22] was an updated version of the two
first meetings, which incorporated certain subjects such as the following:
legal adjustment to the Convention on the Rights of the Child, the issue
of women (violence, labour integration, and equity), gender, the globalization of the economy and the situation of vulnerable groups, among
other subjects (ibid.).

The Lima Accord, Peru, 1996,[23] was held to support and strengthen
the aims set for the decade and to evaluate the advances and difficulties in
achieving the goals, and also to set either local or regional goals seeking
the welfare of children and adolescents in the Region. The "Lima
Agreement" was then signed (ibid.).

The Kingston Consensus, 2000,[24] noted that although significant progress had been made, there was still concern about the un-met goals of the World Summit for Children (1990). There was also concern about children and adolescents were still excluded from participating in economic, political, and social processes, thereby hindering their own development. The Consensus also noted, however, that the situation of children and adolescents of the region had improved remarkably in some ways since 1990 in that, *inter alia*, the CRC had been ratified by most of the countries of the Americas; infant and mortality rates for children under five had been reduced by over 20 per cent in most countries; and net primary school enrolment was over 90 per cent. It acknowledged, however, that there were still weaknesses, and made twenty-three commitments towards advancing the rights of and protecting children, including:

- Making every necessary effort so that children and adolescents had opportunities to fully develop their physical, mental, spiritual, moral and social capacities and to guarantee and promote respect for human rights.
- Developing and implementing integrated policies and actions aimed at breaking the inter-generational cycles of poverty.
- Promoting actions and mechanisms to maximize the participation of children and adolescents in decision-making in all matters that directly and indirectly affect them.
- Ensuring the protection of children and adolescents from all forms of abuse, including injury, violence, neglect, sexual abuse, commercial exploitation, sale and trafficking and forced labour.
- Ensuring the protection of children and adolescents from all forms of discrimination and harm, and supporting policies, plans and programmes to advance equality and respect for them.[25]

The Kingston Accord[26] endorsed the Belize Commitment and outlined priority actions which required immediate action. Signatories were to

1. secure political, administrative and public consensus to shift the development agenda from welfare to social development orientation,

putting children first as an investment in breaking the inter-generational cycle of poverty;
2. have a holistic approach to commitments giving primacy to integration of service delivery to children and families;
3. institute participatory mechanisms involving the public sector and
civil society, as well as children themselves in decision-making, implementation and evaluation; and
4. promote equity in resource allocation so the needs of poor children
and families are addressed.

There was also policy attention given to early childhood development.
In 1997, at the Second Caribbean Conference on Early Childhood
Education (ECE) in Barbados, the Caribbean Action Plan (1997–2002)
for Early Childhood development was adopted.[27] The Caribbean Action
Plan for Early Childhood Education Care and Development was to be
adapted to individual country priorities, and fully implemented within
six years (1997–2002). It provided a policy framework for developing
comprehensive and coordinated early childhood services from birth, and
focused on development of:

1. service delivery—access, quality and coverage particularly for the
disadvantaged;
2. policy standards and legislation;
3. management/administrative strengthening;
4. communication, advocacy and social mobilization to increase awareness and encourage appropriate parental care;
5. training, to improve the capacity of ECD workers to deliver services;
6. materials, to address the standards, range and quality of provisions;
7. integration between all agencies, ministries and so on, involved in service at the early childhood level;
8. adequate financing; and
9. research and monitoring.

Specific commitments were also made by CARICOM to ensure the
adherence to common standards in early childhood development. In
2006, the CARICOM Secretariat developed, on behalf of governments,

a set of "Regional Guidelines for Developing Policy Regulation and Standards in Early Childhood Development Services,"[28] which includes Draft Early Childhood Development (ECD) Minimum Service Standards for the Caribbean. The Minimum Service Standards document outlines the requirements for service providers to ensure standards in twelve areas as follows[29]:

1. The development of healthy, strong and well-adjusted children;
2. the development of a child's ability to communicate effectively;
3. the development of a child who values his/her own culture and that of others;
4. the development of a child who is a critical thinker and independent learner;
5. the development of a child who respects him/herself, others and the environment;
6. the development of a resilient child;
7. the profile and preparation of persons providing care and learning experiences for children;
8. the management of challenging child behaviours and the use of positive discipline practices;
9. provision of safety, security, health and beneficial nutrition;
10. the inclusion of children with different needs and abilities;
11. the protection of children from harm and neglect; and
12. the involvement of parents and communities.

These standard areas are significant, in light of the fact that all entities in the sector, including early childhood institutions are expected to adopt practices which contribute to their attainment. Of particular note, in relation to the construction, refurbishment and upgrading of early childhood infrastructure and administrative processes are the standards on the

- inclusion of children with different needs and abilities;
- provision of safety, security and health;
- protection of children from harm and neglect; and
- involvement of parents and communities.[30]

As is evidenced, the consolidation of the international framework has taken place at the regional level with countries in the Caribbean Community (CARICOM) adopting special commitments to the region's children via its ongoing agenda on youth development. In 2002, the Council for Human and Social Development meeting in Guyana placed the rights of children at the heart of its agenda for pursuing a sustainable approach to human resource development (CARICOM Secretariat 2002). Furthermore, in 2007, CARICOM Heads of Government mandated a full-scale analysis of the situation of youth in the Community and adopted the recommendations of the CARICOM Commission on Youth Development (CCYD) in 2010 (CCYD 2010). Cognizant of the fact that some 64 per cent of the region's population was under thirty years and over 35 per cent were children under eighteen years of age, Heads of Government adopted the Declaration of Paramaribo on the Future of Youth in the Caribbean Community.[31] The CCYD Report and the Declaration reinforced commitments to a life-cycle approach to the development of the region's human resources, including a strategic emphasis on financial and technical investment in the education and health of children and youth.

This is the context in which Caribbean children attempt to enjoy their childhood. These are countries which are politically independent but whose economies, social development and culture continue to be influenced by the ex-mother countries. The analysis of the international and regional contexts reveals an increasing attention on children. The impetus began internationally, and the Caribbean Region developed their plans and programmes to focus on children. In the next section, we examine some of the challenges to childhood on the national level

National Commitments to Children

All four countries under review ratified the Convention in the 1990s and promised to provide, protect and allow children to participate in policy decision-making processes (Table 1.1). Since the ratification of the Convention on the Rights of the Child, all four countries have implemented

Table 1.1 Dates for the ratification of the Convention of the Rights of the Child (CRC) for selected Caribbean countries

Country	Date of political independence[a]	Date the CRC ratified[b]
Barbados	November 30, 1966 (from the UK)	October 9, 1990
Haiti	January 1, 1804 (from the French)	January 26, 1990
Jamaica	August 6, 1962 (from the UK)	May 14, 1991
St. Lucia	February 22, 1979 (from the UK)	June 16, 1993

[a]http://www.silvertorch.com/dates-of-independence.html
[b]http://unchildrights.blogspot.com/2011/01/chronological-order-ratifications-crc.
  html (Accessed April 2, 2018)

programmes or passed legislation to support adherence to Child Rights. Even before the ratification, there was some general protection of children although the focus was not so intense.

Barbados

The Barbados Constitution recognizes and protects the fundamental rights and freedoms of the individual, including children, and protects them from discrimination on the grounds of race, place of origin, political opinion, colour or creed. The Status of Children Reform Act 1979 specifically provides for the equal status of children whether born in or out of wedlock (Government of Barbados, 19). Some of the main pieces of child-related legislation in Barbados include the following:

  i. The Status of Children Reform Act 1979, Chapter 220
 ii. The Education Act 1981, Chapter 41
iii. The Protection of Children Act, 1990 Chapter 146 (A)
 iv. The Domestic Violence (Protection Order) Act, 1992 Chapter 130 (A)
  v. The Films Act 1993 Chapter 299
 vi. The Technical and Vocational Education and Training Council Act, 1993
vii. Technical and Vocational Education (Misc. Provisions) Act 9/2000
viii. Convention on the Rights of Persons with Disabilities in 2007 (Government of Barbados May 2015, 9)

The business of taking care of the nation's children has been covered by at least three ministries in Barbados: the Ministry of Family, Culture, Sports and Youth; the Ministry of Social Care, Constituency Empowerment and Community Development; and the Ministry of Social Transformation. The Barbadian Government set up a Committee for Monitoring the Rights of the Child in September 1998. The committee is made up of ten members from the government, non-government organizations, the youth, social services, the media, and persons with disabilities. It has been advocating for a Child's Act to harmonize all legislation regarding children (Barbados government). There is a Child Care Board which monitors the children in need of care and there are plans to establish a Children's Desk in the Ombudsman's office.

As in many Caribbean countries, there are problems with the definitions of the Child; the CRC defines a child as an individual who has not attained the age of eighteen years, but there are conflicts in the Barbados legislation for the minimum age for adherence to rights. For example,

(a) the age of majority (18 years);
(b) legal and medical counselling without parental consent (generally considered to be 16 years);
(c) end of compulsory education (16 years);
(d) employment: part time/full time (16 years);
(e) sexual consent (16 years);
(f) marriage (16 years);
(g) voluntary enlistment and conscription in the armed forces (18 years);
(h) voluntarily giving testimony in court (7–14 years);
(i) criminal liability (11 years);
(j) deprivation of liberty (11 years);
(k) Imprisonment (16 years); and
(l) consumption of alcohol and other controlled substances (16 years). (Government of Barbados, 16)

The Child Care Board is responsible for the care and protection of children. Children who are removed from their families in their best interests are placed in the Board's residential care facilities. In addition, the Board receives and investigates cases of child abuse and maltreatment. One of the responsibilities of the Child Care Board is to ensure that both public and private institutions with responsibility for the care and protection of children adhere to established standards (Government of Barbados, 21).

Jamaica

The Convention on the Rights of the Child was ratified in Jamaica in 1991. The definition of a child is a person who is under the age of 18 and is thereby considered a minor. Laws that sought to protect children prior to ratification of the Convention on the Rights of Children include the following:

i. The Custody and Guardianship Act, which took into account the best environment for children when deciding which parent/guardian should have custody of a child.
ii. The Juvenile Act, which established the responsibilities of parents who have juveniles or minors in their care, such as providing food, clothing and shelter.
iii. The Family Court was also established to ensure that there would be legal recourse for children who had been ill-treated or abused by their parent/guardian.

After the ratification of the CRC, many other laws were put into place to ensure that children are treated fairly and protected under the law. Some of these acts included

i. the Child Care and Protection Act (2004), which sought not to stop the practice of corporal punishment, but instead wanted to ensure that children were not being harmed or abused in the administering of such punishment by their parents; and
ii. the Law Reform Act (2013), which repealed several provisions from older laws, related to flogging and whipping for criminals. Below are some of the main legislative pieces that support the CRC:

1. The Early Childhood Commission Act, 2003
2. Child Care and Protection Act, 2004
3. National Health Policy (2006–2015)
4. Child Care and Protection (Children's Homes) Regulations, June 2007
5. National Strategic Plan on HIV/AIDS (2007–2012)
6. National Strategic Plan for Early Childhood Development (2008–2013)
7. Child Pornography (Prevention) Act of October 2009
8. Sexual Offences Act, 2009
9. Cybercrimes Act, 2010
10. Victim's Charter of 2006
11. National Development Plan: Vision 2030 Jamaica
12. The National Parenting Support Commission Act, 2012 (Act 7/2012)
13. National Plan of Action on Child Labour (2013)
14. The Child Diversion Act, 2018

(Government of Jamaica March 2015, 2, and https://cabinet.gov.jm/resources-category/legislation-programmes/)

St. Lucia

The Convention on the Rights of the Child was ratified in St. Lucia in 1993. St. Lucia, too, has developed several plans and legislative pieces. There is no singular definition for a child in St. Lucia's law, as depending on the specific law being examined a child can be defined as being no more than twelve years old or someone younger than eighteen years old. Laws that sought to protect children before the Convention on the Rights of Children was ratified include:

i. the St. Lucia Criminal Code (1957), which protected children from abuse (emotional, sexual and physical); and
ii. the Children and Young Persons Act (1972), which established basic protection for children against violence and mistreatment.

After the ratification of the CRC, many other laws and policies were put into place to ensure that children were treated fairly and protected. These included

i. putting in place a Family Court in 1994 so that children could have a voice in the legal system and have their concerns heard;

ii. the Domestic Violence Act (1995), which put into law protections for children that were overlooked in previous laws, by defining what parents can and cannot do to their children and allowing the government to remove children from their homes if the child's life is deemed to be in danger; and

iii. revising the Criminal Code in 2003 to take into account a more general definition of sexual offences against children, as the previous codes had looked primarily at female cases of sexual abuse and had ignored the male victims.

Haiti

In Haiti, the Convention on the Rights of the Child was ratified in 1995. The definition of a child as presented in Article 16.2 of the Haitian Constitution is any person who has not yet reached the age of majority, which is 18. Before the CRC was ratified by Haiti, there were very few laws that sought to strongly protect the rights of children. The primary protection that children received from the legal system came out of the Haitian Constitution of 1987 which stated that "all children are entitled to love, affection, understanding and moral and physical care from its father and mother."

After the ratification of the CRC, many other laws were put into place to ensure that children were treated fairly and protected. Some of these acts included the following:

i. In 2001, Haiti amended many of its Acts that dealt with Family Law, so that the State could remove children from unstable homes and bring criminal charges against parents who neglected their children.

ii. In 2003, a law was passed that helped improve the lives of *restaveks*, many children from rural areas whose parents sent them to live with relatives in urban areas. These children ended up working for no money and tended to live in squalor. The 2003 law stated that the working age for children would be increased and that the living conditions of these children must be improved.

iii. In 2005, a Children's Code was presented before the Haitian Parliament that sought to strengthen child protection laws and make the rights of children a major priority of the Haitian government.

Each nation has responded to the international and regional guidelines set for children. In the next chapter, we review some of the current theories of childhood and determine their adequacy for explaining childhood in SIDS.

Notes

1. http://www.unicef.org/sowc2016/ (Accessed June 28, 2016).
2. http://www.un.org/en/development/devagenda/population.shtml (Accessed July 17, 2018).
3. Ibid.
4. http://www.un.org/womenwatch/daw/beijing/otherconferences/Mexico/Mexico%20conference%20report%20optimized.pdf (Accessed July 15, 2018).
5. Ibid.
6. Ibid.
7. http://www.unicef.org/wsc/declare.htm (Accessed May 2, 2018).
8. Ibid.
9. http://www.un.org/ga/search/view_doc.asp?symbol=A/RES/50/107 (Accessed May 2, 2018).
10. http://www.un.org/events/youth98/yforum98/bragayap.htm (Accessed July 15, 2018).
11. Ibid.
12. Ibid.
13. http://www.sids2014.org/samoapathway (Accessed July 15, 2018).

14. https://www.opanal.org/en/treaty-of-tlatelolco/ (Accessed May 15, 2018).
15. UNICEF and Colombia Government (1994), Nariño Accord. Second American Meeting on Children and Social Policy, Agenda 2000: Children Now, Santafé de Bogotá, Colombia, on 5–6 April 1994 (Accessed May 2, 2018).
16. http://iin.oea.org/DECLARACIONES/Cumbres%20e%20 Infancia%20-%20Ingles.htm (Accessed July 15, 2018).
17. Ibid.
18. https://archive.crin.org/en/library/publications/kingston-consensus-fifth-ministerial-meeting-children-and-social-policy-america (Accessed July 15, 2018).
19. https://www.unicef.org/easterncaribbean/spmapping/Planning/ Regional/general/Belize_1996.doc (Accessed April 22, 2018).
20. https://www.opanal.org/en/treaty-of-tlatelolco/ (Accessed July 15, 2018).
21. UNICEF and Colombia Government (1994), Nariño Accord. Second American Meeting on Children and Social Policy, Agenda 2000: Children Now, Santafé de Bogotá, Colombia, on 5–6 April 1994.
22. http://iin.oea.org/DECLARACIONES/Cumbres%20e%20 Infancia%20-%20Ingles.htm (Accessed July 15, 2018).
23. Ibid.
24. https://archive.crin.org/en/library/publications/kingston-consensus-fifth-ministerial-meeting-children-and-social-policy-america (Accessed July 15, 2018).
25. Ibid.
26. Ibid.
27. http://www.pitt.edu/~ginie/caribbean/Plan-Act.pdf (Accessed May 2, 2018).
28. https://caricom.org/media-center/communications/statements-from-caricom-meetings/declaration-of-paramaribo-on-the-future-of-youth-in-the-caribbean-community (Accessed July 15, 2015).
29. https://caricom.org/documents/12069-regional_guidelines_-_early_ childhood_development_services.pdf (Accessed July 15, 2015).
30. Ibid.
31. https://caricom.org/media-center/communications/statements-from-caricom-meetings/declaration-of-paramaribo-on-the-future-of-youth-in-the-caribbean-community (Accessed July 15, 2015).

References

Ansell, N. (2004). *Children, youth and development*. London: Routledge.

Bruno, S. (n.d.). The issue of children, adolescents and family at summit meetings. Retrieved January 12, 2019, from http://iin.oea.org/DECLARACIONES/Cumbres%20e%20Infancia%20-%20Ingles.htm.

CARICOM Commission on Youth Development (CCYD). (2010). Eye on the future-investing in youth now for tomorrow's community. Report of the CARICOM Commission on Youth Development January 2010. Retrieved March 15, 2018, from http://www.youthjamaica.com/sites/default/files/CCYD%20Report.pdf.

CARICOM Secretariat. (2002). Communique issued at conclusion of sixth meeting of the Council for Human and Social Development (COHSOD), April 17–19, 2002, Georgetown, Guyana. Retrieved October 24, 2018, from https://caricom.org/communications/view/communique-issued-at-conclusion-of-sixth-meeting-of-the-council-for-human-and-social-development-cohsod-17-19-april-2002-georgetown-guyana.

Goodman, J., & Cook, B. (2019). Shaming school children: A violation of fundamental rights? *Theory and Research in Education, 17*(1), 62–81.

Government of Barbados. (2015). Report to the International Committee on the Rights of the Child, May 2015.

Government of Jamaica. (2015). Report to the International Committee on the Rights of the Child, March 2015.

Hendricks, A. (2007). UN Convention on the Rights of Persons with Disabilities. *European Journal of Health Law, 14*, 273–280. https://doi.org/10.1163/092902707X240620

Humanium. (2015). Criticisms of children's rights. Retrieved March 23, 2019, from http://www.humanium.org/en/criticisms-of-childrens-rights/.

International Council for Science. (2015). Review of targets for the Sustainable Development Goals: The science perspective. Retrieved March 23, 2019, from https://www.researchgate.net/publication/272355248_Review_of_Targets_for_The_Sustainable_Development_Goals_The_Science_Perspective.

Khoo, S. M. (2005). The Millennium Development Goals: A critical discussion. *Trocaire Development Review, 2005*, 43–56.

Korang-Okrah, R., Haight, W., Gibson, P., & Black, J. (2019). Solutions to property rights 'violations' experienced by Ghanaian (Akan) widows and their children: The role of international social workers in addressing human rights. *International Social Work, 62*(1), 405–418.

Melamed, C., & Scott, L. (2011). After 2015: Progress and challenges for development. Overseas Development Institute 2011. ISSN 1756-7610. Retrieved February 20, 2018, from http://www.odi.org/sites/odi.org.uk/files/odi-assets/publications-opinion-files/7061.pdf.

Mycoo, M. (2018). Achieving SDG 6: Water resources sustainability in Caribbean Small Island Developing States through improved water governance. *Natural Resources Forum, 42*(1), 54–68.

Pare, M. (2004). Educating marginalized children: The challenge of the right to education in Brazil. *International Journal of Children s Rights, 12*(3), 217–257.

United Nations. (2012). Review of the contributions of the MDG Agenda to foster development: Lessons for the post-2015 UN development agenda. Retrieved January 15, 2018, from http://www.un.org/millenniumgoals/pdf/mdg_assessment_Aug.pdf.

United Nations Children's Fund (UNICEF). (2014). 20 years after the Convention on the Rights of the Child. Retrieved January 15, 2018, from https://www.unicef.org/jamaica/CRC20_in_Jamaica.pdf.

United Nations Development Programme. (2017). Financing the SDGs in the Pacific Islands—Opportunities, challenges and the ways forward. Retrieved March 1, 2019, from https://www.unescap.org/sites/default/files/Financing%20the%20SDGs%20in%20the%20Pacific%20Islands%2D%2DOpportunities,%20Challenges%20and%20Ways%20Forward%20(2).pdf.

2

Childhood in Caribbean Small Island Developing States (SIDS)

The study of childhood has presented much fascination for writers. Fiction writers, historians, sociologists, anthropologists, psychologists and several others have expounded on the "child" and put forward all manner of explanations and descriptions for what childhood was, is and should be. Children pose an enigma and through the decades, the depiction of childhood has changed from first regarding them as "adult-like" to "innocent fragile beings" to "equal citizens" in society. Currently, we are still attempting to understand that period of the life cycle and although many books have been written and will continue to be written, children will remain mystifying for many centuries to come. Notwithstanding the discipline, most writers will agree that investment in this group is very important, and there are few who would not accept that children are the foundation in any society.

However, this societal group is not a globally homogeneous group. It presents various characteristics across countries and within countries. Some sub-groups include children with disabilities, refugee children, children of immigrants, children in conflict with the law and teenage parents. Each sub-group presents unique features and has to be understood based on its depiction at the time of study. Also, there are marked

© The Author(s) 2020   **27**
A. Henry-Lee, *Endangered and Transformative Childhood in Caribbean Small Island Developing States*, Studies in Childhood and Youth,
https://doi.org/10.1007/978-3-030-25568-8_2

differences between children in developed countries and those in developing countries. The study of children, childhood and the impact on adulthood remains as complex as ever:

> We know nothing of childhood: and with our mistaken notions the further we advance the further we go astray. The wisest writers devote themselves to what a man ought to know, without asking what a child is capable of learning. They are looking for the man in the child, without considering what he is before he becomes a man. (Rousseau 1979)[1]

Given the peculiar characteristics of their countries, children in Small Island Developing States (SIDS) are more vulnerable than those in developed countries. While current childhood theories describe and explain childhood in developed countries, they only partially explain the nature of childhood in SIDS in the Caribbean. They do not take account of the particular historical, environmental, cultural and socio-economic conditions that shape the nature of childhood in this region. This book attempts to fill these theoretical gaps. It puts forward a theory of "endangerment" which explains the current nature and characteristics of childhood in SIDS.

Small Island Developing States (SIDS)

Caribbean countries are members of that group called Small Island Developing States (SIDS)[2] which are characterized by significant susceptibility to economic and environmental shocks; small labour markets, limited skilled labour, high unemployment; limited productive sectors and heavy reliance on imports; tourism as a driving force of the economy; an impending large increase in the size of the elderly population and high levels of poverty and inequality (Williams et al. 2013, 9).

There is much debate about the advantages and disadvantages of "smallness." Many small states have good natural resources with small and more cohesive populations allowing them to adapt better to change (Easterly and Kraay 2000). Small states have jurisdiction over globally significant ocean areas providing them with valuable economic, social and cultural resources that support their economic and social well-being (The Commonwealth 2014).

Some of the issues in small states are self-inflicted. In an increasing globalized economy, ease of doing business must be of paramount importance to governments. However, it is not easy to do business in Latin America and the Caribbean as shown by its ease of doing business index in 2019 (58.97). The ease of doing business score ranges from 0 to 100 with the latter being the best performance. The ease of doing business was calculated for 190 countries. Among the countries under discussion, Jamaica is the best for doing business with an index of 67.47 and Haiti is the worst (38.52). Barbados recorded an index of 56.78 and St. Lucia, 63.02.[3]

Corruption can also increase the challenges that small states face. In 2018, out of 175 countries, Barbados, Haiti, Jamaica and St. Lucia were 25th, 161st, 70th and 50th respectively (https://tradingeconomics.com). Haiti was the most corrupt and Barbados, the least. This self-inflicted characteristic retards economic growth.

SIDS also suffer from several other deficiencies. Their small economies may be more vulnerable to terms of trade shocks because of their sizes which prevent them from diversifying into a broader range of activities (Easterly and Kraay 2000). Growth volatility and volatility of terms of trade shocks as a percentage of GDP is higher in small states primarily due to their greater trade openness. However, the net benefits of openness on growth can be positive (Easterly and Kraay 2000).

Briguglio and Kisanga (2004) list the current economic vulnerabilities of the small states which are well documented, and include:

(a) a very high degree of economic openness due to their dependence on exports and imports, mostly because of their small domestic markets and lack of natural resource endowments;
(b) a high degree of export concentration, mostly due to their small economic size, leading to diversification constraints; and
(c) high dependence on strategic imports, such as fuel and food. These vulnerabilities render a country highly exposed to external shocks (Briguglio and Kisanga 2004).

Caribbean countries remain members of a group of "developing countries" which seems unable to change its status. Many are denied access to international arenas. Small states are generally excluded from the real discussions mainly because they are not knowledgeable or are not perceived to be knowledgeable; hence they are deemed to be unable to contribute constructively (ACUNS 2009).

Small states are also impacted negatively due to poor location; that is, they are either remote, landlocked, or both. Some small states are in regions prone to hurricanes and other natural disasters (Srinivasan 1986 cited in Easterly and Kraay 2000). "Small states are less able than large states to cope with environmental degradation, natural disasters and the impacts of global climate change" (The Commonwealth 2014, 2).

The issues of SIDS first gained global attention in 1992 at a UN Conference. The conference participants highlighted the vulnerability of some nations to global warming and sea level rises. By 1994, a programme to deal with the needs of SIDS was adopted at the UN Global Conference on the Sustainable Development of Small Island Developing States. The programme, called the Barbados Programme of Action, outlined strategies to deal with climate change and sea-level rise, natural and environmental disasters, energy resources, tourism, biodiversity, marine resources, transport and communication, and science and technology. Specific actions were agreed to be taken at the national, regional and international levels in support of the Small Island Developing States.

SIDS received significant international attention in 1999, when the UN recognized that progress was uneven in the fulfilment of goals which had been set in the Barbados Programme of Action. They observed that increasing globalization, widening inequalities in income and a continued deterioration of the global environment were impeding the fulfilment of developmental goals for these states.

Since the adoption of the Barbados Programme of Action,[4] the vulnerability of the islands has not decreased significantly. They still suffer from many problems such as the increasing negative impacts of climate change on islands, growing national debt and income inequality, and weakening competitiveness in the main economic sectors—tourism and financial services. In the 2014 Samoa International Conference on SIDS, there was a reaffirmation of a commitment to the sustainable development of

Small Island Developing States through the broad alliance of people, governments, the civil society and the private sector.[5] Many small states have good natural resources with small and more cohesive populations allowing them to adapt better to change (Easterly and Kraay 2000).

Now in 2019, Caribbean SIDS are un likely to fulfil the SDGS and progress in the implementation of the CRC remains slow. We insist that given the very nature of SIDS, childhood is endangered, and deliberate actions by all are needed to transform the processes that shape the quality of childhood currently experienced by large numbers of children in these states.

Problematizing Childhood

The UN Convention on the Rights of the Child (1989) defines a child as an individual aged less than eighteen years. It is indisputable that nations must invest in children. There are economic, legal and ethical reasons why we should pay some attention to those members of the society. Economically, we will get significant returns on investment in children (Kjørholt 2013), which will ensure that the society benefits from productive adults and social stability. Legally, we are obligated by international law and the many Conventions that we have ratified to invest in children. Ethically, our moral compass propels us to provide protection for this most vulnerable group. As researchers of Child Studies, we need to understand childhood and children in order to formulate more effective and efficient policies for their benefit.

While we accept that children are vulnerable, they are a curious set of individuals and there are not many persons who will profess expertise in effectively interacting with all kinds of children. As mentioned before, they do not form a homogenous category, and our perception of them depends on our own background and past experience with them. The outcome of any social interaction with a child will depend on our preconceived expectations, the age of the child and our prior exposure to children. It is quite possible that the same child will be considered "alert and assertive" by one individual and "rude" by another. Children are complex and multifaceted.

For child advocates, it is sometimes difficult to explain to opponents, children's social worth and importance. While it is understood that children are the adults of the future and the foundation of society, they are in fact fragile, and the natural tendency is to protect them at all costs. Yet, to complicate matters, there is a movement to seek the participation of children in decision-making processes. How much freedom is allowable and how to facilitate free expression by all the various groups of children? At what age? On what issues? What is the line between free expression and irresponsible behaviour? Childhood and the behaviours expected of children are continually evolving. It is generally accepted that we can manage children when they are "silent," compliant, and do not demand too much of us. In this book, we attempt to explain the enigma that is childhood in Caribbean SIDS.

Some Main Theories of Childhood

There are numerous theories of childhood and the entire book could be dedicated to the exposition of these. The study of this group continues to fascinate theorists, several of whom provide explanations for the type of childhood a child experiences. These theorists can be divided by their micro or macro focus. The former set focuses on the attributes of the individual child or family, while macro theorists emphasize the community, society and nation. Still there are others who try to cover all bases and provide explanations at both the micro and macro levels. We will focus on a few of the main theories.

Micro Theories

We begin with the micro theories as childhood is first experienced in the home and extends to other social institutions such as the school or church. Chris Jenks (2005, 2), a pioneer of the Sociology of Childhood asserts that even after centuries of debate and discussion, there is no consensus on what constitutes childhood. Handel et al. (2007) outline the various types of childhood theories and we focus on some of them.

Biological and Evolutionary Theories of Childhood assert that childhood is a stage of human evolution, necessary for the survival of the human species. Here, biology is the main explanation for childhood, and physiology, psychology and cognitive mapping determine child development. For example, G. Stanley Hall (1904) believed in evolutionary processes and used both age-related averages of children's growth and behaviours, to account for development:

> Individual growth recapitulates the history of the race—Rate of prenatal growth in height and weight—Statistical methods—Prenatal growth in animals Causes that favor and hinder it—Lessened rate at eight to twelve, also at seventeen and eighteen—Delay and compensation—Last stages of growth Advantages of size—What is growth?—National differences—New genetic theories of retardation and the period of increment—Augmented size and power of the human race—A later, higher, new story superposed on the older foundations now represented in boyhood. (Hall 1904, 1)

S. A. McLeod (2015) presents a critique of many of the theories. He finds that the Biological Theories provide clear predictions of, for example, the effects of neurotransmitters on the behaviours of persons who are genetically related. These can usually be tested and proven. However, the biological explanations are reductionist and do not fully explain the impact of non-physiological factors on human behaviour (McLeod 2015).

Psychoanalytical Theories focus on the formation of the personality. For example, Sigmund Freud (1910) presents childhood as central to the adjustment of the individual to mature well-being. Freud (1910) also developed the Psychosexual Theory and emphasized that a child's personality is formed by the strategies his parents use to manage his sexual and aggressive drives.

Mentioning McLeod (2015) states that after assessing the Psychoanalytical Theories, they concluded that some components would be rejected, and others accepted while others could be "reshaped." The case study approach used by psychoanalytical theories is criticized, as generalizations, he says, could not be made using that methodology. Referring to Anthony Starr, McLeod (2015) also says that the procedures used by psychoanalytical theorists could be contaminated by subjective personal opinion and could not be considered scientific.

Erikson (1950) put forward the Psychosocial Theory and identified eight stages of human development:

- Basic trust vs. mistrust (birth–1 year)
- Autonomy vs. shame and doubt (ages 1–3)
- Initiative vs. guilt (ages 3–6)
- Industry vs. inferiority (ages 6–11)
- Identity vs. identity confusion (adolescence)
- Intimacy vs. isolation (young adulthood)
- Generativist vs. stagnation (middle adulthood)
- Integrity vs. despair (the elderly)

Erikson's theory under-plays the importance of non-psychosocial factors in shaping childhood in any society.

Another group of micro theories includes the Cognitive Development Theories. Jean Piaget (1936) developed a theory of intellectual development that included four distinct stages: the sensorimotor stage, from birth to age two; the pre-operational stage, from age two to about age seven; the concrete operational stage, from age seven to eleven; and the formal operational stage, which begins in adolescence and extends into adulthood.

According to McLeod (2015), Piaget's concentration on the universal stages of cognitive development and biological maturation fails to consider the effect of the social setting and culture on cognitive development. While clinical interviews provide an opportunity to learn more about the client, he says, the interpretation of the data is open to bias. For example, children who have short attention spans may try to please the experimenter and give expected answers. McLeod also noted that Piaget's sample was too small and included his own children. Quoting McLeod states that Piaget is wrong to identify language as being secondary to action. Language and action are intricately linked, and the origin of reasoning has more to do with our ability to communicate with others than with our interaction with the material world (McLeod 2015).

Macro Theories

At the macro level, there are the Behavioural and Social Learning Theories. They explain the importance of the environment and nurturing to the growth of a child. Behaviourism was developed between the 1920s and the 1960s, as a response to psychoanalytical theories. For example, the father of Behaviourist theory—psychologist John Watson—claimed that children were passive beings who could be moulded by controlling their stimulus-response associations. In one of his pieces of research, he conditioned a baby "Albert" to fear certain items (Watson and Rayner 1920).

Watson believed children could be conditioned by their different experiences of learning. He famously said:

> Give me a dozen healthy infants, well-formed, and my own specified world to bring them up in and I'll guarantee to take any one at random and train him to become any type of specialist I might select—doctor, lawyer, artist, merchant-chief and, yes, even beggar-man and thief, regardless of his talents, penchants, tendencies, abilities, vocations and the race of his ancestors. (Watson 1924, 104)

Another Social Learning Theorist, Albert Bandura, also a psychologist, states that children learn by observation and imitation, and over time, children would be more selective in what or who they imitate (Bandura 1977).

According to McLeod, although, they can explain some quite complex behaviour, Social Learning Theories cannot adequately explain why we develop a range of thoughts and feelings. Limiting the explanation of behaviour to the imitation of behaviour cannot be accepted if the individual has no role model. McLeod further points out that criticism of the Social Learning Theory led Bandura in 1986 moved to rename his Social Learning Theory "Social Cognitive Theory" (McLeod 2015).

Other macro theories include the Developmental and Social Constructionist Models such as those of Margaret Mead (1961). They claim that childhood is socially constructed and state that there is no one universal view of children. They stress that the answers to such questions as what is a "child?" or what is "childhood?" are dependent on the society, time, place, the expectations of the child, and society's definitions of a child's roles and responsibilities. Successive generations out of a mix of tradition, social intercourse and technological advancement define the notion that is childhood.

Burke (2008) laments that social constructionist models are too casual in the explanations of historical processes that impact human behaviour. More attention needed to be paid to the origins of those constructions that people developed. These were usually from real personal and collective experiences and prior knowledge.

Macro-level cultural theorists posit that age and physical maturity are not the only important factors defining childhood, but that culture is also key in its formation. Childhood is a stage of innocence and absence of sin or corruption and adulthood is characterized by anxieties, concerns and needs (Burke 2004). Giroux (2001) speaks of the "politics of culture" through which childhood has been constructed, experienced and struggled over, while Cross (1997) focuses on the changing types of toys, portraying the child as consumer, as being socially constructed. Qvortrup (1994) speaks of the plurality of experiences that is childhood. Kincheloe and Steinberg (1997) speak to "the dilemma of postmodern childhood" characterized by a democratization in family life which changed the expectations of children and the concept of childhood, resulting in conflict with many of society's established institutions such as the traditional family or the authoritarian school. Postman (1994) notes that with the twenty-first century-information revolution, there has been a disappearance of childhood.

Urie Bronfenbrenner put forward the Ecological Systems Theory based on the belief that no one feature could explain child behaviour (Bronfenbrenner 1979). There are various systems in the environment, and their interrelations shape child development. There are bi-directional influences as the environment affects the child and the child influences the environment (ibid). He outlines five systems:

The *microsystem*—closest to the child, which includes activities and interactions in the child's immediate environment such as parents, school and friends;

the *mesosystem*—the layer which provides the connection between the structures of the individual's microsystem, such as parents' interactions with teachers, a school's interactions with the daycare provider;

the *exosystem*—social institutions which affect children indirectly—the parents' work settings and policies, extended family networks, mass media, community resources;

the *macrosystem*—broader cultural values, laws and governmental resources; and

the *chronosystem*—changes which occur during a child's life, both personally, like the birth of a sibling, and culturally, like the Iraqi war (ibid.).

Human development takes place through processes of progressively more complex reciprocal interaction between an active, evolving biopsychological human organism and the persons, objects, and symbols in its immediate external environment (Bronfenbrenner and Morris 1998, 996). To be effective, the interaction must occur on a fairly regular basis over extended periods of time. Such enduring forms of interaction in the immediate environment are referred to as proximal processes (Bronfenbrenner and Morris 1998, 996).

Neal and Neal (2013, 2) state that though Bronfenbrenner's ecological theory is widely recognized for underscoring the importance of interdependent and multilevel systems on individual development, the precise relationships of systems to one another remain elusive. They further claim that Bronfenbrenner's original description of ecological systems at different levels, being nested within one another, giving rise to the classic graphic portrayal as a set of concentric circles, obscures the relationships between them. Neal and Neal (ibid.) suggest instead that ecological systems should be conceptualized as networked, not nested, whereby each system is defined in terms of the social relationships surrounding an individual, and where systems at different levels relate to one another in an overlapping but non-nested way.

Current Post-Modernist Macro Theories of Childhood declare that a plurality of childhood is experienced across cultures. They affirm that childhood encompasses a diversity of experiences according to class, ethnicity, gender, and culture, place of residence, health or disability (Jenks 2005; Qvortrup 1994). Post-Modernists reviewed the impact of globalization, the media, and technology on childhood. David Elkind (1981) describes the hurried child and Postman (1994) laments the disappearance of childhood in this rapidly globalizing world.

The Impact of the SIDS Experience

All these current theories emphasize the importance of the nurturing of children and highlight the role of adults and the environment in shaping the type of lives that children experience. What is missing from these theories is an explanation of the impact of the peculiarities of the natural, economic and social environments that children experience in the SIDS. As much of the research informing the theories is carried out in the developed countries, the realities of SIDS are not accounted for and given any relevance. The nuances that exist (such as cultural practices) and the voices of these children are absent in many current sociological discourses on childhood. A unique theory is needed to explain childhood in the SIDS.

We turn our attention to the examination of childhood in Caribbean SIDS. Many Caribbean writers speak of various risks and issues that face children in the Caribbean, but none has systematically examined all the main issues in a single document. Just recently, the Caribbean Human Development Report (UNDP 2016) highlighted some challenges facing youth in the Caribbean: underachievement at the secondary level; high proportions of males are victims and perpetrators of violence; and high rates of youth unemployment except in Trinidad and Tobago where it is 10 per cent. *Caribbean Journal* (2015) outlined three major issues youths faced in the region—poverty, crime and drugs. High levels of poverty inevitably lead to high levels of youth unemployment which give rise to illegal/criminal activities including drug use and distribution (sale).

Others have also recently noted issues facing young persons in the Caribbean:

1. In 2012, in Haiti, one out of four females and one out of five males aged 18 to 24 experienced at least one incident of sexual abuse as a child; and among females and males in the same age range, almost

two-thirds had experienced physical violence by adult household members or authority figures in the community, prior to age 18.[6]

2. The youth unemployment rates in Barbados, Jamaica and Trinidad and Tobago in 2013 were 29.6 per cent, 34 per cent and 9.2 per cent respectively.[7]

3. The number of children aged 0 to 14 infected with HIV/AIDS in Jamaica stood at 1000 and in Trinidad and Tobago the number was 500.[8]

4. The prevalence of HIV among the 15–49 age group as a percentage of the population in Jamaica is 1.8 per cent, in Barbados 0.9 per cent and in Haiti 2.0 per cent as at 2014.[9]

5. In 2014, 6.5 per cent of the prison population in Jamaica was under eighteen years old. It was 1.4 per cent in Barbados, 6.9 per cent in St. Lucia and 4.85 per cent in Trinidad and Tobago.[10]

6. There were 2671 reported cases of sexual abuse in Jamaica in 2011 and 256 in Barbados in 2012.[11]

Brathwaite's study on Youth Risk in the Caribbean pointed to several issues that were likely to affect youths in the region. Included were stress, victimization, death, paranoia or lack of trust. isolation from family and friends, low motivation, academic failure, pregnancy, HIV/AIDS, STDs and STIs as well as youth poverty were also found to be significant issues (Brathwaite 2009, 6).

In examining challenges to Adolescent and Youth Development in the Caribbean, Bailey and Charles (2008, 20) emphasized the following:

1. *Health.* The spread of HIV/AIDS is of particular concern, especially as a by-product of specific cultural practices, including early sexual initiation, incest and sexual abuse.

2. *Education.* Disparities in access to quality education and gendered perceptions of its usefulness remain a challenge for youth in the Caribbean. This is coupled with high drop-out rates among adolescents.

3. *Poverty.* Socio-economic disabilities of youth prevent many older youths from establishing their independence from their parents, thereby retarding their transition to adulthood.

4. *Crime and violence.* Exposure to violent and abusive circumstances has led to high levels of rage among young people.
5. *Recreation.* Throughout the region the lack of leisure facilities geared towards the development of youth decreases the opportunities for their social involvement.

There are several Caribbean researchers (e.g. Jones 2013; Barrow 2011; Henry-Lee and Meeks-Gardner 2008) who discuss the status of children in the Caribbean and highlight the many dangers and risks they face, but there has been no systematic and comprehensive discussion of the risks peculiar to children in SIDS at the micro, meso and macro levels. No attempt has been made to develop a theory of childhood in Caribbean SIDS. Even issues identified almost ten years ago are still relevant. While children everywhere face some of these risks, because of the peculiarities of SIDS, the extent and depth of endangerment these children face prove more extensive.

Elements of an "Endangerment Theory"

While all theories have some relevance to children everywhere, including in the small island developing states (SIDS) of the Caribbean; none have captured the history, vulnerabilities and resilience that Caribbean children display.

We now put forward elements of a theory of endangerment which will attempt to take account of the general features of childhood in SIDS in the Caribbean. This endangerment theory draws on Bronfenbrenner's theory which discusses levels of influence. In the discussion of risks that children face at an early age, we also draw from the Social Risk Management Model proposed by the World Bank (Holzmann et al. 2003). In the Endangerment Theory, the influences are discussed at the macro, meso and micro levels. Let us begin with a definition of endangerment. We argue that while "endangerment" exists in all countries, it is particularly intense in SIDS.

The *Oxford Online Dictionary* defines "endangerment" as the action of putting someone or something at risk or in danger. Children of the SIDS in Caribbean are an endangered species; at risk in private and public spaces. Child endangerment is the process of exposing the younger generation to risks such as inadequate provision of basic necessities; insufficient protection and insufficient facilitation of opportunities for child participation. Endangerment takes place by both primary and secondary agents of socialization and at the macro, meso and micro levels. Some children have done well in spite of this endangerment and they have displayed a resilience that needs to be explored. However, radical transformation is needed to ensure that all children in Caribbean SIDS fulfil their potential and contribute to the sustainable development of their societies.

The theory of "endangered childhood" proposes that at the macro, meso and micro levels, good-quality childhood in SIDS is endangered and is at risk of becoming extinct. We seek to answer the following questions:

- Where does the process of endangerment begin?
- Who are the actors in this process?
- Who is responsible for endangering, and are all children being endangered?
- What is the role of the "endangered" in the process?
- Who is responsible for ending the endangerment?

Good-quality childhood can be defined as that which prepares children from birth to eighteen years, for participation as productive adults. To ensure their positive involvement in the development of their nations, we need to reduce and remove the risks and vulnerabilities that they face in SIDS.

Endangered Childhood in SIDS

Just as SIDS are vulnerable, so too are the children living there. The current theories do not explain these vulnerabilities. Explaining childhood is no easy task:

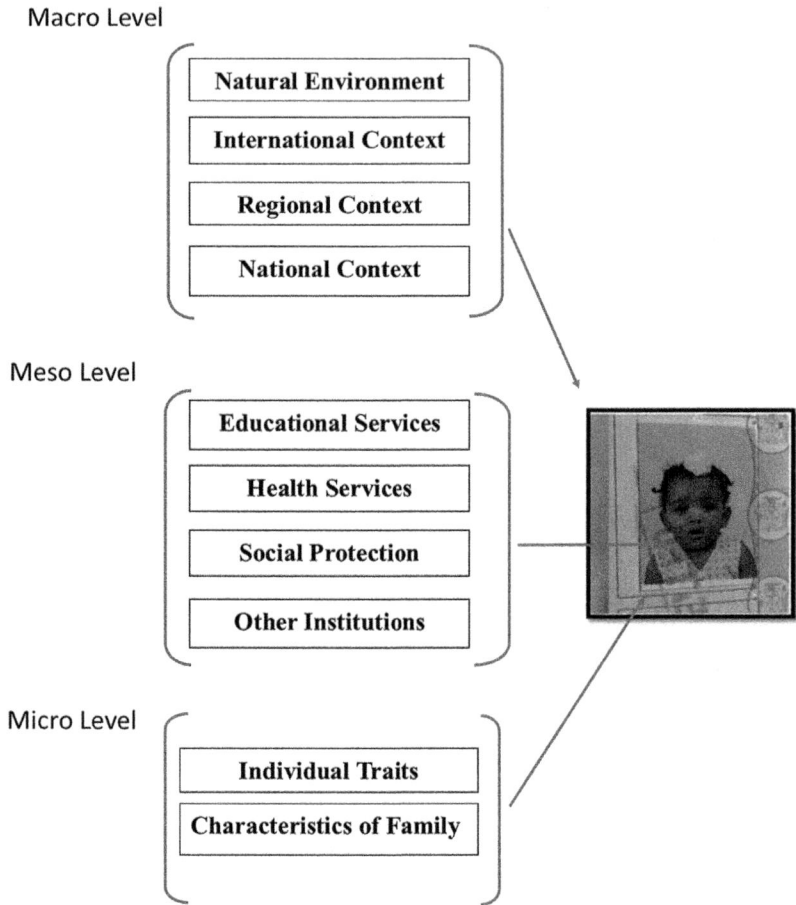

Macro Level

Natural Environment

International Context

Regional Context

National Context

Meso Level

Educational Services

Health Services

Social Protection

Other Institutions

Micro Level

Individual Traits

Characteristics of Family

Fig. 2.1 Main factors affecting the quality of childhood. (Source: Author's formulation, picture of author's daughter)

> Those who attempt to better understand children's social lives and socialization cannot study them in all their diversity and complexity, simultaneously. They must selectively focus on factors they consider most important and most revealing. (Handel et al. 2007, 11)

Figure 2.1 and Table 2.1 outline the risks of endangerment at each level. The process of endangerment of childhood begins at the *macro* level.

Table 2.1 Types of risks faced by children at various levels

	Factors	Risks
MACRO	Natural	Loss of life, shelter, food, education and health.
	International	Global economic crisis, unfavourable international trading terms and markets; nations' ability to influence global governance systems.
	Regional	History of the region leaves citizens scarred by remnants of slavery, colonialism and neo-liberalism.
	National	High levels of indebtedness, slow economic growth, high levels of public and private poverty, business failure and high levels of unemployment.
MESO	School	Access to poor-quality education reduces opportunity to realize full potential.
	Health services	Access to poor-quality health services reduces ability to realize full potential. Illness, injury, concerns all social groups.
	Social protection	Inadequate social protection for the poor and vulnerable.
MICRO	Individual traits	Individual traits (genes, disability, etc.) can influence the quality of childhood.
	Characteristics of the family	Large household size, poverty, low investment in education and health, etc.

Source: Author's outline

Vulnerabilities of SIDS impact on their citizens, especially those most vulnerable. There are influential factors in the natural environment, as well as in the historical international, regional and local contexts. The very islands in which these children are born are very vulnerable. The islands are very susceptible to climate change and external global influences and suffer significantly from their negative effects. This vulnerability is further compounded by the fact that the islands are sensitive to any changes at the global level. Such is the effect of globalization that a decision taken at a board meeting in Washington can have a negative impact on a factory worker and his children in one of the Caribbean SIDS. Apart from their vulnerabilities to external economic shocks and natural disasters, Caribbean SIDS are highly indebted and record high levels of poverty. They are usually unable to provide adequate access to good-quality social services such as health and education for their people. Smith and

Haddad (2002) note that even if there is growth, the benefits may not trickle down to the poor or those suffering deprivation. These constraints inhibit their investment in children. When there are economic recessions and structural adjustment programmes, these usually result in a reduction in expenditure on basic social services and negatively impact the quality of life for childhood in Caribbean SIDS.

The history of the societies also defines the quality of childhood that is experienced. Caribbean SIDS are scarred by their history of slavery and colonialism.

The understanding of childhood in any society cannot be pursued without considering the history of that society. According to slavevoyages.org, 4,930,389 of 9,405,034 African slaves ended up in the Caribbean islands over the course of the slave-trading era. Barbados was the first Caribbean country in which the enslavement of Africans began. The effects of the slave trade are devastating. The development of the Caribbean has been retarded by hundreds of years as the countries have tried to recover from its paralysing effects. The developed countries have advanced economically through the enslavement and exploitation of blacks.

This is a region whose history has slowed down the upward social mobility of blacks. Even now, after years of advancement of blacks, there is still what Bob Marley has labelled in his song "mental slavery." The society still sees colour as being important in some sectors. Bleaching the skin to get as near to the white man's colour as possible is deemed necessary, especially among the lower social classes. While there have been several models of black success, black Caribbean children struggle for self-identity as evident by the recent news of numerous cases of skin bleaching by Caribbean children.

Colonialism too has left its scars. And even today, while politically independent, the Caribbean countries are still controlled by their ex-colonial masters. Caribbean countries are among the most highly indebted market economies in the world (Drakes et al. 2012). Jamaica is still under IMF rule and the current administration based its 2016 political campaign on the economic stability gained by adhering to the IMF's advice and guidance.

use non-developmental strategies to cope with their deprivation. These strategies include hustling, delay in seeking medical care, heavy borrowing, crime and several informal activities. These non-developmental coping strategies often increase their dependence on the State and their own levels of deprivation.

It is not the first time that the term "endangered childhood" has been used. Comparing children of today with those of twenty-five years ago, Joan Almon (1998) spoke of "endangered childhood." She found that today's children tended to be thinner, paler and far more nervous; much more likely to have asthma, allergies, or sleeping or eating disorders; more likely to be diagnosed as hyperactive and much less likely to be able to play than children in the past. She did note, however, that some children of today were extremely bright; many being very skilled at the computer at a young age, while others were reading fluently by age four or five. She concluded that it was perplexing to understand what was happening and to know how best to help children (Almon 1998).

Jennifer Hill used the term "endangered childhood" in reference to the impact of consumerism on child and youth identity. Using research on children in North America, she showed that they were increasingly experiencing the effects of consumer culture at unprecedented levels of involvement. The author asserted that young Americans were receiving an endless barrage of material messages encouraging purchasing behaviour and consumption that impacted the self-image. She claimed that children from the ages of four to twelve were increasingly being defined and viewed by their spending capacity. Girls especially were targeted by marketers in order to encourage them to buy a whole line of products they "needed" to emulate a feminine ideal and bemoaned the fact that the structure of childhood was being eroded and children were suffering from serious physical, emotional and social deficits directly related to consumerism (Hill 2011).

Lee also labelled children as almost an endangered species and noted that some parents believed that if children were not playing the violin at three and reading at five, they would not be successful in life. The education system by its very rigorous nature was stealing childhood (Lee 2014).

We plan to go beyond these perspectives of endangered childhood and present a comprehensive deconstruction of "endangered childhood" from birth to youth. While Handel et al. (2007) caution against trying to explain everything about children, we attempt in this book to review the influences on children at the macro, meso and micro levels. We believe that processes at these three levels can determine the quality of childhood that children experience (see Fig. 2.1 and Table 2.1).

It would be extremely difficult to examine childhood in all SIDS, so childhood is explored in Barbados, Jamaica, Haiti and St. Lucia. Although these countries vary in geographical size and population, and currently report varying levels of human development and economic growth, their common history of slavery, colonialism and their global positioning have resulted in large numbers of their children being exposed to what can be termed "endangerment." This "endangerment" presents at various levels, but the end result is that there are large groups of children whose childhood is not adequately preparing them for their roles as adults in their societies. Unless childhood is transformed, children in these Caribbean SIDS are not guaranteed realization of their full potential.

Vulnerability at the National Levels

We are discussing childhood in four Caribbean SIDs. We purport that the very vulnerabilities that they experience on the macro level as SIDS impact negatively on the quality of children that citizens experience in these countries. These vulnerabilities result in an "endangered childhood" for thousands of children.

The four countries under discussion record varying levels of vulnerability from Higher Medium (Barbados, Haiti and Jamaica) to High Vulnerability (St. Lucia) based on the Commonwealth Vulnerability Index which takes into account several economic, environmental and insularity variables (CARICOM Secretariat 2000). These countries were specially chosen because they represent islands of different geographical size, GDP per capita, Human Development Indices (HDI) and levels of poverty.

Barbados boasts the highest HDI with Haiti, the lowest. It can be demonstrated that even if some countries may appear to be "better off" than others, they all suffer from "endangered childhood" as the

Table 2.2 Socio-economic data for selected Caribbean countries

Indicator	Barbados	Jamaica	Haiti	St. Lucia
Geographical size (Area-sq. km.)[a]	431	10,990	27,750	539
Population (million)[a]	0.3	2.9	11.1	0.2
GDP per capita, PPP (current international $)[b]	18,520	9046	1815	13,956
GDP per capita (current US$) (2013)[a]	15,975	4879	705	7848
HDI value (2014)[c]	0.8	0.7	0.5	0.7
HDI rank (2014)[c]	60	96	168	91
Population in severe multidimensional poverty[c]	0.0	0.8	22.5	0.0
Languages spoken[d]	English (official) Bajan Creole	English (official) Jamaican Creole	French (Official) French Creole	English (Official) French Creole
Urban population (%)[a]	31.1	55.7	55.3	18.7
GDP: Gross domestic product (million current US$) (2013)[a]	4553	14,057	7647	1397
GDP growth rate at constant 2005 prices (annual %) (2012)[a]	1.7	1.4	1.4	0.7
Gross Public debt as a % of GDP (2018)[b]	123.6	97.4	33.3	71.8
Unemployment rate (2018)[a]	9.5	12.3	13.9	20.4
Youth unemployment rate (2017)[c]	28.95	29.74	35.95	45.01
Intentional homicide rate (2018)[a]	10.9	47	10	19.3
Gini coefficient		0.3803[d] (2015)	0.411[e] (2012)	0.512[e] (2016)

[a]http://data.un.org/Default.aspx (Accessed April 2, 2018)
[b]https://www.gfmag.com/global-data/economic-data/public-debt-percentage-gdp (Accessed April 2, 2018)
[c]https://www.theglobaleconomy.com/rankings/Youth_unemployment/ (Accessed April 2, 2018)
[d]Planning Institute of Jamaica (2015) Jamaica Survey of Living Conditions
[e]https://data.worldbank.org/indicator/SI.POV.GINI (Accessed April 2, 2018)

vulnerabilities of the SIDS at the macro, meso and micro impact negatively on children, more so than do conditions in developed countries.

High levels of debt and low economic growth characterize Caribbean SIDS (Table 2.2). In Barbados, payment of debt represents 124 per cent of GDP. High levels of unemployment also plague these countries, with St. Lucia recording the highest at 20.4 per cent. Multi-dimensional poverty[12] is highest in Haiti at 22.5 per cent. Youth unemployment is high in all countries and the homicide rate is high especially in Jamaica (Table 2.2). Available data show that there exist high levels of inequality, especially in St. Lucia (Table 2.2).

Profile of Children in the Caribbean SIDS

Children form a significant proportion of the Caribbean population with at least 19 per cent of the population in Barbados aged under fifteen years. In Haiti, 33 per cent of the national population is aged less than fifteen years; with 19 per cent in St. Lucia and 23 per cent in Jamaica as at 2017.[13]

In spite of the unimpressive economic performance, life expectancy is at seventy-five years or over, in three of the countries under discussion (Table 2.3). This is close to the rates of two developed countries (UK, 81 years; US, 79 years).[14] However, Haiti is lowest at sixty-three years and generally presents the worst child welfare data, such as with the under-5 mortality rate (76 per 100 live births) and maternal mortality (at 350 per 100,000). While Barbados boasts the highest level of human development as suggested by the HDI (0.785), the country has not fulfilled the MDG Goal 4 of reducing the infant mortality rates by two-thirds, and is far from the rates of Norway with three, and the United States of America with six.[15] Thirty years after the adoption of the Convention on the Rights of the Child (CRC), children in the Caribbean SIDS face many challenges. There are still high levels of child poverty.

Table 2.3 Some child-related data for selected Caribbean countries

Indicator	Barbados	Jamaica	Haiti	St. Lucia
% of population aged 0–14 years (2018)	19	23	33	19
Life expectancy (2016)	76	76	63	75
Fertility rate (2016)	1.8	2.0	2.9	1.5
Under-5 mortality rate (per 1000 live births) 2017	12	15	72	17
Maternal mortality ratio (per 100,000 live births)	27	89	359	48
Births attended by skilled health personnel (%)	99 (2015)	99 (2011)	42 (2017)	99 (2012)
Measles immunization (% of 1 year olds) (2017)	92	95	53	87
Low birth weight babies % of births (2011)	11.5	11.3	23 (2012)	10.1
Children 0–14 living with HIV (2017)	–	500	7600	–
Children 0–14 newly infected with HIV (2017)	–	100	950	–
Prevalence of HIV, total % of population ages 15–49	1.6	1.8	1.9	–
Enrolment at primary schools–gross) (2017)	92	99.4 (2015)[a]	(2012) Male: 77 Female: 78[b]	(2012) Male: 94 Female: 92[c]
Percentage of repeaters (primary) (2017)	–	2.9	17 (1997)	3.4
Persistence to grade 5 (2016)[a]	94 (2010)	94	–	94
Progression to secondary school, % (2016)	99 (2008)	95	Na	97

Source: https://data.worldbank.org (Accessed February 2, 2019)
[a]http://statinja.gov.jm/demo_socialstats/education.aspx (Accessed February 2, 2019)
[b]https://www.unicef.org/infobycountry/haiti_statistics.html (Accessed April 3, 2019)
[c]https://www.unicef.org/infobycountry/stlucia_statistics.html (Accessed April 2, 2019)

Perceptions of Childhood in a Caribbean SID: Jamaica

National data analysis has highlighted the status of children in these four Caribbean SIDS. We now examine the perceptions of some senior citizens and children about childhood in one Caribbean SID. One's perception of life will affect one's well-being and self-realization. In this section, we examine the primary exploratory qualitative data from 10 senior citizens and the data collected from 103 high school students from two urban schools in Jamaica. Similar studies were not completed for the other countries. These data in Jamaica were collected in 2013–2014. Four schools were targeted but only two principals gave their consent for their students to be interviewed. Written consent was received from the parents and the children were interviewed at school to ensure non-interference from parents. There were eighty-two girls and thirty-one boys enrolled in Grades 11 and 12.

The students were asked about their perceptions on the following:

- The quality of life living in Jamaica,
- Parents' treatment of children,
- Teachers' treatment of children,
- Protection of children,
- Quality of education and health facilities, and
- Children's well-being.

Ten exploratory in-depth face-to-face interviews were held with senior citizens who lived in a nearby urban community. They were chosen based on convenience and ease of contact. This was done to reduce cost and length of the exploratory study. The respondents provided written consent. Fifteen senior citizens were targeted but only those who were in good health were interviewed. The main aim of this exploratory study with the senior citizens was to obtain their views on the quality of their childhood and the issues children face today. Table 2.4 provides details on the ten senior citizens interviewed during the exploratory study.

Table 2.4 Senior citizens interviewed for exploratory study on childhood in Jamaica

Sex	Age	Parish where respondent spent most of his or her childhood
F	92	Kingston (urban)
F	60	St. Elizabeth (rural)
F	80	Clarendon (rural)
F	103	St. Elizabeth (rural)
M	81	St. Elizabeth (rural)
F	100	Westmoreland (rural)
F	61	Kingston (urban)
M	75	Portland (rural)
M	61	Hanover (rural)
F	78	St. Andrew (urban)

Source: Primary data, 2013

Past Childhood: Nostalgic Memories

All ten senior citizens were of the view that their childhood was better than what children of today experience. There was communal raising of children in both the rural and the urban areas. These statements reflected their sentiments:

- "They (the neighbours) treated you as their own; people would look out for you … you knew them well. We would spend all day outside with our neighbours and the children were basically shared." (Senior citizen, female, 60 year old, raised in St. Elizabeth [rural area])
- "Our neighbours were interested in them (children). They see that the children were ok and that no one interfered with us. If someone troubled you; they would speak to that person." (Senior citizen, female, 92 year old, raised in Kingston [urban area])

The communities were safer and "there was no place that people avoided" (senior citizen, female, 80 year old, raised in Clarendon [rural area]). They all agreed that communities were less safe for the children today and communal raising of children had ended.

A wide generational gap exists. These senior citizens were not impressed by the behaviour of the children today. When asked how they would describe today's children, the common theme among the female senior citizens was that children were badly behaved and rude:

- "No manners—not even in school—throwing lick back on teachers—assaulting teachers." (Senior citizen, female, 103 year old, raised in St. Elizabeth [rural area])
- "So rude and badly behaved." (Senior citizen, female, 78 year old, raised in St. Andrew [urban area])
- "Different. The change of time caused this because they were more orderly and better behaved as well as more respectful in my day." (Senior citizen, female, 92 year old, raised in Kingston [urban area])

The senior males pointed to the high intelligence of the children today and the better facilities that they are exposed to:

- "Dem bright; quick to learn." (Senior citizen, male, 61 year old, raised in Hanover [rural area])
- "Exposed to what we were not exposed to." (Senior citizen, male, 75 year old, raised in Portland [rural area])
- "They have better facilities now." (Senior citizen, male, 81 year old, raised in St. Elizabeth [rural area])

They all decried the poverty that they had to endure during childhood but said that life was fun. The main problem highlighted was parenting (especially by both male and female senior citizens):

- "Parents don't have time for them, so they get rude." (Senior citizen, female, 92 year old, raised in Kingston [urban area])
- "Father and mother abandonment—children begging on the streets." (Senior citizen, male, 81 year old, raised in St. Elizabeth [rural area])
- "Not enough love." (Senior citizen, female, 103 year old, St Elizabeth [rural area]).
- "Parents cannot parent: children having children." (Senior citizen, 61 year old, raised in Hanover[rural area])

One senior male highlighted the negative impact of technology:

- "Children are too influenced by technology, the media and all the negative influences." (Senior citizen, male, 75 year old, raised in Portland [rural area])

They all lamented that violence was the problem that children faced in Jamaica, every day.

There was no discussion about rights during their childhood but there was no need to speak about rights. The common view was:

- "Our parents were loving; they treated us well, sent us to school and gave us lots of love; there was no need for rights." (Senior citizen, female, 92 year old, raised in Kingston [urban area])

Consequently,

- "As a child, you don't think you have more rights than everyone else; you don't think you have rights. As a matter of fact; you just know that it is a privilege to be there and to do something. Looking back, you can see that you had a right, but you did not know at the time; it wasn't obvious and there was no need really to have rights." (Senior citizen, male, 75 year old, raised in Portland [rural area])

Above all,

"Children should be seen and not heard." (Senior citizen, female, 80 year old, raised in Clarendon [rural area])

Children's Voices

We introduce some of the views of the 103 Jamaican high school children in this chapter. Their views will further be discussed in most of the subsequent chapters. We focus now on their views on the quality of their childhood. Unlike the senior citizens, these children did not have any previous reference point and 72 per cent of them rated the quality of life in Jamaica as fair to very good (Table 2.5). This is in spite of the poor economic context and the high levels of crime discussed earlier in this chapter.

While the senior citizens highlighted the issue of poor parenting, the children themselves (79.6 per cent of them) gave their parents high ratings from 4 to 5 (Table 2.6).

Those who rated their parents less than 4 gave some of the following reasons:

- *Mom is not a good Mom; Grand Mom take care of me.*
- *My father treats me very badly; he treats his step children better than me.*
- *At home, my voice is not heard, I am shouted; sometimes, one meal per day.*
- *They over-exaggerate for the simplest things and don't allow me to go out.*

Table 2.5 Rating of quality of life among 103 children living in urban areas in Jamaica (*N* = 103)

Rating	%
Excellent	11.7
Very good	10.7
Good	12.6
Fair	36.9
Bad	20.4
Very bad	7.7

Source: Primary data, 2013

Table 2.6 Perceived treatment by parents

Ratings	Frequency	Percentage
1	4	3.88
2	5	4.85
2.5	3	2.91
3	5	4.85
3.5	4	3.88
4	30	29.13
4.5	5	4.85
4.7	2	1.94
5	45	43.69
	103	100.00

Source: Primary data, 2013

The negative effect of migration was mentioned:

"My parents left my sister and me with a lady and go Bahamas and she put us in a children's home."

Poverty of course has deleterious effect on parenting as parents are usually

"[g]ood but economic crisis causes bad to come out."

The children themselves revealed the main problems that they face in Jamaica today (Table 2.7). The main problem that children face today is abuse/neglect/violence (33.1 per cent) and financial problems (29.1 per cent). While the senior citizens had pointed out that parenting was a serious problem, for the children themselves, family issues was the third main problem children in Jamaica faced today.

All the elite interviewees noted that children in Caribbean SIDS were under threat:

- "We do not value children; it is all talk and no action." (Child advocate: Jamaica)
- "In the family, by the State, most people do not treat children right." (Child advocate: St. Lucia)

These are some of the main findings from the analysis of the qualitative and quantitative data in Jamaica. While the samples are small, the findings indicate the high level of vulnerability that children face. The children see abuse/neglect/violence as the main problem that they confront,

Table 2.7 Problems that children face today in Jamaica

Issue	Percentage
Abuse/neglect/violence	33.1
Financial problems	29.1
Family issues	19.0
Nobody to talk to/cannot express/make decision	13.3
Others (e.g. jealousy, peer pressure)	5.5
Total (N = 103)	100

Source: Primary data, 2013

and they highlight the issue of financial deprivation. The senior citizens noted the changing nature of childhood and the loss of communal parenting and safe environments.

In the previous chapter and this one, we examined the international, regional and local contexts which shape childhood in Caribbean SIDS. In the next chapter, we examine the endangerment to childhood posed by the high vulnerability of SIDS to climate change. This is in keeping with Fig. 2.1, discussed earlier.

Notes

1. https://history.hanover.edu/courses/excerpts/165rouss-em.html (Accessed February 23, 2016).
2. https://sustainabledevelopment.un.org/topics/sids/memberstates (Accessed February 23, 2016).
3. http://www.doingbusiness.org/content/dam/doingBusiness/country (Accessed May 13, 2019).
4. www.un.org/esa/dsd/dsd_aofw_sids/sids_pdfs/BPOA.pdf.
5. http://www.SIDS2014.org/samoapathway (Accessed February 23, 2016).
6. Violence against children in Haiti-findings from a national survey 2012. http://www.cdc.gov/violenceprevention/pdf/violence-haiti.pdf (Accessed February 23, 2016).
7. http://data.worldbank.org/indicator/SL.UEM.1524.NE.ZS (Accessed February 23, 2016).
8. http://data.worldbank.org/indicator/SH.HIV.0014 (Accessed February 23, 2016).
9. http://www.who.int/gho/countries/en/index.html (Accessed February 23, 2016).
10. http://www.prisonstudies.org/map/caribbean (Accessed February 23, 2016).
11. Extract from UNICEF (2012). Sexual violence against children in the Caribbean. http://www.unicef.org/easterncaribbean/ECAO_Sexual_Violence_againstChildren_in_the_Caribbean.pdf (Accessed June 1, 2018).

12. The index identifies deprivations across the same three dimensions as the HDI and shows the number of people who are multi-dimensionally poor (suffering deprivations in 33 per cent or more of weighted indicators) and the number of deprivations with which poor households typically contend. Source: http://hdr.undp.org/en/content/multidimensional-poverty-index-mpi (Accessed April 2, 2019).

13. https://data.worldbank.org/indicator (Accessed April 2, 2019).

14. http://data.worldbank.org/indicator/SP.DYN.IMRT.IN (Accessed April 3, 2019).

15. http://data.worldbank.org/indicator/SP.DYN.IMRT.IN (Accessed April 3, 2019).

References

Academic Council on the United Nations System (ACUNS). (2009). Challenges facing small states at the UN. Speech by Ambassador Vanu Gopala Menon, Permanent Representative of Singapore to the United Nations.

Almon, J. (1998). Endangered childhood. *The Online Waldorf Library*. Retrieved May 21, 2018, from http://www.waldorflibrary.org/journals/22-research-bulletin/484-june-1998-volume-03-2-endangered-childhood.

Bailey, B., & Charles, S. M. (2008). *The missing generation: A situational analysis of adolescents (10–14) in the Caribbean Community*. UNICEF and CARICOM.

Bandura, A. (1977). *Social learning theory*. Englewood Cliffs, NJ: Prentice Hall.

Barrow, C. (2011). Caribbean early childhoods. Socialization, motherhood, poverty and rights. Sir Arthur Lewis Institute of Social and Economic Studies, Mona Campus, Kingston, Jamaica.

Brathwaite, B. (2009). An exploration of Youth Risks in the Caribbean, through the voices of youth. Retrieved June 28, 2008, from http://sta.uwi.edu/conferences/09/salises/documents/B%20Brathwaithe.pdf.

Briguglio, L., & Kisanga, E. J. (2004). *Vulnerability and resilience of small states*. Malta: Commonwealth Secretariat and Islands and Small States Institute of the University of Malta.

Bronfenbrenner, U. (1979). *The ecology of human development*. Harvard College.

Bronfenbrenner, U., & Morris, P. A. (1998). The ecology of developmental processes. In W. Damon & R. M. Lerner (Eds.), *Handbook of child psychology, Vol. 1: Theoretical models of human development* (5th ed., pp. 993–1023). New York: John Wiley & Sons Inc.

Burke, C. (2004). Theories of childhood. *Encyclopaedia of children and childhood in history and society*. Encyclopedia.com, February 16, 2016. Retrieved June 21, 2018, from http://www.encyclopedia.com/doc/1G2-3402800409.html.

Burke, T. (2008). The problem with social construction. Retrieved May 1, 2018, from https://blogs.swarthmore.edu/burke/blog/2008/11/03/the-problem-with-social-construction/.

Caribbean Journal. (2015). 12 challenges facing Caribbean Small Island Developing States. Retrieved May 1, 2018, from http://caribjournal.com/2015/03/08/12-challenges-facing-caribbean-small-island-developing-states/#.

Commonwealth Secretariat. (2000). *A commonwealth vulnerability index for developing countries*. Retrieved May 1, 2018, from http://www.thecommonwealth-ilibrary.org/commonwealth/economics/a-commonwealth-vulnerability-index-for-developing-countries/the-commonwealth-vulnerability-index-cvi_9781848597167-4-en.

Cross, G. S. (1997). *Kids'stuff: Toys and the changing world of American childhood*. Cambridge, MA: Harvard University Press.

Drakes, M. L., Thomas, M. C., Craigwell, R., & Greenidge, K. (2012). *Threshold effects of sovereign debt: Evidence from the Caribbean* (No. 12–157). International Monetary Fund.

Dubois, D., & Prade, H. (2012). *Possibility theory* (pp. 2240–2252). New York: Springer.

Easterly, W., & Kraay, A. (2000). Small states, small problems? Income, growth, and volatility in small states. *World Development, 28*(11), 2013–2027.

Elkind, D. (1981). *The hurried child: Growing up too fast too soon*. Reading, MA: Addison-Wesley.

Erikson, E. H. (1950). *Childhood and society*. New York: Norton.

Freud, S. (1910). The origin and development of psychoanalysis. *American Journal of Psychology, 21*(2), 196–218.

Giroux, H. A. (2001). *Stealing innocence: Youth, corporate power, and the politics of culture*. New York: Palgrave.

Girvan, N. (2012, November). Colonialism and neo-colonialism in the Caribbean: An overview. In *IV International Seminar Africa, the Caribbean and Latin America; St. Vincent and the Grenadines*.

Hall, G. S. (1904). *Adolescence, its psychology and its relations to physiology, anthropology, sociology, sex, crime, religion and education*. New York: D. Appleton.

Handel, G., Cahill, S., & Elkin, F. (2007). *Children and society: The sociology of children and childhood socialization*. Roxbury Publishing Company.

Henry-Lee, A., & Meeks-Gardner, J. (Eds.). (2008). *Promoting child rights: Selected papers from the Caribbean Child Research Conference 2006, Volume 1*. Sir Arthur Lewis Institute of Social and Economic Studies, Mona Campus, Jamaica.

Hill, J. (2011). Endangered childhoods: How consumerism is impacting child and youth identity. *Media, Culture and Society, 33*(3). University of British Columbia, Canada. Retrieved October 19, 2018, from http://mcs.sagepub.com/content/33/3/347.abstract

Holzmann, R., Sherboune-Benz, L., & Tesliuc, E. (2003). The World Bank's approach to social protection in a globalizing world. Retrieved November 21, 2018, from http://siteresources.worldbank.org/SOCIALPROTECTION/Publications/20847129/SRMWBApproachtoSP.pdf.

James, C. (2015). *Childhood sexual and physical abuse in Caribbean Young Adults and its association with depression, PTSD and skin bleaching*. Paper presented at the Sir Arthur Lewis Institute of Social and Economic Studies, Mona Campus, Kingston, Jamaica, December 1, 2015.

Jenks, C. (2005). *Childhood*. London and New York: Routledge.

Jones, A. D. (2013). *Understanding child sexual abuse perspectives from the Caribbean*. London: Palgrave Macmillan.

Kincheloe, J. L., & Steinberg, S. R. (Eds.). (1997). *Kinderculture: The corporate construction of childhood*. Westview Press.

Kjørholt, A. T. (2013). Childhood as social investment, rights and the valuing of education. *Children & Society, 27*, 245–257.

Lee, G. (2014). Endangered childhood. Retrieved December 10, 2018, from http://www.thechildrensforum.com/downloads/news/Childhood%20an%20endangered%20species%20gil%202014.pdf.

Mead, M. (1961). *Coming of age in Samoa: A psychological study of primitive youth for Western civilization*. New York: Morrow.

McLeod, S. A. (2015). Biological psychology. Retrieved December 10, 2018, from www.simplypsychology.org/biological-psychology.html.

Neal, J. W., & Neal, Z. P. (2013). Nested or networked? Future directions for ecological systems theory. *Social Development, 22*(4), 722–737.

Piaget, J. (1936). *Origins of intelligence in the child*. London: Routledge & Kegan Paul.

Postman, N. (1994). *The disappearance of childhood*. New York: Vintage Books.

Qvortrup, J. (Ed.). (1994). *Childhood matters: Social theory, practice, and politics.* Aldershot, UK: Avebury.

Smith, L. C., & Haddad, L. (2002). How potent is economic growth in reducing undernutrition? What are the pathways of impact? New cross-country evidence. *Economic Development and Cultural Change, 51*(1), 55–76.

The Commonwealth. (2014). Small states and the commonwealth—Strengthening resilience for sustainable development. Commonwealth Secretariat.

United Nations Development Programme (UNDP). (2016). Caribbean Human Development Report: Multidimensional progress: Human resilience beyond income. Retrieved April 9, 2019, from http://hdr.undp.org/sites/default/files/undp_bb_chdr_2016.pdf.

Watson, J. B. (1924). *Behaviorism.* New York: People's Institute Publishing Company.

Watson, J. B., & Rayner, R. (1920). Conditioned emotional reactions. *Journal of Experimental Psychology, 3*(1), 1–14.

Williams, A., Cheston, T., Coudouel, A., & Subran, L. (2013). Tailoring social protection to Small Island Developing States—Lessons from the Caribbean. In *Social Protection and Labor Discussion Paper*, No. SP 1306. Washington DC: World Bank. Retrieved May 21, 2018, from http://documents.worldbank.org/curated/en/2013/08/18086868/tailoring-social-protection-small-island-developing-states-lessons-learned-caribbean.

World Bank. (1990). *World Bank development report.* Oxford: Oxford University Press.

3

Climate Change, Childhood and Caribbean SIDs

Even the natural environment in which children in SIDS experience childhood endangers them. Based on the conceptual framework presented in Chap. 1, we examine the endangerment of children in their natural environments. While all countries are affected by climate change, poor, developing countries are likely to be more severely affected, as they already have fewer resources and are typically tackling severe socio-economic problems which usually accompany slow development. Climate change and natural disasters therefore exacerbate the vulnerabilities of these countries, putting extra pressure on their already ravaged economies, and their health and education sectors.

Caribbean SIDS are susceptible to the negative impact of climate change and urgent climate action is needed to reduce their vulnerability:

Global emissions, the main cause of human induced climate change, are rising at their fastest rate in history, even as we bear witness to massive and accelerating ice loss from the ice sheets of Greenland and Antarctica, and a doubling of the rate of sea level rise. We are at a major turning point in the history of mankind. Are we willing to sacrifice the most vulnerable members of the international

© The Author(s) 2020
A. Henry-Lee, *Endangered and Transformative Childhood in Caribbean Small Island Developing States*, Studies in Childhood and Youth,
https://doi.org/10.1007/978-3-030-25568-8_3

community? This is the stark choice we face. But after the islands disappear, who will be next? Inaction or inadequate action is inexcusable and morally indefensible, given the level of certainty of the scientific evidence before us, and the technological and financial tools at our disposal to effect the necessary change. While some useful progress was made at the Durban Climate Change Conference in December last year, we are not close to finding a solution to this problem. (Former Minister of Foreign Affairs, Barbados)[1]

Children in SIDS are particularly vulnerable physically and emotionally. They are especially sensitive to climatic changes as they are less able physiologically and metabolically to adapt (Akachi et al. 2009). The increase in natural disasters is associated with climate change. Using secondary data on past natural disasters, this chapter examines the impact of climate change on children in Barbados, Jamaica, Haiti and St. Lucia. There are not much data on the direct impact on children as the data are usually presented on the national level and on adults, but wherever possible, the direct impact on children is discussed. The data analysis shows that great losses have been incurred by these islands and children in poorer households were more negatively affected and endangered.

Climate Change and Its Impact

The *Oxford Dictionary* defines "climate change" as follows:

A change in global or regional climate patterns, in particular a change apparent from the mid- to late 20th century onwards and attributed largely to the increased levels of atmospheric carbon dioxide produced by the use of fossil fuels.[2]

There are several negative impacts of climate change. The rising temperatures result in many heat-related illnesses and even death. The long periods of drought and deluges and warming temperatures have contributed to more outbreaks of malaria, fevers—such as dengue, tick-borne encephalitis, and diarrhoeal illnesses.[3] It is known that the warmer temperatures facilitate the survival of disease-carrying insects, animals and microbes, while colder weather destroys them. Majumder (2015, 21) noted that in 2003, extreme heat waves caused more than 20,000 deaths in Europe and more than 1500 deaths in India. The World Health Organization (WHO) reported that climate change may have caused more than 150,000 deaths in 2000 alone and warned of a likely increase in death in the future.[4] There is an association between climate fluctuation and many prevalent human maladies, for example, cardio-vascular mortality and respiratory illnesses due to heat waves to altered transmission of infectious diseases and malnutrition as a result of crop failure.[5]

Climate change also has a negative impact on world economies. A British government report notes that climate change could cost between 5 and 20 per cent of the annual global gross domestic product.[6] Another report out of the United States warns that an increase in floods and hurricanes could cost billions of dollars in property and infrastructure. "Property and infrastructural damage can cause major costs and inconvenience to members of the society and slow down the economy."[7]

Climate change also causes an increase in intense hurricanes and storms. It is estimated that between 1980 and 2011, more than 5.5 million people were affected by floods, which caused direct economic losses of more than €90 billion.[8] Industries such as agriculture, forestry, energy and tourism are particularly vulnerable to climatic changes.[9]

Food supply and security are also negatively impacted, especially in developing countries, as they depend heavily on their natural environment, and they are already grappling with the problem of having the least resources to cope with the changing climate. Children are also usually most at risk when food supply is restricted, and it is noted that food insecurity is associated with a range of adverse health outcomes among young children.[10]

The World Health Organization also noted the importance of access to water and how access would be diminished by climatic changes.[11] There are scarcities of water, which is essential for hygiene, and excess water due to more frequent and torrential rainfall. Lack of access to safe water will increase the incidence of diarrhoeal disease, which is spread through contaminated food and water. Currently, diarrhoeal disease is already the second leading infectious cause of childhood mortality and accounts for a total of approximately 1.8 million deaths each year.[12]

International Response to Climate Change Issues

There have been several international responses to climate change issues. We will examine some of them. In June 1992, the United Nations Framework Convention on Climate Change (UNFCCC) was adopted at the Earth Summit in Rio de Janeiro, Brazil, and entered into force on March 21, 1994.[13] This was the first global political response to climate change. Parties came to the agreement recognizing and acknowledging the role of humans in substantially increasing the atmospheric concentrations of greenhouse gases; that developed countries are the primary contributors of global emissions of greenhouse gases; and that the contribution of same by developing countries is relatively low. The Convention also acknowledged that small island developing countries are particularly vulnerable to the adverse effects of climate change.

Having acknowledged the above, the parties agreed that the ultimate objective of the Convention was to stabilize greenhouse gas concentrations "at a level that would prevent dangerous anthropogenic (human induced) interference with the climate system."[14] This level "should be achieved within a time frame sufficient to allow ecosystems to adapt naturally to climate change, to ensure that food production is not threatened and to enable economic development to proceed in a sustainable manner."[15]

Developed countries which are Parties to the Convention are charged with taking the lead in combatting climate change and its adverse effects. Full consideration is also to be given to the specific needs and special circumstances of developing country Parties, "especially those that are particularly vulnerable to the adverse effects of climate change … especially developing country Parties that would have to bear a disproportionate or abnormal burden under the Convention."[16] Developed country

Parties under the Convention also agreed to provide financial support for action on climate change to their developing nation Parties counterparts, and for those which are particularly vulnerable to the adverse effects of climate change, in meeting the costs associated with such effects. Technological support should also be given to developing courses to help them fulfil the provisions of the Convention. It also established the Conference of the Parties (COP) as its supreme body, charged with periodic review of these and subsequent commitments, further stipulating that after its first session to be held by its interim secretariat, the Conference would meet annually.

COP meetings were held in Berlin, Germany, and Geneva, Switzerland, in 1995 and 1996 respectively; however, it was not until COP 3 in Japan that another major agreement on climate change was reached, the Kyoto Protocol.

On December 11, 1997, the Kyoto Protocol was adopted, and it entered into force on February 16, 2005.[17] It was linked to and expanded the agreements of UNFCCC 1992. The Protocol recognized that developed countries are primarily responsible for the high levels of greenhouse gas emissions because of their historical industrial activity, and "places a heavier burden on developed nations under the principle of "common but differentiated responsibilities."[18]

The Protocol commits Parties to "pursue limitation or reduction of emissions of greenhouse gases"[19] through national policies and measures and in accordance with their national circumstances. These measures should be done in "such a way as to minimize adverse effects, including the adverse effects of climate change, effects on international trade, and social, environmental and economic impacts on other Parties, especially developing country Parties such as small island countries and countries with areas prone to natural disasters."[20]

Parties called for the actual emissions to be monitored and also agreed to formulate and update national, and where appropriate, regional programmes, containing measures to mitigate and to facilitate adequate adaptation to climate change. Developed country Parties could also provide, and developing country Parties could avail themselves of, the financial resources for the implementation of these measures. The Protocol also called for the first commitment period for the Protocol to start in 2008 and end in 2012.[21]

The sixth COP was held in Bonn, Germany, in 2001. In these so-called Bonn Agreements, accord was reached on a special climate change fund, which would be established to finance activities and programmes related to climate change in areas such as adaptation, technology transfer, waste management, and very importantly, activities to assist developing country Parties in diversifying their economies.[22] Specifically, three market-based mechanisms were agreed on, with the objective of achieving emissions reductions as cost-effectively as possible encompassing "emissions trading (the buying and selling of emissions credits among countries with binding emission targets); joint implementation (allowing one country with a target to receive emissions credit for a specific project undertaken in another country with a target); and the Clean Development Mechanism (CDM), (allowing developed countries to receive emissions credit for financing projects that reduce emissions in developing countries)."[23]

In New Delhi in 2002, the eighth COP adopted the Delhi Ministerial Declaration on Climate Change and Sustainable Development. This reiterated that all countries, particularly developing and small island developing states, faced an increased risk of the negative effects of climate change, and that the specific needs and concerns of developing country parties arising from these negative effects should be given full consideration.[24]

The Bali Road Map was adopted at the 13th Conference of the Parties in December 2007. It includes the Bali Action Plan, which is "a comprehensive process to enable the full, effective and sustained implementation of the UNFCCC through long-term cooperative action, up to and beyond 2012."[25] This was to be accomplished through cooperative action, and included a long-term global goal for emission reductions, aimed at achieving the ultimate objective of the UNFCCC, particularly in accordance with the principle of common but differentiated responsibilities.

At the United Nations Climate Change Conference held in Cancun, Mexico, in December 2010, a most comprehensive agreement was adopted to help developing nations deal with climate change. This package included finance, technology and capacity-building which would serve to better help developing countries in adapting to climate change. The Parties also agreed to reducing global greenhouse gas emissions in order to limit the increase in global average temperature to below 2 degrees Celsius above preindustrial levels, and that Parties should take urgent action to meet this long-term goal. It also acknowledged that Parties, especially developing country Parties, were to be given full consideration as they would have to bear a disproportionate or abnormal burden under the long-term cooperative action of the UNFCCC.

The 21st Conference of the Parties (COP) to the United Nations Framework Convention on Climate Change (UNFCCC)—the United Nations body which is responsible for climate change—took place from November 30 to December 15, 2011, in Paris, France. The country parties, in recognizing that climate change increasingly threatened development, poverty eradication efforts and the welfare of their citizens, reached a landmark agreement and accompanying decision on December 12, 2015, to stop or mitigate the natural consequences of climate change.

This agreement which culminated a four-year negotiating round, called for countries to limit temperature rise to well below 2, maybe even 1.5 degrees. It required "all countries to take action, while recognizing their differing situations and circumstances. Under the Agreement, countries are responsible for taking action on both mitigation and adaptation."[26]

The agreement and accompanying decisions[27] were to

- reaffirm the goal of limiting global temperature increase well below 2 degrees Celsius, while urging efforts to limit the increase to 1.5 degrees;
- establish binding commitments by all parties to make "nationally determined contributions" (NDCs), and to pursue domestic measures aimed at achieving them;
- commit all countries to report regularly on their emissions and "progress made in implementing and achieving" their NDCs, and to undergo international review;
- commit all countries to submit new NDCs every five years, with the clear expectation that they will "represent a progression" beyond previous ones;
- reaffirm the binding obligations of developed countries under the UNFCCC to support the efforts of developing countries, while for the

first time also encouraging voluntary contributions by developing countries; and

• extend the current goal of mobilizing $100 billion a year in support by 2020 through 2025, with a new, higher goal to be set for the period after 2025.

The agreement paved the way for implementing the current 2030 Sustainable Development Agenda, particularly the goals which spoke to ending poverty, building stronger economies and safer, healthier, and more liveable societies everywhere.[28] Twelve of the seventeen Sustainable Development Goals (SDGs) directly involve taking action on climate change.

The agreement, open for signature from April 22, 2016, to April 21, 2017, would only enter into force if approved through ratification, acceptance, approval or accession (whichever method a country uses for deciding whether to join an international agreement) by at least 55 Parties to the Convention accounting for at least 55 per cent of total global greenhouse gas emissions.

These are just some of the international agreements that have been made to reduce the negative impact of climate change, especially on the developing countries.

Climate Change and Caribbean SIDS

As discussed before, the developing countries are particularly susceptible to the impact of climate change. In SIDS, hundreds of poor households live in poorly constructed buildings made from inferior material. Women and children are particularly vulnerable as they are more exposed to physical harm and injury during and after natural disasters. Homeless children and those with disabilities are even more susceptible to the negative impacts of natural disasters.

The damage caused by natural disasters has been tremendous as evident in Table 3.1.

The increase in natural disasters is associated with climate change. The Caribbean islands, because of their geology, location and geography, are

Table 3.1 Economic costs for selected SIDS countries experiencing severe natural disasters, 2000–2017

Country economic	Year	Disaster	Cost ($)	Damage % of GDP
Barbados@	2010	Tropical Storm	US$37,000	n.a.
Jamaica[a]	2017	Rainfall	J$4 billion	0.2
Haiti	2010	Earthquake	US$8 billion	121
St. Lucia	2011	Hurricane		34
Caribbean				

Sources: @; Evanson (2014, 51–52)
Extracted from IMF Policy paper available at https://www.imf.org/external/np/pp/eng/2016/110416.pdf (Accessed September 15, 2017) and Caribbean Human Development Report, 2016
[a]http://www.pioj.gov.jm/Portals/0/Sustainable_Development/Macro%20Socio-economic%20and%20Environmental%20Impact%20Assessment%20of%20the%20Damage%20and%20Loss%20caused%20by%20the%20March%20to%20June%202017%20Rains.i.pdf

prone to several natural hazards. The major threats include hurricanes, floods, landslides, droughts and earthquakes. According to the Association of Caribbean States, for the period 1990–2008, the Caribbean experienced 165 natural disasters. The total impact including damage and losses for this period was estimated at US$136 billion, with the economic impact being the highest at US$63 billion (46 per cent). It is estimated that the impact of the 2004 hurricane season in the Caribbean (measured by the sum of indirect losses and damages) totaled more than US$3 billion. This translated into significant proportions of GDP, ranging from approximately 10 per cent in Jamaica to more than 200 per cent in Grenada Association of Caribbean States.

In the analysis of the economic impact of disasters on imports and external debt, the period 1990–2008 saw increases in imports in the Caribbean between the year prior to, and the year of the natural disaster (Association of Caribbean States n.d.). From 2003 to 2004 when Hurricane Ivan occurred, there was a 4 per cent increase in the Bahamas; in Belize and Grenada, a 7 per cent increase; and in Jamaica an increase of 2 per cent (Association of Caribbean States n.d.). In 2010, St. Lucia suffered damages in excess of 50 per cent of the GDP as a result of the impact of Hurricane Tomas (UNICEF 2011, 34). The impact of hurricane Sandy on Haiti in 2012 was devastating, with 52 confirmed deaths, at least a dozen missing and some 200,000 people left homeless

[29](*Guardian*, 2012). In Cuba, Hurricane Sandy left 11 dead and 137,000 damaged homes. Caribbean countries have suffered great loss from natural disasters.[30]

A prevalent Vulnerability Index (PVI) was calculated for some Caribbean SIDS (Sarmiento and Hoberman 2011, 16). This index discusses the vulnerability conditions by measuring exposure and susceptibility (ES), socio-economic fragility (SF), and lack of social resilience (LR) in disaster-prone areas. According to the Inter-American Bank for Development (IABD), PVI varies between 0 and 100; a value of 80 indicates very high vulnerability, 40 to 80 indicates high, 20 to 40 indicates a medium value, and less than 20 indicates a low value (Sarmiento and Hoberman 2011). The authors reveal that the individual contributions of the three components (exposure and susceptibility, socio-economic fragility, and lack of social resilience) to the PVI (Sarmiento and Hoberman 2011). The data show a reduction in vulnerability until 2005, which is more evident in Barbados and much less intense in the other countries discussed in the table. The data reveal that, in 2007, a slight increase occurred in the indicator of lack of resilience in the four countries (Sarmiento and Hoberman 2011). This increase signifies that no risk prevention/mitigation investments occurred during that period. Comparing the three indicators, the lack of resilience makes the greatest contribution to prevalent vulnerability.

The occurrence of natural disasters in Barbados takes the form of hurricanes or tropical storms. As in other countries, when such disasters occur, they can impact on children's education and their parents' livelihoods when income-generating sectors or crops are affected (UNICEF 2009, 12). Natural disasters also affect other social systems that provide a sense of stability, normalcy and protection for children. Between 1900 and 2010, there were 8428 people affected and total damage for storms alone cost up to US$106,700,000 (Sarmiento and Hoberman 2011). There is no doubt that whatever affects a nation and individual households, affects children.

In Jamaica, the impact of natural disasters can be narrowed into four main categories: child protection, health, food and nutrition and education (Edwards and Morris 2008, 3–4). They noted that among the issues faced by children during and after a natural disaster, was the need for protection against becoming victims of violence, sexual abuse, or drugs. They also noted that the need for identification, tracing and reunification of families may arise if family members are separated. Among the health-related issues discussed by Edwards and Morris are acute respiratory infections and diarrhoeal diseases as well as increased psychosocial needs. They also noted that food and nutrition needed for growth and development were also affected. The normally balanced diets were prone to disruptions, food preparation could be less than adequate in places of shelter and prolonged periods of nutritional disruption could cause malnutrition and diseases. They observed that the education system might be interrupted by natural disasters since schools were often used as shelters, and that texts, uniforms and other essential school needs were often lacking in these times. Of great concern too was the lack of stimulation for pre-school children in shelters (Edwards and Morris 2008, 3–4).

Jamaica has experienced an increase in the frequency of natural disasters over the past 25–30 years. The impact of these hazards has resulted in significant social and economic losses. Between 1998 and 2004, there were approximately ten major weather-related disastrous events with significant economic implications. In 1998, there were three events totalling just under J$200 million in damage; in 2001, Hurricane Michelle resulted in damage valued at 0.8 per cent of GDP and cost 2.8 per cent of government revenue and grants. In 2002, damage was valued at 0.7 per cent of GDP while in 2004, Hurricane Ivan resulted in damages of J$35 billion.[31]

If you want to put the worst-case scenario together in the Western hemisphere (for disasters), it's Haiti. There's a wide variety of factors working against Haiti. One it is the hurricane track. The second is tectonics. Richard Olson, Florida International University Richard Olson International University, highlighted the environmental degradation and poverty which exacerbated Haiti's vulnerability.[32]

Haiti, the poorest country in the Caribbean, has been the worst hit by natural disasters. The year 2008 is an unforgettable one for many persons there. There were four storms, Fay, Gustav, Hanna and Ike. Three of them hit Haiti in twenty-one days. Masters (2008) estimated that 22,702 homes were damaged, about 84,625 homes were affected, 793 persons were killed, 593 injured and 310 missing after the storms. Some of the major natural disasters to impact Haiti are listed as follows:

i. 1770: Strong earthquake devastates Port-au-Prince in then French colony.

ii. 1842: Earthquake destroys Cap-Haitien and other cities in northern Haiti and in the Dominican Republic.

iii. 1935: Unnamed storm kills more than 2000 in Haiti before moving on to Florida as hurricane, where 400 die.

iv. 1946: Magnitude-8.1 quake strikes Dominican Republic and Haiti, causing tsunami that kills 1790 people.

v. 1954: Hurricane Hazel kills hundreds in Haiti.

vi. 1963: Hurricane Flora leaves more than 6000 dead in Haiti and Cuba.

vii. 1994: Hurricane Gordon blamed for hundreds of deaths in Haiti.

viii. 1998: Hurricane Georges destroys 80 per cent of Haiti's crops while killing more than 400.

ix. May 2004: Three days of heavy rains cause floods that kill more than 2600.

x. September 2004: Tropical Storm Jeanne causes flooding and landslides that kill 1900 and leave 200,000 homeless in Gonaives, Haiti's third-largest city.

xi. October 2007: Tropical Storm Noel triggers mudslides and floods, killing at least fifty-seven Haitians.

xii. August and September 2008: Three hurricanes and tropical storm kill some 800 in Haiti, devastate crops and cause $1 billion in damage.

xiii. January 12, 2010: Magnitude-7.0 quake levels buildings in Port-Au-Prince, raising fears of tens of thousands of deaths.
(http://www.seattletimes.com/nation-world/timeline-of-haitis-natural-disasters/)

Before they could recover from the 2008 disasters, Haitians were struck by a devastating earthquake with a magnitude of 7.0 according to the United Nations Evaluation Group (2010, 28). In 2010, a cholera epidemic affected more than 87,735 people and caused the deaths of more than 700 between January and October 2012. Similarly, the passage of Hurricane Sandy in October 2012 damaged and/or destroyed more than 6000 homes, 30 water networks and 150 schools, leaving some 54,000 people in need of shelter, 830,000 suffering from an interruption in access to water and some 50,000 children in need of education support (UNICEF-HAITI 2013).

A UNICEF-HAITI 2013 report points to an estimated 357,785 people (138,000 children) who were still living in crowded temporary settlements, dependent on aid and at higher risk of exposure to abuse and exploitation in 2013. These children will continue to have need for access to humanitarian and social services, while their families and caregivers are helped to make a sustainable move to communities of return (UNICEF-HAITI 2013). In Jamaica, during Hurricane Dean, 300,000 people affected, and up to 90,000 of those are children[33]

As their counterparts in the other Caribbean islands, children and their families in St. Lucia live under increased threat of natural and man-made hazards. These include hurricanes, storms, and volcanic eruptions (UNICEF 2009, 37). The 1700s–1800s saw heavy hurricanes/storms/floods occurring in St. Lucia with as much as 824 deaths as a result (National Emergency Management Organization 2014, 58). In the 2000s, there were reports of six hurricanes/storms/floods which accounted for a total of loss of eight lives (National Emergency Management Organization 2014, 58). As we are aware, natural disasters are dangerous, especially for those families who reside in low-lying coastal areas. In 2008, St. Lucia's coastal areas were severely affected by Hurricane Omar. Whatever the natural disaster, they all impact negatively on children. They all disrupt children's education, their parents' livelihoods and other social systems that provide stability and a sense of normalcy (UNICEF 2009, 37).

Natural Disasters can occur outside the hurricane season as St. Lucians learnt recently. On December 24 and 25, 2013, (well outside the hurricane season), a tropical trough passed over St. Lucia and produced extraordinarily heavy rains. The rainfall produced intense and rapid flash flooding. Based upon an initial assessment of impacts to each affected sector, that flood event resulted in total damage and loss of US$99.88 million (EC$267.76 million), equivalent to 8.3 per cent of St. Lucia's gross domestic product.[34] Transport infrastructure sustained the majority of damage (72 per cent), followed by infrastructure for agriculture (13 per cent), water and sanitation (6 per cent), and housing (4 per cent). Out of a total population of 180,870, 6 persons were confirmed dead, over 550 were displaced, and approximately 19,984 were directly impacted by the event.[35] In less than 24 hours, the lives of thousands of persons were impacted in a significant way.

Conclusion

Climate change has led to the intensification and increase in frequency of natural disasters. While there has been increasing global attention on the impact of climate change, developing countries are experiencing and will continue to experience the greatest negative impact of climate change. Children and their childhoods in Caribbean SIDS are constantly endangered as the very natural environment in which they live is susceptible to all kinds of natural disasters. These small islands with weak economies cannot recover quickly from the negative impact of these disasters.

When disasters occur, the greatest impact is on children, though there are indaequate data on this. However, given the analysis presented in this chapter, we see that all the islands under discussion have suffered great loss from natural disasters. Whatever the impact on the national level, children would be affected. Already vulnerable in normal times, their vulnerability is intensified by the impact of natural disasters as they are physically less able to fend for themselves and are more exposed to abuse and exploitation both during and after these occurrences. They usually suffer more trauma, attend school less and become more vulnerable to infectious diseases. Natural disasters disrupt childhood and may have long-lasting effects.

Before, during and after natural disasters, countries are duty bound to take care of their children and ensure that they are adequately provided for and protected from all harm. This is what we promised with the several international agreements that bind us. In the next chapter, we examine the deficiencies in the provision and in Chap. 5, we assess the levels of protection that we afford our children.

Notes

1. http://www.unmultimedia.org/radio/english/2012/10/184152/ (Accessed February 28, 2018).
2. http://www.oxforddictionaries.com/definition/english/climate-change (Accessed February 28, 2018).
3. http://www.nrdc.org/globalwarming/fcons/fcons2.asp (Accessed February 28, 2018).
4. http://www.nature.org/ourinitiatives/urgentissues/global-warming-climate-change/threats-impacts/human-health.xml (Accessed June 28, 2018).
5. http://www.nature.org/ourinitiatives/urgentissues/global-warming-climate-change/threats-impacts/human-health.xml (Accessed June 28, 2018).
6. http://www.nature.com/nature/journal/v438/n7066/pdf/nature04188.pdf . *Nature*—international weekly journal of science.
7. http://webarchive.nationalarchives.gov.uk/20130129110402/http:/www.hm-treasury.gov.uk/d/Executive_Summary.pdf (Accessed January 28, 2018).
8. http://ec.europa.eu/clima/change/consequences/index_en.htm (Accessed February 28, 2019).
9. http://ec.europa.eu/clima/change/consequences/index_en.htm (Accessed February 28, 2019).
10. http://ipcc.ch/pdf/assessment-report/ar5/wg2/WGIIAR5-Chap11_FINAL.pdf (Accessed June 2, 2018).
11. http://www.who.int/mediacentre/news/statements/2008/s05/en/ (Accessed March 20, 2018).
12. http://www.who.int/mediacentre/news/statements/2008/s05/en/ (Accessed March 20, 2018).
13. Information on the framework taken from: http://unfccc.int/essential_background/convention/items/6036.php (Accessed March 20, 2018).
14. Information on the framework taken from: http://unfccc.int/essential_background/convention/items/6036.php (Accessed March 20, 2018).
15. http://unfccc.int/files/essential_background/convention/background/application/pdf/convention_text_with_annexes_english_for_posting.pdf (actual agreement) (Accessed March 20, 2018).
16. Ibid.

17. Information on this protocol is taken from: http://unfccc.int/kyoto_protocol/items/2830.php (Accessed February 28, 2019).

18. Information on this protocol is taken from: http://unfccc.int/kyoto_protocol/items/2830.php (Accessed February 28, 2019).

19. United Nations Framework Convention on Climate Change—Kyoto Protocol. http://unfccc.int/kyoto_protocol/items/2830.php (Accessed February 28, 2019).

20. http://unfccc.int/resource/docs/convkp/kpeng.pdf (Accessed February 28, 2019).

21. Ibid.

22. http://www.c2es.org/international/negotiations/cop-6-bis (Accessed February 28, 2019).

23. http://www.c2es.org/international/negotiations/cop-6-bis (Accessed February 28, 2019).

24. http://unfccc.int/cop8/latest/1_cpl6rev1.pdf (Accessed February 28, 2019).

25. http://unfccc.int/resource/docs/2007/cop13/eng/06a01.pdf (Accessed February 28, 2019).

26. http://www.un.org/sustainabledevelopment/climate-change/ (Accessed March 20, 2018).

27. http://www.c2es.org/international/negotiations/cop21-paris/summary (Accessed March 20, 2018).

28. http://www.un.org/sustainabledevelopment/climate-change/ (Accessed March 20, 2018).

29. https://www.theguardian.com/world/2012/oct/30/sandy-superstorm-flooding-power-cuts (Accessed May 2, 2018).

30. Responding to Natural Disasters in the Caribbean http://www.mona.uwi.edu/cardin/virtual_library/docs/1145/1145.pdf (Accessed February 29, 2016).

31. http://www.mona.uwi.edu/cardin/virtual_library/docs/1091/1091.pdf (Accessed March 20, 2018).

32. http://www.azcentral.com/news/articles/20100113why-disasters-hit-haiti13-ON.html#ixzz41xN6RDaZ (Accessed May 19, 2018).

33. https://www.unicef.org/jamaica/emergencies_9570.htm (Accessed May 19, 2018).

34. http://www.drrinacp.org/sites/drrinacp.org/files/publication/St%20Lucia_JRDNA_pdf.pdf (Accessed May 19, 2018).

35. http://www.drrinacp.org/sites/drrinacp.org/files/publication/St%20Lucia_JRDNA_pdf.pdf (Accessed May 19, 2018).

References

Akachi, Y., Goodman, D. L., & Parker, D. (2009). Global climate change and child health: A review of pathways, impacts and measures to improve the evidence base. UNICEF Innocenti Research Centre.

Association of Caribbean States. (n.d.). Natural hazards in the Caribbean: Too costly to ignore? Retrieved January 23, 2018, from http://www.acs-aec.org/index.php?q=disaster-risk-reduction/natural-hazards-in-the-caribbean-too-costly-to-ignore.

Edwards, M. T., & Morris, K. A. N. (2008). Disaster Risk Reduction and vulnerable populations in Jamaica: Protecting children within the comprehensive disaster management framework. *Children Youth and Environments, 18*(1), 389–407.

Evanson, D. (2014). Country documentation for disaster rick reduction: Barbados, 2014. Department of Emergency Management (DEM). Retrieved January 23, 2018, from http://dipecholac.net/docs/files/784-documento-pais-barbados-web.pdf.

Hurricane Sandy News Blog. (2012). Hurricane Sandy: High winds and flooding hit US East Coast—Monday, October 29. *The Guardian*. Retrieved February 1, 2018, from http://www.theguardian.com/world/us-news-blog/2012/oct/29/hurricane-sandy-new-york-live-blog.

Majumder, M. (2015). *Impact of urbanization on water shortages in face of climatic aberrations*. London: Springer.

Masters, J. (2008). *Hurricanes and Haiti: A tragic history*. Ann Arbor, MI: WeatherUnderground. Retrieved February 21, 2018, from https://www.wunderground.com/hurricane/haiti.asp.

National Emergency Management Organization. (2014). St. Lucia: Country document for Disaster Risk Reduction. Retrieved July 11, 2019, from http://dipecholac.net/docs/files/869-documento-pais-saint-lucia-para-la-web.pdf.

Sarmiento, J. P., & Hoberman, G. (2011). Disaster risk management disparity in the Caribbean: Evidence from Barbados, Dominican Republic, Jamaica and Trinidad and Tobago. Latin American and Caribbean Center, Disaster Risk Reduction project, Florida International University.

United Nations Children Fund (UNICEF). (2009). Children in Barbados and the Eastern Caribbean: Child rights: The unfinished agenda. Retrieved March 21, 2018, from http://www.unicef.org/easterncaribbean/Child_Rights_-_The_Unfinished_Agenda.pdf.

United Nations Children Fund (UNICEF). (2011). Situation analysis of children and their families in the Eastern Caribbean. Retrieved February 10, 2018, from http://www.unicef.org/easterncaribbean/SITAN_Bdos.pdf.

United Nations Children Fund-Haiti (UNICEF-HAITI). (2013). Haiti. Retrieved March 21, 2018, from http://www.unicef.org/appeals/files/Haiti_HAC_2013_26_Dec.pdf.

United Nations Evaluation Group. (2010). Haiti earthquake response—Context analysis. Retrieved February 1, 2019, from https://www.alnap.org/system/files/content/resource/files/main/haiti-context-analysis-final.pdf.

4

Human Capital Investment in Children

Introduction

The case for adequate investment in children has repeatedly been made and is hardly disputed. Duty bearers have a responsibility to provide adequately for children (Article 4, Convention on the Rights of the Child [CRC]). They made that commitment by the adoption of the CRC. However, public and private deprivation could limit the quantity and quality of that provision. In the case of the SIDS, sluggish economic growth, high levels of indebtedness, poverty and inequality (see Chap. 2 for more discussion on characteristics of SIDS) can negatively impact the quality and quantity of the social investment in children. Inadequate and poor-quality provision by social institutions adversely affects quality of life and endangers childhood.

One cannot reasonably dispute that the quality of childhood has improved since emancipation and independence in Caribbean SIDS. A child is now less likely to die at childbirth; life expectancy has improved, and children have improved access to basic social services. Yet, inequities exist. Large proportions of children have limited access to good quality education; are leaving school too early and many of them with little or no

© The Author(s) 2020
A. Henry-Lee, *Endangered and Transformative Childhood in Caribbean Small Island Developing States*, Studies in Childhood and Youth,
https://doi.org/10.1007/978-3-030-25568-8_4

certification. Teenage pregnancy, high levels of drug use, attempted suicide and related mental health issues have a deleterious impact on childhood. Too many children experience an "endangered childhood" due to inadequate provision by duty bearers. While we are aware that there are several types of provision for children, we focus mainly on health, and education as the critical foci for the attainment of sustainable development, bearing in mind that research has shown:

> An investment in a child's well-being is an investment that generates returns over the long term and affects the prosperity and viability of society well into the future. (Berlinski and Schady 2015, 1)

The Right to Health

Health is a state of complete physical, mental and social well-being and not merely the absence of disease or infirmity.[1]

SDG 4: *Ensure healthy lives and promote well-being for all at all ages.*

All four Caribbean SIDS under discussion have implemented policies and programmes to provide health care to all their citizens. There are several ministries and departments to implement health policies and policies. In Barbados, a draft National Strategic Plan for Health (NSPH) for the period 2017–2022 is currently awaiting finalization. Some of the policies in Jamaica are National Strategic and Action Plan for the Prevention and Control of Non-Communicable Diseases in Jamaica 2013–2018 and the National Infant and Young Child Feeding Policy (2014). In Haiti, there is the Plan Stratégique de Nutrition (Strategic Nutrition Plan) and the Haiti's Health Sector Strategic Plan (July 2015–2020); and in St. Lucia, there was a National Strategic Plan for Health 2006–2011 (NSPH).

The World Health Organization (WHO) recommends that countries allocate at least 6 per cent of GDP to health. Barbados and Haiti recorded the highest proportions of health expenditure (percentage of GDP), exceeding the WHO recommendation for many years between 2007 and 2015 (Table 4.1). However, in Haiti, there has been a reduction in health expenditure since 2011; which may be due to its recovery efforts after the

Table 4.1 Expenditure on health since 2000 in selected Caribbean countries

| | Current health expenditure (% of GDP) | | | | | | | | |
| | Years | | | | | | | | |
Countries	2007	2008	2009	2010	2011	2012	2013	2014	2015
Barbados	6.25	6.78	6.98	6.93	7.40	8.32	8.15	7.68	7.46
Jamaica	5.09	5.49	5.25	5.38	5.48	5.26	5.83	5.51	5.93
Haiti	6.78	7.66	8.69	10.22	10.64	10.09	7.24	7.18	6.87
St. Lucia	6.03	6.14	6.16	6.62	6.87	6.95	7.26	5.78	5.96
Latin America and the Caribbean	6.7	6.6	7.1	6.9	6.8	6.7	6.8	6.9	7.4

Source: https://data.worldbank.org/indicator/SH.XPD.CHEX.GD.ZS (Accessed April 10, 2019)

2010 earthquake. In some years under review, Barbados' health expenditure as a percentage of GDP exceeded the Latin America and Caribbean figure (Table 4.1). Jamaica has never met the WHO recommendation and in St. Lucia, health expenditure as a percentage of GDP has been increased since 2000 but has fluctuated and was 5.96 of GDP in 2015. Haiti has exceeded the recommendations in all the years under review.

Among the four countries, per capita total expenditure on health is highest in Barbados with Haiti recording the lowest (Table 4.2). Private health expenditure as a percentage of current health expenditure (CHE) is also highest in Barbados and lowest in St. Lucia. For all other indicators of health provision, Barbados is highest; this is not surprising since the country has the highest HDI. For most of the indicators of health provision, Barbados exceeds the averages for the Latin America and the Caribbean region (Table 4.2).

Health Outcomes

Barbados has the best returns on its investment in health as it enjoys the best health outcomes (Table 4.3). Barbados boasts the highest life expectancy, together with Jamaica (Table 4.3). It is not surprising that Haiti with the lowest current health per capita records the worst health indicators in most instances. For example, life expectancy is at 63; under 5 mortality rate per 1000 is 72; maternal mortality ratio per 100,000 live

Table 4.2 Health provision in selected Caribbean countries

Indicator	Barbados	Jamaica	St. Lucia	Haiti	Latin American and the Caribbean
Current health expenditure (CHE) per capita in PPP, current US$ (2015)	1160.2	294.3	481.6	53.6	636.5
Domestic general government health expenditure (GGHE-D) as percentage of general government expenditure (GGE) (%), 2015	7.4	12.6	8.5	3.4	10.3
Domestic private health expenditure (PVT-D) as percentage of current health expenditure (CHE) (%), 2015	52.5	40.5	39.2	52.6	47.5
Population using improved drinking-water, 2018 (%)[a]	99.9 (u) 99.7 (r)	97.5 (u) 89.4 (r)	99.5 (u) 95.6 (r)	64.9 (u) 47.6 (r)	97.4 (u) 83.9 (r)
Population using improved sanitation facilities, 2018[a]	96.2 (u) 96.2 (r)	79.9 (u) 84.1 (r)	89.7 (u) 91.9 (r)	33.6(u) 19.2 (r)	87.9 (u) 64.1 (r)
Psychiatrists working in mental health sector (per 100,000)[b]	4.29 ('11)	1.11 ('14)	1.09 ('14)	0.07 ('14)	NA

Source: https://data.worldbank.org/indicator/ (Accessed April 10, 2019)
Key: u: urban and r: rural
NA: No data available
[a]http://data.un.org/en/index.html (Accessed April 10, 2019)
[b]http://apps.who.int/gho/data/view.main.HWF11v (Accessed April 10, 2019)

births at 359 and low weight as a percentage of live births (2008–2012) is 23 (Table 4.3). Measles immunization rates are lowest in St. Lucia and Haiti. Access to skilled health personnel is high for all the countries under review except Haiti. Barbados fared best among the four countries when compared to its Latin American and Caribbean countries.

Table 4.3 Health outcomes in selected Caribbean countries

Indicator	Barbados	Jamaica	St. Lucia	Haiti	Latin America and the Caribbean
Life expectancy (2016)	76	76	75	63	76
Fertility rate (2016)	1.8	2.0	1.5	2.9	2.1
Under-5 mortality rate per 1000 live births (2017)	12	15	17	72	18
Maternal mortality ratio per 100,000 live births (2015)	27	89	48	359	67
Births attended by skilled health personnel (%)[a]	99	99	99	42	–
Measles immunization (% of children ages 12–23 months) (2017)	92	95	87	53	92
Low birth weight % live births (2008–2012)	11.5	11.3	10.1	23	8.9
Prevalence of HIV among adults aged 15–49 years (2017) %	1.6	1.8	–	1.9	0.5

Source: https://data.worldbank.org/indicator (Accessed April 10, 2019)
[a]http://apps.who.int/gho/data/node.imr (Accessed April 10, 2019)

HIV/AIDS

Children are being left behind. The good news is that 1.4 million new HIV infections have been averted since 2010, but I am distressed by the fact that, in 2017, 180,000 children became infected with HIV, far from the 2018 target of eliminating new HIV infections among children.[2] (Michel Sidibe, UNAIDS Executive Director, 2018)

UNAIDS (2018) noted that globally, a reduced number of persons are dying from AIDS; an increased number of persons are accessing antiretroviral therapy and three out of four persons know their HIV status. However, the number of new cases of HIV is not falling fast enough and there is a growing complacency in the fight against HIV/AIDS (UNAIDS 2018).

The Caribbean has made strides in reducing the mother-child transmission. The Caribbean and Latin America is committed to jointly fighting the HIV epidemic and improving the lives of people living with the illness.[3] Labelled the "90-90-90" targets, Latin America and the Caribbean and their partner organizations have set new goals for expanding diagnosis and antiretroviral treatment (ART) and reducing patients' viral loads by 2020. These targets include increasing the proportion of people with HIV who know their status by 90 per cent; increasing the proportion of people receiving antiretroviral treatment by 90 per cent and increasing the proportion of people under treatment who have an undetectable viral load also by 90 per cent.[4]

Children in the Caribbean live in a region with the highest incidence of reported AIDS cases in the Americas and which has an adult HIV prevalence rate between 1.9 per cent and 3.1 per cent, second only to Africa (7.5 per cent and 8.5 per cent).[5] There are between 350,000 and 590,000 Caribbean people living with HIV/AIDS in the region.[6] UNAIDS 2018 reports that nearly 90 per cent of new infections in the Caribbean in 2017 were reported in four countries—Cuba, the Dominican Republic, Haiti and Jamaica—while 87 per cent of deaths from AIDS-related illness occurred in the Dominican Republic, Haiti and Jamaica. Haiti accounts for nearly half of new HIV infections and deaths due to AIDS-related illness and is one of the few countries in the region that does not provide comprehensive sexuality education in primary and secondary schools (UNAIDS 2018).

On the positive side, the rate of mother-to-child transmission in the Caribbean was 13.3 per cent (2017), among the lowest in the world and was lower than the 2010 rate of 18.7 per cent (UNAIDS 2018). Seven countries in the Caribbean have eliminated mother-to-child transmission of HIV: Anguilla, Antigua and Barbuda, the Cayman Islands, Cuba, Montserrat and Saint Kitts and Nevis (UNAIDS 2018). UNAIDS (2018) notes that stigma and discrimination hinder progress in the elimination of HIV. Of concern is the prevalence rate for the age group 15–19 years old in some countries. For example, in Jamaica, the HIV prevalence rate increased five-fold to between 0.4 and 0.5 per cent.[7]

Child Health Endangerment

There are certain other phenomena that endanger childhood in the Caribbean. In addition to under-nutrition, there is the increasing problem of obesity among children (Healthy Caribbean Coalition 2017; Malecka-Tendera and Mazur 2006; Shivpuri et al. 2012). One in every three children in the Caribbean is overweight or obese and this figure is growing (Healthy Caribbean Coalition 2017). There are deleterious effects of obesity that will impact the quality of life that these children enjoy. If uncontrolled, obesity will lead to many chronic illnesses.

There is a significant number of children who engage in risky behaviour. Among the 13–15 year olds, a third of them have engaged in sexual intercourse (Table 4.4). Of that number a third of them did not use a condom the last time that they had intercourse (Table 4.4). Boys report a higher incidence of sexual activity than girls (Table 4.4). At least one-third of the students interviewed had had sexual intercourse without using a condom and teenage pregnancy rates are high ranging from 72 per cent in Jamaica to 49.3 per cent in St. Lucia (Table 4.4).

Many have noted the increasing problem of unstable mental health among children (Loeber et al. 1998; Kieling et al. 2011; Schulte-Körne 2016). Socialization with close friends is an indicator of healthy relationships and healthy child development. However, some children aged 13–15 years have no close friends (Table 4.4). The incidence is higher in Jamaica and St. Lucia. Except for St. Lucia, a slighter larger proportion of boys are reporting having no close friends (Table 4.4). Suicidal ideation is higher in St. Lucia and high among girls in the countries with available data (Table 4.4).

St. Lucia reported the higher levels of violence among students aged 13–15 years (Table 4.5). A larger proportion of boys reported being in a physical fight one or more times during the twelve months before the survey (Table 4.5). Boys have reported higher levels of physical injury in the previous twelve months and they were also the target of bullying during that same time period (Table 4.5). All these are examples of at-risk behaviour that endanger childhood.

Table 4.4 Some at-risk indicators in selected Caribbean countries (aged 13–15 years old)

Country	Percentage of students who were obese			Percentage of students who ever had sexual intercourse			Among those who had sexual intercourse, the percentage of those who used a condom, the last time, they had sexual intercourse			Teenage pregnancy rates (2006–2010)[a] %	Percentage of students with no close friends			Percentage of students who ever considered attempting suicide in the last 12 months		
	Total	Boys	Girls	Total	Boys	Girls	Total	Boys	Girls		Total	Boys	Girls	Total	Boys	Girls
Barbados (2011)	14.2	13.9	14.6	33.5	44.0	23.1	64.9	65.3	64.6	49.5	6.2	8.0	4.3	NA	NA	NA
Jamaica (2017)	10.1	10.3	9.9	36.8	60.6	15.5	65.0	66.0	NA	72	8.8	9.6	8.0	24.8	17.5	31.5
St. Lucia (2007)	NA	NA	NA	26.1	38.0	16.8	53.5	48.0	NA	49.3	8.8	8.6	9.0	18.0	15.6	20.1

Source: World Health Organization Global School-based Student Health Survey. http://www.who.int/chp/gshs/datasets/en/ (Accessed March 25, 2014)

Note: Students aged about 13–15 years

NA: No data available

Data not collected in Haiti

[a]https://www.unicef.org

Table 4.5 Violence and unintentional injury (students aged 13–15 years old)

Country	Percentage of students who were in a physical fight one or more times during the 12 months before the survey			Percentage of students who were seriously injured one or more times during the 12 months before the survey			Percentage of students who were bullied on one or more days during the 30 days before the survey		
	Total	Boys	Girls	Total	Boys	Girls	Total	Boys	Girls
Barbados (2011)	38.4	47.9	28.3	41.3	46.4	35.9	13.3	15.4	11.0
Jamaica (2017)	34.5	44.3	25.4	39.6	45.4	34.0	25.5	26.3	24.8
St. Lucia (2007)	40.7	52.4	31.1	47.8	55.0	42.3	25.1	25.2	25.1

Source: World Health Organization Global School-based Student Health Survey.
  http://www.who.int/chp/gshs/datasets/en/ (Accessed April 13, 2019)
Note: Students aged about 13–15 years
No data collected for Haiti

Substance abuse among secondary school students has been flagged as a major concern (Oshodi et al. 2010; Arrazola et al. 2015). Tables 4.6 and 4.7 present prevalence rates (alcohol and marijuana) among secondary school students in the Caribbean. Of all the secondary school students interviewed, 67.9 per cent of them had a lifetime prevalence for alcohol (Table 4.6). Dominica and St. Lucia reported the highest levels of lifetime use of alcohol among its secondary school students while Guyana recorded the lowest. Dominica, St. Vincent and the Grenadines and St. Lucia have the highest past year prevalence while St Vincent and the Grenadines, St. Lucia and Dominica recorded the highest past month prevalence rates for alcohol use (Table 4.6). Guyana recorded the lowest past month prevalence use of alcohol (16.5 per cent) (Table 4.6).

While there have been proven benefits of marijuana use, it is not recommended that children use it without any supervision or medical guidance. Some of the negative effects of marijuana use include elation, anxiety, tachycardia, short-term memory recall issues, and sedation.[8] The highest lifetime prevalence rates for marijuana use among secondary school students aged 13–15 years was recorded in Dominica and Antigua

Table 4.6 Prevalence of alcohol and marijuana use among secondary school students in the Caribbean

Country	Alcohol			Marijuana		
	Lifetime prevalence	Past year prevalence	Past month prevalence	Lifetime prevalence	Past year prevalence	Past month prevalence
Antigua and Barbuda	71.1	56.0	36.2	31.0	22.4	16.7
The Bahamas	67.4	46.0	27.5	12.0	8.1	4.3
Barbados	71.2	56.3	32.8	22.0	16.9	11.0
Belize	65.1	47.6	32.2	23.9	15.7	10.5
Dominica	81.2	59.2	36.6	31.4	19.6	12.5
Grenada	72.0	54.7	35.0	19.5	12.9	7.0
Guyana	54.0	32.8	16.5	7.1	4.2	2.4
Haiti	56.6	35.4	23.0	3.2	2.4	1.2
Jamaica	65.0	45.0	24.1	21.1	11.9	6.3
St. Kitts and Nevis	65.5	44.5	25.9	24.2	16.1	11.6
St. Lucia	74.8	57.2	39.9	28.8	17.2	10.7
St. Vincent and the Grenadines	71.9	58.4	46.9	26.4	19.4	14.0
Trinidad and Tobago	66.9	49.4	27.6	16.6	10.7	6.2
Average	67.9	49.4	31.1	20.6	13.7	8.8

Source: OAS and CICAD 2016, 24 and 59

Notes: Lifetime prevalence: those who had used the substance anytime in the past

Last year or past year prevalence: Those who had used the substance in the past year before the survey was administered

Last month or past month: Those who had used the substance in the past month before the survey was administered and Barbuda with the lowest rate reported in Haiti (Table 4.6). Haiti also recorded the lowest past year and past month prevalence rates (Table 4.6).

Inequities in Health

At the macro level, the health data are fairly reasonable (except for Haiti) but these indicators mask some inequities. These inequities have negative implications for the quality of childhood that a child enjoys. Inequities in access persist with individuals (and ultimately children) in the rural areas having less access to safely managed sanitation services (Table 4.7). Rurality and poverty are intricately linked, with the highest proportions of persons living below the poverty line found in the rural areas (see Chap. 7 for further discussion on children living in poverty).

The most recently available data indicate that inequities in access exist in Jamaica with the poorest quintile having the least access to indoor taps/pipes and WCs linked to sewer. (Planning Institute of Jamaica. Survey of Living Conditions. 2016.)

Children with disabilities are also disadvantaged (see Chap. 7 for further discussion on challenges facing this group). For example, in its 2014

Table 4.7 Percentage of population using safely managed sanitation services, 2015

	Rural	Urban	Total
Bahamas	NA	NA	92
Barbados	NA	NA	96
Belize	84	91	87
Cuba	88	92	91
Dominican Republic	74	85	83
Grenada	NA	NA	88
Guyana	85	89	86
Haiti	22	37	31
Jamaica	87	84	85
St. Lucia	92	86	91
St. Vincent	NA	NA	87
Trinidad and Tobago	NA	NA	92

Source: http://apps.who.int/gho/data/view.main.GSWCAH52v (Accessed February 1, 2019)
NA: No data available

Report to the UN, Jamaica noted more needed to be done to help children with disabilities get improved access to a broader range of social services and reduce discrimination and stigma that these children face.

The Right to Education

SDG 4: *Ensure inclusive and equitable quality education and promote lifelong learning opportunities for all*

Article 28 of the CRC and SDG 4 call for UN members advocate for focussed attention to be paid on access to good quality education. Indisputably, investment in education is key to sustainable development. Good quality education impacts positively on the individual, the home/family and the society. There have been great improvements in the education system in the Caribbean in the last decades. An increased number of persons have access to school at all levels and completion rates have improved at all levels. However, access to inclusive and equitable good quality education remains elusive for several groups of children. Without access to good quality education, the quality of childhood and adulthood are compromised.

Since 2010, Barbados has experienced a decline in the percentage of total government expenditure on education while St. Lucia experienced a sharp increase from 2015 to 2016 (Table 4.8). The decline for Barbados may be due to the economic issues facing the country in recent years. Debt remains high at 123.6 per cent of GDP in 2018 (Table 2.2). Haiti also experienced a decline in education expenditure in 2017.

The largest proportion of the education budget is allocated to the secondary schools in Barbados and St. Lucia (Table 4.9). Barbados spends a fairly large proportion of its education budget on university education while St. Lucia spends the smallest proportion of its budget on that level. Primary school education receives the largest proportion of the education budget in Jamaica and St. Lucia. Even though research shows that investment in early childhood education yields the best returns on investment, available data show that these countries spend very little on that level.

Table 4.8 Expenditure on education in selected Caribbean countries

Government expenditure on education, total (% of government expenditure)

Countries	Years										
	2007	2008	2009	2010	2011	2012	2013	2014	2015	2016	2017
Barbados	18.1	15.6	16.1	18.1	–	16.7	14.8	17.5	–	14.1	12.9
Jamaica	17.2	19.1	17.6	16.1	18.6	18.8	20.6	21.8	20.1	19.1	18.4
Haiti	–	–	–	–	–	–	–	–	–	14.4	13.1
St. Lucia	–	19.9	13.9	14.2	13.8	12.2	13.8	15.3	16.5	22.4	–
Latin America and the Caribbean	16.4	18.1	17.3	17.1	15.9	16.8	16.9	16.8	18.1	18.0	

Source: https://data.worldbank.org/indicator/SH.XPD.CHEX.GD.ZS (Accessed April 10, 2019)

Table 4.9 Distribution of total education expenditure

% of total education expenditure	Barbados (2016)	Jamaica (2017)	Haiti (1991)	St. Lucia (2016)
Pre-primary/early childhood	NA	3.8	NA	1.4 (2015)
Primary	29.6	37.9	58.9	26.4
Secondary	39.3	36.3	21.1	30.8
University	31.1	19.3	10.2	5.0 (2011)

Source: https://data.worldbank.org/indicator/ (Accessed April 11, 2019)
NA: Not available

Education Outcomes

Cuba has recorded the highest pre-primary enrolment rate in the Caribbean (102 per cent) with Bahamas registering the lowest rate (32 per cent) in the 2012–2017 period.[9] For the countries under review and for which data are available, St. Lucia reported the highest pre-primary enrolment rate (82 per cent), with Jamaica reporting the lowest (76 per cent).[10] In Haiti, pre-school gross enrolment in 2007 was estimated at 67 per cent and almost all pre-schools were privately owned (Wolff 2008).

Samms-Vaughan (2016) noted that while enrolment was fairly high, the early childhood sector was in need of improvement:

1. The comprehensive review of current laws, policies and programmes to improve educational outcomes
2. Increased investment in early childhood sector was needed.

Primary school enrolment rates are fairly high in the Caribbean with the Dominican Republic recording the lowest (86.1 per cent) and Belize (96 per cent), the highest.[11] Jamaica and St. Lucia reported primary school enrolment rates of 88 and 93.4 per cent respectively. For Barbados, 90.8 per cent was recorded when compared with Trinidad and Tobago's enrolment rate of 95.2 per cent.[12]

Child Educational Endangerment

In spite of the fairly reasonable investment in education, there is evidence that educational outcomes are not as desired in the Caribbean. The education system is failing its children and not preparing them adequately for life above the poverty line. Approximately 11,000 pupils across the region who wrote the Caribbean Examination Council's Secondary Education Certificate (CXC/CSEC) Exam in May/June 2018 got no passes (Grades 1–3).[13] It should be noted that only 20 per cent of the eligible Caribbean population are allowed to write the CSEC Exam and of this cohort some 13 per cent pass no subjects. Those who receive no passes in the secondary school exit examinations are more likely to become minimum wage earners in adulthood.

The overall CSEC passes for Jamaica and St. Lucia were 68.4 per cent and 73.3 per cent respectively (Table 4.10). In Barbados, CSEC results showed a 68 per cent pass rate in 2015–2016 (Table 4.10). Primary to Secondary transition rates were relatively high. Jamaica recorded a transition rate of 95.39 and St. Lucia 96.81 (Table 4.10). Data on the number of students eligible to sit the exams and the number who actually sit the exams in these countries were not available.

Persistence to Grade 5—measured by share of children enrolled in the first grade of primary school who eventually reach Grade 5—was equally

Table 4.10 Educational outcomes in selected Caribbean countries

	Jamaica	St. Lucia	Barbados
CSEC pass rate–overall[a]	68.4 (2018)	73.3 (2017)	68 (2015/16)[d]
Drop-out rates–to the last grade of secondary (2016)[b]	3.98	3.17	NA
Persistence to Grade 5 (2013)[c]	95.39	92.14	94.46 (2010)
Primary to secondary transition rate (2016)[b]	94.52	96.81	

NA: No data available
[a]https://jis.gov.jm/increase-in-csec-passes;https://www.htsstlucia.org/saint-lucia-cxc-results-show-1-increase-in-pass-rates/
[b]http://data.uis.unesco.org/index.aspx?queryid=150
[c]https://data.worldbank.org/indicator/SE.PRM.PRS5.ZS?locations=BB-JM-LC
[d]https://www.google.com/search?q=2015%E2%80%932016_statistics_on_education_in_barbados_at_a_glance.pdf&rlz=1C1GCEA_enJM825JM825&oq=2015%E2%80%932016_statistics_on_education_in_barbados_at_a_glance.pdf&aqs=chrome..69i57.1316j0j7&sourceid=chrome&ie=UTF-8. Retrieved October 15, 2019

high in the three countries. For St. Lucia, the persistence rate in 2013 was 92.14 per cent and in Jamaica, it was 95.39 per cent. Barbados recorded a 94.46 persistence rate in 2010. However, some students do not even get to sit the secondary exit exams. Dropout rates (secondary) were higher for Jamaica (4 per cent) (Table 4.10).

Potential employers and college administrators look for passes in Mathematics and English to accept applicants in their businesses or colleges. However, not all children in the Caribbean are able to obtain passes in these two subjects. An assessment of the performance of students at the secondary exit showed that over the last three years, the percentage of passes in the core subjects (English Language, Mathematics and Information Technology) has fluctuated. Jamaica, for example, in the area of Mathematics showed a 14.3 percentage point drop from 2015 to 2016 sittings, with performance improving slightly to 50.2 per cent in 2017 and then declining again (Table 4.11). In St. Lucia, core subject passes did not surpass 70 per cent (Table 4.11). For Barbados, most recent available data reveal that the percentage passes for Mathematics and English Language were 56 per cent and 79 per cent respectively (Table 4.11).

Low academic performance may be caused by what transpires in the classroom. An analysis of primary data collected in a survey of 103 secondary school students in 2013 in Jamaica, showed that some children (25 per cent) felt that their teachers treated them very badly to fair at school (Table 4.12).The reasons for the low ratings of their teachers were: pay little attention to me/disrespect me (51 per cent); they don't like me (35 per cent) and they like to punish students (14 per cent).

While the sample is too small to generalize to the national level, these findings indicate that some students are not happy with the way they are treated by their teachers.

When asked if they were allowed to ask questions; some said:

- *dem teachers don' listen to anybody*
- *You cannot ask any question*
- *Teacher always shouting at us*
- *Teacher call we slow* (Responses of students, 2013)

Table 4.11 Passes at the secondary school level in three subjects in Jamaica, St. Lucia and Barbados

Jamaica					St. Lucia				Barbados
Percentage Passes									
Subjects	2015	2016	2017	2018[a]	Subjects	2015	2016	2017	2015/16
English Language	65	71.2	70.8	68.7	English Language	66.2	NA	NA	79
Mathematics	62	47.7	50.2	46.5	Mathematics	55.2	45.8	NA	56
Information Technology	85.5	75.2	82.6	–	Information Technology	NA	NA	NA	–

Sources: Jamaica-Planning Institute of Jamaica-ESSJ report 2017
St-Lucia: https://www.stlucianewsonline.com/csec-results-continue-to-improve-in-saint-lucia/; https://thevoiceslu.com/
  2016/08/s-j-c-tops-csec-exams/
Barbados: https://mes.gov.bb/Resources/Publications/
NA: No data available
[a]https://jis.gov.jm/increase-in-csec-passes/

Table 4.12 Perceived treatment of children by teachers in Jamaica

Rating	N	%
Very poorly	7	7
Poorly	10	10
Fairly	11	11
Well	49	47
Very well	26	25
Total	103	100

Source: Primary data collected by author

Students revealed that they generally liked their schools (72 per cent) but 28 per cent did not. For those who did not the reasons proffered were:

- *The work is too hard*
- *Teacher don' explain properly*
- *Too much tests* (Responses of students, 2013)

Inequities in Education

Disparities exist in private education expenditure with the poorest quintile investing the least in education. In Jamaica, the richest quintile invests three times as much in extra lessons for their children than the poorest quintile ($J33,883.00; J$12,509.00).[14] This higher expenditure prepares the children for their exit exams and increases their chances of performing well. The children in the poorer quintile without these extra lessons are less likely to perform well.

A child may be enrolled and not attend school regularly. Poverty impacts negatively on attendance. Using the most recent available data from Jamaica, we note that the children from the poorest quintile had the largest proportion of children who could not attend school because of financial issues (Planning Institute of Jamaica, 2017 p.31). Verner (2008) noted that children in rural areas in Haiti often faced a long travel time to go to school and for the poor, this was especially so, as they went to school on foot. Verner further revealed that of the youth aged 18–24, only 39.1 per cent attended formal education in Haiti, but the variation across location was large. A larger proportion of children from the urban areas were in school; of 18–24 year olds, 46.6 per cent were in school in the metropolitan area compared to only 32.8 per cent in the rural areas (Verner 2008).

Child advocates who were interviewed in these countries stated that poverty, poor parenting, inadequate financing, the lack of trained teachers and facilities in the rural areas and the urban poor areas; the shortage of spaces in the upper secondary schools and the levels of violence in schools were some of the reasons children were not performing better in the education system in the Caribbean.

Poor quality education endangers childhood and limits individual choice and upward mobility in the labour market. Large groups of under-educated and badly trained individuals will impact negatively on our societies and jeopardize the fulfilment of the UN2030 Agenda. Gender differentials exist and research reveals that girls are outperforming boys at all levels of the system (Jackson et al. 2010; Parry 1997). A larger proportion of incarcerated are males. These educational outcomes indicate that the children are not performing and that there are systemic problems in the education sector.

Earlier in this chapter, we saw that several at-risk behaviours, mental health issues and high levels of teenage pregnancy and HIV prevalence rates make it difficult for all children to enjoy their childhood and become productive adults. Analysis of both primary and secondary data reveals that child endangerment exists in health and education sectors in the Caribbean.

Notes

1. https://www.who.int/about/who-we-are/constitution (Accessed April 9, 2019).
2. http://www.unaids.org/sites/default/files/media_asset/unaids-data-2018_en.pdf (Accessed April 13, 2019).
3. http://www.paho.org/hq/index.php?option=com_content&view=article&id=9655%3A2014-90-targets-controlling-epidemic-america-caribbean&catid=740%3Apress-releases&Itemid=1926&lang=en.
4. http://www.paho.org/hq/index.php?option=com_content&view=article&id=9655%3A2014-90-targets-controlling-epidemic-america-caribbean&catid=740%3Apress-releases&Itemid=1926&lang=en.

5. https://caribbean.unfpa.org/en/node/19856 (Accessed April 13, 2019).
6. https://caribbean.unfpa.org/en/node/19856 (Accessed April 13, 2019).
7. United Nations' Children Fund (2018) Situation Analysis of Jamaican Children.
8. https://www.livescience.com/24558-marijuana-effects.html (Accessed April 12, 2019).
9. http://hdr.undp.org/en/indicators/133006.
10. Ibid.
11. Sources: https://data.worldbank.org/indicator/SE.PRM.NENR. http://www.pioj.gov.jm/Portals/0/Economic_Sector/OVERVIEW%202012.pdf (Accessed April 1, 2019).
    Notes: Cuba 2015, Guyana 2012, Jamaica 2012, St. Lucia 2007, Trinidad and Tobago 2010.
    (Accessed April 12, 2019).
12. https://data.worldbank.org/indicator/SE.PRM.NENR (Accessed April 12, 2019).
13. https://newsday.co.tt/2018/08/12/cxc-11000-pupils-got-zero-passes/ (Accessed November 26, 2018).
14. Planning Institute of Jamaica (2017), JSLC 2015, 33 http://hdr.undp.org/en/indicators/133006.

References

Arrazola, R. A., Singh, T., Corey, C. G., Husten, C. G., Neff, L. J., Apelberg, B. J., … McAfee, T. (2015). Tobacco use among middle and high school students—United States, 2011–2014. *Morbidity and Mortality Weekly Report (MMWR), 64*(14), 381.

Berlinski, S., & Schady, N. (2015). *The early years: Child well-being and the Role of Public Policy.* Retrieved April 28, 2019, from https://publications.iadb.org/en/early-years-child-well-being-and-role-public-policy.

Healthy Caribbean Coalition. (2017). Preventing childhood obesity in the Caribbean—Civil society action plan 2017–2021. Retrieved April 5, 2019, from https://www.healthycaribbean.org/preventing-childhood-obesity-caribbean-civil-society-action-plan-2017-2021/.

Jackson, J. F. L., Moore, J. L., III, & Leon, R. A. (2010). Male underachievement in education across the globe: A shift in paradigm for gender disparities regarding academic achievement. Retrieved April 7, 2019, from https://

www.researchgate.net/publication/286112301_Male_Underachievement_
in_Education_Across_the_Globe_A_Shift_in_Paradigm_for_Gender_
Disparities_Regarding_Academic_Achievement.

Kieling, C., Baker-Henningham, H., Belfer, M., Conti, G., Ertem, I., Omigbodun, O., … Rahman, A. (2011). Child and adolescent mental health worldwide: Evidence for action. *The Lancet, 378*(9801), 1515–1525.

Loeber, R., Farrington, D. P., Stouthamer-Loeber, M., & Van Kammen, W. B. (1998). *Antisocial behavior and mental health problems: Explanatory factors in childhood and adolescence.* Psychology Press.

Malecka-Tendera, E., & Mazur, A. (2006). Childhood obesity: A pandemic of the twenty-first century. *International Journal of Obesity, 30*(S2), S1.

Organization of American States (OAS) and Inter-American Drug Abuse Control Commission (CICAD). (2016). A report on students' drug use in 13 Caribbean countries: Antigua and Barbuda, The Bahamas, Barbados, Belize, Dominica, Grenada, Guyana, Haiti, Jamaica, St. Kitts and Nevis, St. Lucia, St. Vincent and the Grenadines, Trinidad and Tobago. v.; cm. (OAS. Official records; OEA/Ser.L/XIV.6.46). Retrieved April 10, 2019, from http://www.cicad.oas.org/oid/pubs/FINAL%20SCHOOL%20SURVEY%20REPORT%202016.pdf.

Oshodi, O. Y., Aina, O. F., & Onajole, A. T. (2010). Substance use among secondary school students in an urban setting in Nigeria: Prevalence and associated factors. *African Journal of Psychiatry, 13*(1), 52–57.

Parry, O. (1997). 'Schooling is fooling': Why do Jamaican boys underachieve in school? *Gender and Education, 9*(2), 223–232.

Planning Institute of Jamaica. (2017). Jamaica Survey of Living Conditions (JSLC), 2015.

Samms-Vaughan, M. (2016). *Social policy and early childhood development in Aldrie Henry-Lee (editor) pathways to action.* Kingston, Jamaica: Ian Randle Publishers.

Schulte-Körne, G. (2016). Mental health problems in a school setting in children and adolescents. *Deutsches Ärzteblatt International, 113*(11), 183.

Shivpuri, A., Shivpuri, A., & Sharma, S. (2012). Childhood obesity: Review of a growing problem. *International Journal of Clinical Pediatric Dentistry, 5*(3), 237.

UNAIDS. (2018). UNAIDS data 2018. Retrieved April 13, 2019, from http://www.unaids.org/sites/default/files/media_asset/unaids-data-2018_en.pdf.

Verner, D. (2008). *Making poor Haitians count* (Vol. 4571). World Bank Publications.

Wolff, L. (2008). *Education in Haiti: The way forward.* Washington, DC: PREAL.

5

Children in Violent Circumstances

2013:
Dem not stop kill the children dem.
Senior citizen talking about child murders in Jamaica (with author), 2013
2019:
Anguish in Sterling Castle After Eight-Year-Old Girl Found Murdered
Jamaica Gleaner, *April 16, 2019 (http://jamaica-gleaner.com/article/*
news/20190416/anguish-sterling-castle-after-eight-year-old-girl-found-
murdered (Accessed April 19, 2019)).

Introduction

Nature has determined that the young should be protected by their parents and the other members of the community. However, analysis of both primary and secondary data shows that children in SIDS are at risk physically and emotionally in private and public spaces. The findings reveal that many children are exposed to adverse childhood experiences (ACEs), and that abuse in the home, school and wider community is at a high

© The Author(s) 2020
A. Henry-Lee, *Endangered and Transformative Childhood in Caribbean Small Island Developing States*, Studies in Childhood and Youth,
https://doi.org/10.1007/978-3-030-25568-8_5

level. In these SIDS, childhood is under threat and many children live in violent circumstances.

Definitions of violence are formulated depending on the focus and approach taken by the writer; it may be defined for legal, medical, sociological or other purposes. Article 19 of the Convention on the Rights of the Child (CRC) defines violence as "all forms of physical or mental violence, injury and abuse, neglect or negligent treatment, maltreatment or exploitation, including sexual abuse."

The World Health Organization (WHO) defines violence as follows:

> The intentional use of physical force or power, threatened or actual, against oneself, another person, or against a group or community, that either results in or has a high likelihood of resulting in injury, death, psychological harm, maldevelopment, or deprivation.[1]

The organization also goes on to outline the types of violence: self-directed violence which one does to oneself, and interpersonal violence that occurs between people. The latter type of violence can be further divided into family and intimate partner violence, partner violence and community violence. There is also collective violence committed by large groups of people which can be categorized into social, political and economic violence.[2]

Violence can be committed by individuals or by the State as well as groups and organizations through their members and their actions. It results not only in fear of/or actual injury but also in the violation of the victim's rights and freedoms.

Violence against children (VAC) is a violation of their rights as stated in the Convention on the rights of the Child (CRC):

> States Parties shall take all appropriate legislative, administrative, social and educational measures to protect the child from all forms of physical or mental violence, injury or abuse, neglect or negligent treatment, maltreatment or exploitation, including sexual abuse, while in the care of parent(s), legal guardian(s) or any other person who has the care of the child.

Such protective measures should, as appropriate, include effective procedures for the establishment of social programmes to provide necessary support for the child and for those who have the care of the child, as well as for other forms of prevention; and for identification, reporting, referral, investigation, treatment and follow-up of instances of child maltreatment described heretofore, and, as appropriate, for judicial involvement (UNCRC 1989, Convention on the Rights of the Child, Article 19).[3]

Yet every day, all over the world, children witness and suffer violence. According to the WHO, globally, up to 1 billion children aged 2–17 years have experienced physical, sexual, or emotional violence or neglect in the past year.[4] Violence against children takes place in private and public spaces and can take several forms, including incest, rape, corporal punishment, emotional and psychological abuse, negligent treatment, or exploitation.

Much research has been completed on the subject in the Caribbean. Children from economically disadvantaged families are considered at higher risk for transactional abuse, but there are a number of interlocking factors which both fuel child sexual abuse and place children at greater risk of being sexually abused (UNICEF 2012a, 17). Jones and Trotman (2009) analysed sexual abuse in the Caribbean and found that intra-familial and non-family sexual abuse are characterized by a higher level of secrecy and silence, while transactional sexual abuse is described as being more visible or as an "open secret."

In this chapter, we focus on interpersonal violence with special emphasis on corporal punishment, sexual abuse of children, violence in schools and communities and self-inflicted violence. We argue that violence impacts negatively on the children in these SIDS and endangers their childhood. Violence against children is a serious problem with contributing factors such as historical precedents of violence for punishment and in addressing conflicts, politically based arming of civilians, and the rise of narco-trafficking, poverty, inequality, family instability and inadequate educational systems (Matthies et al. 2008, 3).

The historical legacy of violence from slavery to the present is so entrenched that eradication of physical violence remains difficult and necessitates drastic cultural changes. Primary data collected from children, seniors and elite respondents and secondary data from various sources show that children are not adequately protected from all forms of violence in private and public spaces. Violence is one of the contributors to an endangered childhood which violates all the rights of children set out in the CRC.

Impact of Violence

There is enough evidence to show that violent circumstances are deleterious on anybody, especially children. Violence can endanger their lives and result in adverse childhood experiences (ACEs). UNICEF (2014) states that exposure to violence has a negative impact on individuals and societies. Both boys and girls suffer from violence, but girls may be more prone to be victims of sexual abuse. Using the life-cycle approach, the writers discussed the impact of violence from the foetus to childhood/early adolescence. Pregnant women who are abused may give birth to babies with low birth weight and other defects (UNICEF 2014, 12). Exposure to violence and abuse can disrupt the development of the brain and may also result in "regressive symptoms in young children" (ibid.). The latter includes increased bedwetting, delayed language development and additional anxiety over separation from parents, which in turn may affect children's ability to learn and to get along with other adults and with peers (UNICEF 2014, 13). Violence against children may also result in lower attendance and performance rates in schools and higher drop-out rates. Girls are at more risk of sexual violence which may result in higher fertility rates, lower health status and a weakened household economy (UNICEF 2014, 13).

Holt et al. (2008, 1) found that children and adolescents living with domestic violence are at increased risk of experiencing emotional, physical and sexual abuse, of developing emotional and behavioural problems and of increased exposure to the presence of other adversities in their lives. The impact may last even after measures have been taken to move them into safety (ibid.).

In Jamaica, exposure to violence was independently associated with poor school achievement among children attending government, urban schools (Baker-Henningham et al. 2009). Focusing on children's experiences of three types of violence—exposure to aggression among peers at school, physical punishment at school, and exposure to community violence—the researchers found that children experiencing higher levels of violence had the poorest academic achievement and children experiencing moderate levels recording poorer achievement than those experiencing little or none (Baker-Henningham et al. 2009, 1). The levels of violence against children have been so high in Jamaica that there have been calls for the State to stem the tide of violence against children (Miller 2014).

Children's Perceptions of Violence

In 2018, there were 1287 persons killed in Jamaica.[5] By the end of the seventh day in 2019, there had been twenty murders.[6] By all accounts, Jamaican children live in a country with high levels of violence. Children are aware of the violent circumstances in which they live and primary data collected from students in Kingston, Jamaica, revealed that a high proportion of them believed that children face high levels of violence in private and public spaces. Of all the respondents, 80 per cent reported that the levels of violence against children in Jamaica were either high or very high (Table 5.1). Of all the respondents, 32 per cent found that levels of violence against children in the community were high or very high. According to sixty-two of the respondents, violence that children faced in the home were at very high/high levels.

Two statements from these students indicate the high level of violence in Jamaica:

> In my community, children don't normally come out to play.
> You cannot walk freely in Jamaica without worrying about an attack.

In Chap. 2, we noted that the senior citizens lamented that children today do not live in safe environments as they did during their childhood. These findings are not too surprising given the national context within which the children live. Jamaica has been ranked one of the most violent countries in the world. In 2006, respondents in a national poll listed "crime and violence" as the number one problem facing Jamaica

Table 5.1 Children's perceptions of levels of violence in Jamaica

Levels	%
Perceptions of levels of violence that children face in the homes in Jamaica (n = 103)	
Very high	37.2
High	24.5
Low	5.3
Very low	3.6
Non-existent	2
Don't know	27.4
Perceptions of levels of violence that children face in the community (n = 103)	
Very high	8.7
High	23.3
Low	25.2
Very low	20.3
Non-existent	5
Don't know	18.4
Perceptions of levels of violence against children in Jamaica (n = 103)	
Very high	52.4
High	27.2
Low	6.8
Very low	5.8
Non-existent	7.8

Source: Primary data collected by author 2013

(*Jamaica Observer* 2006). The crime problem is a complicated and complex one to address and has preoccupied several national governments for decades. *Jamaica Gleaner* (2016, editorial) lists some of the main underlying causes of crime:

> broken families and social decay; neglected and abused children, with early exposure to violence; bad housing, poor education and limited job opportunities; the erosion of moral authority by entrenched systems of political corruption and patronage, links between politics and organised crime, and the maintenance of gang-dominated garrison communities and informal settlements.[7]

with bad housing, poor education and limited job opportunities.[8] The impact of these underlying factors is that childhood in Jamaica is "endangered" and some aspect of violence becomes a daily direct or indirect feature in the life of a Jamaican child. This institutionalization or "normalization of violence" has resulted in 72 per cent of the children in the study discussed earlier, describing their quality of life as "fair to excellent." There appears to be the development of an insensitivity or resilience to violence among the children in Jamaica. This phenomenon needs to be further explored.

Similar studies were not carried out by the researcher in the other countries (Barbados, Haiti and St. Lucia), so comparisons could not be drawn.

Reported Cases of Child Abuse

In violation of the Convention on the Rights of the Child, several children are abused daily in Caribbean SIDS. In Barbados, the Child Care Board (CCB) in conjunction with the Welfare Department works to reduce the incidence of abuse against children. The CCB is charged with the mandate of child care and protection which involves investigating cases of child abuse or child labour and providing counselling, residential placements or foster care. The Welfare Department provides counselling on a wide range of family-related issues (Barbados Human Rights Report 2018). The Barbados Child Care Board recorded over 1000 cases of child abuse in 2017.[9] It was noted that 547 of those reported cases involved neglect in the 5–11 age group. Reports from Guyana, Jamaica and Barbados showed that the main perpetrators of physical abuse in the home were parents/caregivers, particularly mothers, and a significant minority of the physical abuse was perpetrated by children such as older siblings (UNICEF 2006, 17).

Children in Jamaica live in a country that has the highest homicide rate in the Caribbean. It is not surprising therefore that child abuse is a major concern in Jamaica. The Jamaica Office of the Children's Registry (OCR) noted a steady increase in the number of cases reported to their office. In 2014, over 11,400 cases of abuse against children were reported

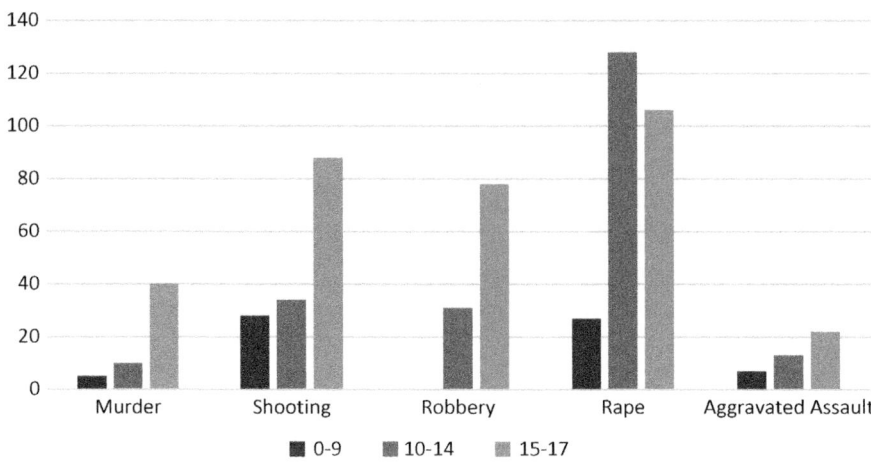

Fig. 5.1 Child victims of selected crimes, Jamaica, 2017, by age group. (Source: Planning Institute of Jamaica, Economic and Social Survey of Jamaica 2017, 378)

to them. Abuse against girls outnumbered that of boys (approximately 6500 to 4900). This figure increased in 2015 to a total of over 13,600 reported cases of abuse (OCR 2015).[10]

Data from Fig. 5.1 revealed that the age group 15-17 have the highest proportion of their members being victims of crime in Jamaica.

In Haiti, hundreds of children serve as *restavèks* (child labourers) who work to earn income. They are usually from poor families and are desperate for food. Over 30 per cent of females and males who were ever *restavèks* in childhood experienced some form of sexual violence before the age of eighteen (Gilbert et al. 2018). Female *restavèks* were more than twice as likely to experience childhood physical and emotional violence and close to twice as likely to experience sexual violence compared to female youth who had never been *restavèks* (Gilbert et al. 2018). For male *restavèks*, they were at approximately 50 per cent greater likelihood of physical violence and over three times more likely to experience emotional violence than non-*restavèk* males (Gilbert et al. 2018). The data revealed that a child can be a *restavèk* from as young as three years, with 51 (18.6 per cent) and 34 (21.7 per cent) of the females and males restavèks respectively starting between age three and six years old (Gilbert et al. 2018).

Table 5.2 Number of cases of child abuse reported 2010–2015 in St. Lucia

	2010	2011	2013	2014	2015
Verbal abuse	25	5	14	28	12
Neglect/abandonment	62	64	87	103	61
Physical	82	100	86	81	84
Sexual	76	87	108	103	73

Source: UNICEF (2017, 44)

Gilbert et al. (2018) also noted that a total of 71 (29.4 per cent) and 26 (13.0 per cent) of female and male children respectively became restavèks between ages 13–17 years.

There were 1341 reported cases of child abuse in St. Lucia with girls accounting for over 70 per cent of the victims between 2010 and 2015 (UNICEF 2017). There has been a decrease in the number of reported cases of child abuse in St. Lucia since 2011 (Table 5.2). Verbal abuse is the least reported type of abuse in St. Lucia.

Some children in the Caribbean have life taken away from them. In 2017, there were fifty-five children murdered in Jamaica (Planning Institute of Jamaica, Economic and Social Survey of Jamaica 2017).

Corporal Punishment

Hundreds of children in the Caribbean are the frequent victims of corporal punishment. The Committee on the Rights of the Child in the General Comment No. 8 defines "corporal" or "physical" punishment as

> any punishment in which physical force is used and intended to cause some degree of pain or discomfort, however light. Most involves hitting ("smacking," "slapping," "spanking") children, with the hand or with an implement … In the view of the Committee, corporal punishment is invariably degrading.[11]

The most recent Multiple Indicator Cluster Surveys (MICS) in the Caribbean revealed that there were high percentages of children who experienced physical punishment or any violent discipline method in Barbados, Jamaica and St. Lucia (Table 5.3). There was no similar study in Haiti.

Table 5.3 Percentage of children aged 4–14 years who experienced physical punishment or any violent discipline method for Barbados, Jamaica and St. Lucia

	Barbados			Jamaica			St. Lucia		
	Physical punishment		Any violent discipline method	Physical punishment		Any violent discipline method	Physical punishment		Any violent discipline method
Quintiles	Any	Severe		Any	Severe		Any	Severe	
Poorest	58.3	12.4	79.8	79.0	9.9	90.1	49.6*	7.1*	74.7*
Second	56.5	4.1	70.7	72.2	6.0	86.6	NA	NA	NA
Middle	56.1	4.8	77.9	68.7	3.7	83.4	NA	NA	NA
Fourth	57.2	3.7	75.4	64.1	5.2	83.3	NA	NA	NA
Richest	50.0	6.3	72.1	51.9	2.3	75.9	39.4**	4.9**	61.6**
Total	55.7	6.1	75.1	68.4	5.7	84.5	43.9	5.9	67.5

Source: MICS reports (2012): Jamaica, Barbados and St. Lucia

Note: *Poorest 40 per cent, **Richest 60 per cent, NA—not available

The data showed that at least 75 per cent of all children in Barbados received at least one form of violent discipline, while in Jamaica and St. Lucia, the proportions were 84.5 and 67.5 per cent, respectively. Higher proportions of children in the poorest quintile received violent discipline (Table 5.3). Children in the poorest quintile are more likely to experience endangered childhood and live in violent circumstances.

Corporal punishment remains culturally accepted in Barbados. Many see it as a necessary form of discipline to keep children "in-line." There is supported by even the religious leaders as the extracts below show:

Lash them!
Senator Durant for using the rod
(Extracts)
FLOG THEM.

If that is what it takes to keep children in line, one of Barbados' leading clerics says there is nothing wrong with the "rod of correction" though he is against brutalising youngsters.

Senator Dr David Durant, whose position runs counter to the growing global trend against any form of corporal punishment, told the Senate yesterday that Barbadians should not be pushed into "dismantling key systems of control" that had worked for the country for so many years.

He was contributing to debate in the Upper House on the Prison Amendment Bill.

Durant, an influential Pentecostal preacher, said that corporal punishment should not be used as a first option but as a last resort. However, he stressed: "I believe it should still be encouraged and it is this **same principle that should be applied in home and in the schools** (emphasis that of author's). We should not be in a hurry or be in a mad rush to dismantle key systems of control that have held this society together for more than 300 years ......"

Durant told the Senate that he believed most of the senators in the chamber got "a licking" when they were young and it made them "better."

"It helped to keep me in line," he pointed out.

—**Support for Corporal Punishment by a Cleric in Barbados**[12] (17 January 2015)

The Clergyman cautioned against dismantling systems of discipline that had worked in Barbados.

In Haiti, while it is unclear whether or not corporal punishment is lawful in the home, but this form of punishment is prohibited in alternative care settings such as institutions, orphanages, children's homes and places of safety (UNICEF 2013b, 1–2). According to a UN report, although there is very little variation in the proportion of children subjected to corporal punishment according to the child's gender, place of residence or even the educational level of the head of household, it was shown that the prevalence was slightly lower for children aged 10–14 (75 per cent) than for younger children (83 per cent or more) (UNCRC Haiti 2015, 24). It was noted that violent forms of corporal punishment were used more frequently against boys (18 per cent) than girls (14 per cent) and against children in urban areas as opposed to rural areas (17 per cent versus 15 per cent) (UNCRC Haiti 2015, 24).

The Center for Disease Control and Prevention (CDC), (2014), found that 38.1 per cent of girls and 36.4 per cent of boys aged 13–17 in Haiti experienced physical violence by an adult household member or authority figure in the community in the twelve months prior to a survey which they conducted. They noted that 90.0 per cent and 85.7 per cent of girls and boys respectively, perceived that their experience of physical violence by adult household members or authority figures was a result of disciplinary action or intended as punishment (CDC 2014).

Corporal punishment remains an intractable feature of Jamaican culture and parenting practice. The UNCRC report noted that this form of punishment begins in the earliest years of a child's life, and children as young as between two and five years commonly experience this, with boys punished more frequently and with more severity than girls (UNCRC Jamaica 2013, 55). The prohibition of corporal punishment is still to be achieved in Jamaica in the homes, schools and day cares (UNICEF 2013a, 1). The report noted that this form of punishment is lawful in the home under the common law right to inflict "reasonable and moderate" punishment. Although corporal punishment is unlawful and prohibited in alternative care settings, it appears to be prohibited in some but not all day care (UNICEF 2013a, 1–2). On the other hand, corporal punishment is lawful in schools, with the exception of "basic schools."

Data revealed that 87 per cent of children in Jamaica between the ages of 2–14 years are subjected to at least one form of psychological or physical punishment in the past six months (UNICEF 2010). This is in tandem with other data which found that only 11 per cent of Jamaican parents practice positive forms of discipline (UNCRC Jamaica 2013, 55). Similarly, data on the patterns of discipline in Jamaican households showed that physical punishment was used more often for children under twelve than for older children, with 60.2 per cent of parents reporting beating or slapping their child under the age of twelve years (Ricketts and Anderson, cited in UNCRC Jamaica 2013, 55).

Members of the Jamaican society have strong views on the use of corporal punishment in the home and at school. Even the young impressed support for corporal punishment. Some views of young people on the use of corporal punishment to discipline children in Jamaica are highlighted below[13]:

QUESTION:

Contrary to the norm in many Jamaican households, corporal punishment is now being labelled as abuse and ineffective, with an ultimatum of total eradication. Where do you stand on this matter?

RESPONSES:

I believe that total eradication is not necessary and where "abuse" and "ineffectiveness" come into play, is where things become extreme. I think the matter should really be where the limit is set because it cannot be that every time a "hard-of-hearing" child does wrong, we are going to nicely say, "Please stop." Actions speak louder than words, and when you spank him, it might be just enough to let him attribute that spanking to the wrong behaviour, so he will walk away from it in the future.—**NOVIA S., 18**

If I didn't face certain penalties that I did while growing up, I don't know what I would be like today. I know that it may work differently for others who will believe that violence is the answer for everything but, for me, it restrained me to the point where I did everything to escape a good licking, so I behave myself. I think if it is eradicated, totally, then it will just give kids leverage to do as they please because if you raise your hand at them, they can have you jailed. Is that the society we're aiming at? **The United Nations doesn't know what we are dealing with here, and this**

First-World thinking may not work for everybody (emphasis is that of the author's).—**ANTHONY D., 16**

   I think I agree that it is abuse because there is no limit to corporal punishment; and when parents are in a rage, they are likely to go to extremes and may not see where they are seriously hurting the child. The child will fear the parent, instead of loving them, and bottle up hate and anger inside, which they will eventually take out on their peers. For me, corporal punishment is never the answer.—**MAYA C., 15**

   Even the State is reluctant to vigorously seek policy change regarding corporal punishment. According to the *Gleaner* online dated May 11, 2015, the then Minister of Youth and Culture Lisa Hanna reported that her ministry was not ready to outlaw corporal punishment for children until the topic was completely ventilated through public discourse. The Minister noted that although, so far, the evidence that had been presented suggested that corporal punishment had a negative effect on the island's children, the ministry was not ready to do away with this form of punishment (*Jamaica Gleaner Online*, May 11, 2015).

   A former Minister of Education, Ronald Thwaites, in February 2015, told journalists that the country was not ready to enact legislation to completely outlaw corporal punishment in response to the UN's appeal. According to him, corporal punishment should be generally discouraged but a total ban was not necessary at this time.[14]

   Only children in State care are exempt from corporal punishment. In Jamaica, according to Section 62 (d) of the Jamaican Child Care and Protection Act, a child in a place of safety, children's home or in the care of a fit person shall have the right to be free from corporal punishment.

   Provided below are some insights into the use of corporal punishment in Haiti (Highlights of Survey on Childhood Physical Violence in Haiti)[15]:

1. Almost two-thirds of females and males aged 18–24 years experienced physical violence by adult household members or authority figures in the community prior to the age of eighteen.
2. Approximately one-third of females and males aged 13–17 years experienced physical violence in the twelve months prior to the survey.

3. Childhood domestic servitude was significantly associated with physical violence among females 13–17 years of age in the twelve months preceding the survey.
4. Nine out of ten females and almost nine out of ten males aged 13–17 perceived that their most recent experience of physical violence perpetrated by an adult household member or authority figure was a result of disciplinary action or intended as punishment in the twelve months prior to the survey.
5. One out of every four females and one out of every six males who experienced any physical injury due to physical violence had a severe injury resulting in either deep wounds, broken bones, broken teeth, blackened or charred skin, or permanent injury or disfigurement.

According to a UNCRC report, prevalence of corporal punishment was noted as slightly lower for children aged 10–14 (75 per cent) than for younger children (83 per cent or more) (UNCRC Haiti 2015, 24). It was noted that violent forms of corporal punishment were used more frequently against boys (18 per cent) than girls (14 per cent) and against children in urban areas as opposed to rural areas (17 per cent versus 15 per cent) (UNCRC Haiti 2015, 24).

In 2019, the St. Lucian government suspended corporal punishment and established a working committee charged with the responsibility of deciding the required initiatives and implementation dates towards the eventual abolition of corporal punishment.[16] According to findings by Owen (2015, 2), in St. Lucia, corporal punishment of children is unlawful as a sentence for crime but it is not prohibited in the home, alternative care settings, day care, schools and penal institutions. The study noted that as originally drafted, the laws did not explicitly prohibit corporal punishment but provided the drive to review national legislation and to ratify new laws which could be used to prohibit corporal punishment. Additionally, corporal punishment is lawful in alternative care settings and in day care, under the right of persons having lawful control or in charge of a juvenile "to administer reasonable punishment" (Owen 2015, 2). Although some schools in St. Lucia are part of the UNICEF child-friendly schools initiative do not use corporal punishment, it remains lawful in these and all schools under the right of teachers "to administer reasonable punishment" as pointed out by Owen (2015, 3).

According to the Humanium Report (2013), the practice of corporal punishment is not legally prohibited in St. Lucia and remains a legal way to discipline children. The report noted that corporal punishment is practised and advised as a preferred form of discipline. Any parent, teacher, or legal guardian is allowed to administer "reasonable" corporal punishment (Humanium 2013). It was also noted that around 30 per cent of parents with children under twelve years administered violent punishment. Most of the time these punishments took the form of spankings with an object (stick, belt, and shoe) (Humanium 2013).

Health Minister Alvina Reynolds cautioned that corporal punishment was too rampant in St. Lucia and those who badly beat their children should understand they could be creating monsters that would return to haunt them in life (*Nationwide News Magazine*, August 17, 2016).[17]

According to the St. Lucia MICS report, 68 per cent of children aged 2–14 years experienced at least one form of psychological or physical punishment from their parents or other adult household members; with male children more likely to be subjected to these forms of punishment than females (UNICEF 2017, 17). Additionally, the use of violent discipline is slightly more prevalent in urban areas (77 per cent) than in the rural areas (65 per cent). The 2–4 year olds are the children most likely to be subjected to violent discipline methods (69 per cent) than the other age groups and children from the poorest households are more likely to be disciplined using a violent method (75 per cent) compared to those from the richest households (62 per cent) (UNICEF 2015a, b, 17).

Alternatives to Corporal Punishment

Children themselves do not always like physical punishment. In an analysis of primary data from 103 students interviewed in two urban schools in Jamaica, 89 per cent were against physical punishment for children as revealed by their negative response when asked "*is it right to beat children?*" They offered alternative forms of punishment: take away privileges (80 per cent); do work/chores (8 per cent); ground them (3 per cent); talk to them (4 per cent); allow children to make mistakes and learn from them (3 per cent); and, do anything that the adults think will work (2 per cent).

Adults have access to alternatives to corporal punishment. According to UNICEF,[18] in order to discipline a child without beating one can do the following

1. Set the right example for your child.
2. Let your children help you as you set the rules for the family.
3. Give them a timeout—that is, make them sit in a quiet place away from others, if they do something wrong.
4. Take away something the child likes, as another option, if your child misbehaved.
5. Praise your child when he or she does well.
6. Spend time with your children.
7. Seek help if you feel that parenting is challenging and that you cannot provide discipline for your child.

Using violence to physically discipline a child will impact negatively on their childhood and the long-term effects may become visible in adulthood when they use violence in resolving conflict in private and public spaces. The physical, psychological and emotional effects of violence contribute to endangerment of childhood in SIDS.

Violence in Schools

Children face several challenges at school. Evans (2001), for example, found that problems at school included indiscipline; poor performance at the examinations level and the negative impact of emigration of hundreds of qualified teachers to schools in North America and Europe. The focus in this section is on violence in schools.

As discussed in the previous section, violence has a deleterious effect on children. Most studies tend to focus on the impact of violence on them in any setting (such as home, school, community). Consequently, studies that investigate the impact on school violence tend to draw heavily on the general impact of violence. In many cases, there is no significant difference in the impact of school violence as opposed to other types of violence perpetrated in the home and community.

Apart from the obvious physical impact, there are also psychological effects. After experiencing the trauma of school violence, children may experience sleep disturbances, nightmares, persistent thoughts of the event, a belief that another event will occur, and other problems (Shen and Sink 2002 in Daniels et al. 2007). Younger children may be particularly affected by experiencing enuresis, increased dependency or re-enactment of the traumatic event through play and other means (Flouri 2005, in Daniels et al. 2007). The impact of school and community violence on children may also be depicted by their aggressive acting-out behaviours. (O'Keefe 1997). School violence not only has a deleterious effect on its victims, but also on those who witness it. Witnessing this may diminish the well-being of children, and their exposure to it makes them more likely to conduct themselves aggressively, dislike school or even avoid it (Janosz et al. 2008).

Notwithstanding the earlier disclaimer that the effect of school violence is similar to that of other types of violence, Flannery et al. (2004) posit that where school violence is prevalent, there is an institutional effect, as the climate of the entire school can be affected and can contribute to the continuation of the cycle of violence exposure, victimization, and perpetration of violence on school grounds. Students may become hyper-vigilant and wary of people around them. This is likely to have a negative effect on teaching and learning.

Bailey et al. (2014) argued that the high rates of interpersonal violence in the Caribbean can be attributed to the culture of violence that is manifested in many ways in schools. They noted the increased vulnerability of Caribbean youth as a threat to their long-term development and point to the continued use of corporal punishment as a form of discipline which is often embedded in the culture, as having a negative impact on children's behaviour and which is often executed by those who have responsibilities for their care and protection.

Bailey et al. (2014) examined the use of corporal punishment in Trinidad and Tobago, St. Kitts and Nevis, Grenada, and St. Vincent and the Grenadines, and highlighted a significant relationship between children's aggression, antisocial behaviours and that of physical punishment (Bailey et al. 2014). Their survey results (teachers $n = 206$ and students $n = 835$) revealed that the most popular methods of discipline used by teachers were "the calling in of the parents" (90 per cent) followed by "the sending of children to the principal's office" (89 per cent). However, corporal punishment was commonly by 82 per cent of the teachers. Although, corporal punishment was widely used in the schools, the frequencies were recorded to be mainly rare or sometimes; 37 per cent and 40 per cent respectively, with the highest prevalence of corporal punishment in St. Kitts and Nevis and the lowest in Trinidad and Tobago. Even while noting the negative impact of corporal punishment, the teachers thought that it was justified with (73 per cent). The teachers highlighted that the negative impact of corporal punishment on children included—psychological effects and aggression—36.4 per cent and 41.8 per cent respectively (Bailey et al. 2014). Of the teachers, 61.7 per cent of them admitted that corporal punishment was not an effective form of discipline and proposed, for example, "extra homework" as more effective way of disciplining children. There was, however, universal support (97.1 per cent) in favour of some form of discipline in schools.

Students were questioned as to whether or not they knew of students who were beaten by a worker at school or whether they themselves were victims of corporal punishment. It was revealed that both scenarios were widespread in all the countries surveyed. Of all the respondents, 94 per cent knew of others who had been victims of corporal punishment whereas 87 per cent admitted to having been victims themselves (Bailey et al. 2014).

The researchers note that there is not much facilitation in the way of eliminating corporal punishment in schools as it is still allowed in most countries and somewhat authorized by ministries once done within the purview of the law. There found mixed emotions as to the effectiveness of corporal punishment. Although some felt that it was not an effective tool, it was still carried out amid the negative impacts (physical injuries, psychological problems, etc.) to children that may arise. Although the Convention of the Rights of the Child was ratified in these countries, strict adherence to international laws was still lacking and as such Caribbean governments needed to bring their policies and practices in accordance with the accepted standards for the treatment of children (Bailey et al. 2014).

Gittens (2008, 8–11) reported on the violence in secondary schools in Barbados. It was revealed that 47 per cent of the students had thought about hurting another student, 44 per cent were worried about being attacked, while 42 per cent had been involved in fights at school. Additionally, in a 2.5 per cent multi-stage random sample of 521 secondary students from five secondary schools ages 11–18 years, students who reported to have been treated badly by either students or staff/teachers at school, stood at 29 per cent and 10 per cent respectively.

Pinheiro (2006 cited in Vince-Whitman 2008, 4–7) pointed out that of the students interviewed in Barbados, 95 per cent of boys and 92 per cent of girls said they had experienced corporal punishment by caning or flogging in school. Vince-Whitman (2008, 7) pointed to the creation of policies as one way to effectively curtail violence in schools noting that for effective learning and social development, learning environments must be safe and free from violence. It was noted however that these policies must go beyond banning violence in schools to fostering positive and respectful standards (Vince-Whitman 2008, 6). Vince-Whitman also noted that the creation of a caring environment by adults would allow students to feel attached to their school and to caring teachers, coaches, or counsellors (Vince-Whitman 2008, 7).

With the increasing use and availability of light weapons and small arms in Barbados, 6.7 per cent of secondary school students have seen guns at school, although scissors, knives, ice picks and cutlasses are more commonly seen in this context (UNICEF 2009b, 10). The issue of violence is also fuelled by psychological dimensions of "dissing" or public humiliation often witnessed by peers and these have become predominant triggers of retaliatory and premeditated youth-on-youth violence (UNICEF 2009b, 10).

The *Nation News* (Barbados) reported that two separate incidents of school violence took place wherein a female teacher and a principal were reportedly attacked by students. This was not confirmed as the principal declined to comment when contacted (Barbados *Nation News*, June 10, 2016).[19]

In Haiti, there has been a ban on corporal punishment in schools from June 2003, but it appears to continue to be a common practice.[20] In 2015, the Ministry of Education and Vocational Training (MENFP) was alarmed by the increase in violence within the schools particularly at the secondary level. It appealed to all stakeholders, especially parents, to better supervise young people to prevent acts of violence (*Haiti Libre*, June 3, 2015) and noted that it was particularly dismayed by the acts of aggression which had been perpetrated recently (March 2015) against students of the Lycée Fritz Pierre-Louis, where two were stabbed by other students. Fortunately, the lives of these students were not in danger based on reports of the medical authorities (*Haiti Libre*, June 3, 2015).

According to the Global Initiative to End all Corporal Punishment of Children Report (2016b), statistics collected between 2005 and 2013 revealed that in the month prior to the survey, 85 per cent of children aged 2–14 experienced violent discipline including physical punishment and/or psychological aggression in the home. Additionally, 79 per cent experienced physical punishment and 64 per cent experienced psychological aggression (being shouted or yelled at, screamed at or insulted). Fifty-two per cent were punished by being forced to kneel and 30 per cent of mothers and caregivers were of the view that physical punishment was necessary in childrearing (UNICEF 2014).

Violence in schools in Jamaica is very high. This is not surprising given the high crime rate in the country and the local newspapers are replete with stories of violence against children. These examples from the *Gleaner* illustrate:

CASE 1: Man Killed Outside Hanover School, Student Reportedly Shot in Mouth
A man was shot and killed, and a child injured in a shooting incident outside the gates of a Hanover school this morning. The man was reportedly shot multiple times at the gate of the Churchill Primary school in Santoy, Hanover, about 8 o'clock this morning. A child was reportedly shot in the mouth and was rushed to hospital.
Source: http://jamaica-gleaner.com/article/news/20161114/man-killed-outside-hanover-school-student-reportedly-shot-mouth (Retrieved December 8, 2018)

CASE 2: Student Shot and Killed Police Searching for Driver of BMW X5

WESTERN BUREAU: Doctors at the Kingston Public Hospital (KPH) worked hard to save 17-year-old Khajeel Mais' life last Friday night, and when nothing seemed to be working, one of the medics held the Kingston College sixth-form student and prayed.

Mais' life was taken from him, his parents, family members and school-mates Friday night by the angry driver of a black/blue BMW X5 whose sport utility vehicle (SUV) had been hit by a taxi in which the 17-year old was a passenger.

The shooting occurred about 7 p.m. along Fairfax Avenue in Havendale, St Andrew, a few metres from where the young man resided. The angry X5 driver, reportedly upset that his vehicle had been struck, retaliated by pulling up alongside the taxi and firing two shots inside it, one of which went through Mais' head.

The driver then sped off.

Source: http://jamaica-gleaner.com/gleaner/20110703/news/news2.html (Retrieved December 8, 2016)

The *Jamaica Observer* noted that in one academic year, 1288 reported incidents of violence in schools took place.[21] The newspaper further stated that these included 915 fights, 160 robberies and 3 murders. School Resource Officers (SROs) reportedly seized 1288 weapons, including 431 knives and 486 pairs of scissors and arrested 201 students, cautioned 2361, monitored 1109 and seized illegal substances on 164 occasions.[22]

Soyibo and Lee (2000, cited in Pottinger 2012, 369) noted that in that country, 61 per cent of high school students reported experiencing violence in schools (based on an epidemiological study of 3124 high school students from 34 randomly selected schools throughout the island). Meeks Gardener et al. (2003, cited in Pottinger 2012, 369) reported that 84 per cent of students knew of other students who carried weapons to school and 89 per cent were worried about violence at school (based on a randomly selected study of 1710 students at secondary schools in the Kingston metropolitan area).

Pottinger (2012, 369–371) acknowledged the prevalence of community, school and home violence among and against children in Jamaica. As a matter of fact, school violence tended to be more prevalent as educators, with some of whom admitting to creating an environment of punishment in schools, were now involved in these acts. Pottinger (2012, 370) also highlighted pinching and thumping, flogging and verbal humiliation as the most popular forms of "disciplining" children in schools. Evans (2001 cited in Pottinger 2012, 370), on the other hand, pointed to corporal punishment and verbal abuse as being more common among educators. She noted however that these were more often meted out to boys than to girls.

Children are also involved in violence against each other. As detailed below, in two separate incidents which occurred in quick succession in Jamaica causing serious injury of children:

Student Stabs Another Repeatedly—Holy Childhood High

According to sources—Two students from Holy Childhood High were injured during a brawl along Half Way Tree Road in St Andrew on Friday.

Details as to what led to the incident, which involved several students of the all-girls school and caused traffic pile up in the busy commercial district, are unclear at this time, but it ended with the two students nursing injuries.

Police have confirmed that students, along with their parents, are now at the Half Way Tree Police Station giving statements.

The incident is the second violent flare up, involving persons associated with an educational institution in the area, this week.

Earlier this week, there was a stabbing and shooting incident at the St Andrew High School for Girls compound which is located just across the road from Holy Childhood. That incident involved two males—a parent and another man. The men were reportedly attending a school leaving ceremony for sixth form students.

Police say the developments have left a dark shadow over the actions of individuals associating themselves to educational institutions that have over the years set very high standards.

Source: https://djpowermixtape.blogspot.com/2016/06/student-stabs-another-repeatedly-at.html (Accessed May 5, 2019)

In another example:

Hundreds of students of the Jamaica College and other stakeholders staged a peaceful protest in front of the school against violence against children.

This protest follows last week's stabbing death of 14-year-old third-form student from the institution. He was killed on a bus during an attempted cellular phone robbery. (*Jamaica Gleaner*, October 31, 2016)[23]

Bullying, according to Pottinger (2012, 370) was also seen as another form of violence in schools in Jamaica. The author noted that this constituted both peer-bullying and educator-bullying. Pottinger and Stair (2009 cited in Pottinger 2012, 370) revealed that the top occurrences of violence reported by students were that of being beaten, robbed and verbally abused. In addition, it was reported that the worst form of bullying was committed by educators (reported by 40 per cent of students). Pottinger also noted that educator-bullying (verbal aggression, physical assault, sexual harassment) could result in oppositional behaviours, loss of trust and depression in children and adolescents. Further, that students who experienced violence at school whether by peer or educator had been victimized resulting in increased poor psychosocial health—poor self-esteem, depression and loss of trust in the system and opposition to authority figures (Pottinger 2012, 370).

Soyibo and Lee reported that 60.8 per cent of students indicated that they had witnessed violence in their schools. For these Jamaican students, the use of hands or feet punching and kicking in the perpetration of violence among students were the most prevalent forms (59.8 per cent/54.5 per cent). This was followed by the use of blunt objects (26.5 per cent), knives (18.4 per cent) and machetes (8.9 per cent). Scissors, forks and guns were also used in these acts of violence in schools (Soyibo and Lee 2000, 232–236).

Several interventions have been implemented to reduce school violence in Jamaica. The officials of the Minister of Education developed a training programme on grief management for teachers and it was successfully piloted in two schools. It was noted that the majority of children exposed to violence did not receive mental health services; as such, this school-based programme was designed to take interventions aimed at loss and grief management into the schools (Pottinger and Stair 2009 cited in Pottinger 2012, 370). The coverage of violence in the media also came under scrutiny. A symposium heightened the awareness of the impact of screen violence particularly on children (Pottinger and Stair 2009 cited in

Pottinger 2012, 371). This sparked several initiatives including a proposed new code of conduct for journalists and media practitioners.

According to the *St. Lucia News Online* dated October 14, 2014, between 2013 and mid-2014, the St. Lucian police confiscated a number of weapons from students (primary and secondary). These weapons included knives (35), scissors (26), penknives (4), cutlasses (91), metal eating forks (8), and wood with nails embedded. Other items confiscated included alcohol, marijuana, a live bullet (0.380 calibre), golf club and rope.[24] Blosnich and Bossarte (2011, 111) noted that the use of surveillance (cameras, security guards or teacher in the hall-way) could serve as a deterrent to high-level violent behaviour including weapon carrying and gang activities.

There is much to be done to reduce school violence and its impact. Meeks Gardener et al. (2003, 102) highlighted the need for increased counselling services as a counter. They noted that this would help students to cope with the high levels of exposure to violence which was evident both in the school environs as well as in their neighbourhoods.

According to the National School Safety Centre (NSSC), the establishment of a strict visitor/trespasser policy in schools is one action that could limit violence in schools (NSSC 2007, cited in Miller 2008, 22). It was also suggested by the NSSC that the acknowledgement of the students' problems immediately and seeking help from local health or mental health professionals and the police could mitigate the influence of problematic behaviours, including the perpetration of violence in schools.

Sexual Abuse

The most common types of child sexual abuse in the Caribbean include intra-familial sexual abuse, non-family sexual abuse, and transactional sexual abuse (UNICEF 2012a, 17). Jones and Trotman Jemmott (2009) analysed sexual abuse in the Eastern Caribbean and found that intra-familial and non-family sexual abuse were characterized by a higher level of secrecy and silence, while transactional sexual abuse was described as being more visible or as an "open secret." Children from economically disadvantaged families are considered at higher risk for transactional abuse, but there are a number of interlocking factors which both fuel child sexual abuse and place children at greater risk of being sexually abused (UNICEF 2012a, 17).

Holt et al. (2008, 1) found that children and adolescents living with domestic violence were at increased risk of experiencing emotional, physical and sexual abuse, of developing emotional and behavioural problems and of increased exposure to the presence of other adversities in their lives. The impact may last even after measures had been taken to move them into safety (ibid.).

Violence and abuse against children continue to be a serious problem in Barbados. According to the Humanium Report (2013), although the age for consensual sex is 16, exploitation of children is still persistent. The government has insufficient policies in place to combat the sexual exploitation of children and although there is no research to document the problem, child pornography and prostitution of children exist. International abduction also poses a serious threat for Barbados and although this is the case, the country is not a party to the 1980 Hague Convention on the Civil Aspects of International Child Abduction.

In 2018, it was reported that aid workers were sexually exploiting women and girls in Haiti.[25] The most recently available data reveal that more victims of sexual abuse are females, and the first sexual encounter for one out of five females was unwanted while it was unwanted for one out of ten males (Table 5.4).

Although the age of sexual consent for boys and girls is sixteen years, there is no independent human rights institution established by law, no protocol approval in cabinet, parliament or other body and no comprehensive national strategy against child sexual abuse in Jamaica (UNICEF 2011, 67–69). There is, however, an independent human rights institution specific for children's rights, a national process for the collection and collation of data from multiple sources as well as a national hotline to counter child sexual abuse (UNICEF 2011, 67–69). A significant majority of children (both males and females) earn money through commercial sex work. The report found that street children who engaged in commercial sexual activity were particularly vulnerable to exploitation and abuse because of the lack of family support and protection (UNICEF 2006, 73–74). However, these children were not the only ones being exposed to

Table 5.4 The prevalence of childhood sexual violence in Haiti

Highlights
1. One out of four females and one out of five males aged 18 to 24 years experienced at least one incident of sexual abuse as a child.
2. Females and males, 18 to 24-year olds who had worked as child domestic servants were more likely to have experienced sexual abuse prior to age 18 than those who had not worked as a child domestic servant.
3. The first experience of sexual intercourse as a child was unwanted for one out of five females and one out of ten males aged 18 to 24 years.
4. Nearly one out of five females and one out of ten males aged 13 to 17 years experienced at least one incident of sexual abuse in the 12 months prior to the survey.
5. About 4 per cent of females and 7 per cent of males aged 18 to 24 years received money, food, gifts, or other favours in exchange for sex prior to age 18.
6. About 2 per cent of females and 3 per cent of males aged 13 to 17 received money, food, gifts, or other favours in exchange for sex in the past 12 months.

Source: Violence against children in Haiti—Findings from a National Survey 2012. Retrieved from http://www.cdc.gov/violenceprevention/pdf/violence-haiti.pdf

violence through commercial sexual activities, some girls as young as ten years were involved in formal prostitution operating from brothels, go-go clubs and massage parlours. Many of these girls were introduced into this type of work by parents and guardians (UNICEF 2006, 73–74). Some mothers even acted as pimps for their children. Both males and females were benefiting in cash or kind from "Sugar daddies/mommies" who would support the children and their families in exchange for sexual favours. Among other abuses the study (UNICEF 2006, 73–74) also identified another category of sex worker called the "Sacrificial Sex Worker." These children were sexually exploited to "cleanse" men of sexually transmitted infections (STIs) as a common myth that virgins can cure men of STIs (UNICEF 2006, 73–74).

There were seventy-three reported cases of child abuse in St. Lucia in 2015 (UNICEF 2017, 44). Based on a self-reported sexual victimization study in 2000 involving 1526 St. Lucian students aged 10–19, one in every ten students reported that they had been abused in the past year. Females were twice as likely to have been abused as males (UNICEF 2009b, 35).

The general consensus in St. Lucia is that delinquency, sexual abuse and sexual exploitation of children are of major concern to the general public and policy makers. The International Centre, University of Calgary (2007) study pointed out that since the signing of the Convention on the Rights of the Child in 1993, St. Lucia has initiated several reforms to existing legislation concerning child rights. However, the country has been slow in enacting amendments and new laws. Also, there is a need to enhance the capacity of social services to respond to the demands of reports of child abuse. Although the Convention was ratified in 1993, the police and the courts have made very few prosecutions of sexual offenders due to parents refusing to testify against perpetrators. St. Lucia has also failed to ratify the Optional Protocol on the sale of children, child prostitution and child pornography (UNICEF 2006).

In Chap. 7, we will explore the issue of human trafficking in the four countries under review.

Suicide

There are some children who do not live to adulthood. They make the decision that they no longer want to try to cope with life's many challenges and they commit suicide. The World Health Organization defines suicide as the act of deliberately killing oneself.[26] It also notes that the risk factors for suicide include mental disorder (such as depression, personality disorder, alcohol dependence, or schizophrenia), and some physical illnesses, such as neurological disorders, cancer, and HIV infection.[27] The most recent data show that there were an estimated 804,000 deaths due to suicide worldwide in 2012; and a global suicide rate of 11.4 per 100,000 (15.0 for males and 8.0 for females) but these figures may be under-reported as suicide remains illegal in some countries.[28] Suicide has a youthful dimension as it is the second leading cause of death among 15–29 year olds and 75 per cent of the cases take place in low- and middle-income countries. Provided below are some facts about suicide on a global scale[29]:

- Over 800,000 people die due to suicide every year.
- For every suicide there are many more people who attempt suicide every year.
- A prior suicide attempt is the single most important risk factor for suicide in the general population.
- Suicide is the second leading cause of death among 15–29 year olds.
- Around 75 per cent of global suicides occur in low- and middle-income countries.
- Ingestion of pesticide, hanging and firearms are among the most common methods of suicide globally.

According to Holder-Nevins et al. (2012), there were twenty-six adolescents aged 9–19 who died by suicide in Jamaica between 2007 and 2010, representing 14 per cent of all suicide cases in the island during the period. The average age of the victims was sixteen, most (76.9 per cent) of whom were males. Most (65 per cent) were students while the others had mainly elementary occupations such as "labourer" and "higgler" (Holder-Nevins et al. 2012).

The first-ever Mental Health Action Plan of the WHO was adopted by the Sixty-sixth World Health Assembly in May 2013, which identified as one of its goals the reducing of the rate of suicide in countries by 10 per cent by 2020.[30]

Bullying and Cyberbullying

Many children suffer in silence from bullying. We examined bullying briefly in the discussion of violence in schools but will now pay a little more attention to bullying and cyberbullying.

The technological revolutions have been both beneficial and detrimental. Hinduja and Patchin (2007, 89–112) point to cyberbullying as a fast-developing segment of violence against children. They note that although this takes place outside of schools, the victims may be at risk for other negative developmental and behavioural consequences including school violence and delinquency (Hinduja and Patchin 2007, 103). They further note that victims of cyber-bullying experience dysphoric emotions that may motivate or induce delinquent behaviours such as school violence or general delinquency (Hinduja and Patchin 2007, 104).

In Jamaica, a UNICEF 2015 survey found that 64.9 per cent of students interviewed reported having ever been bullied."[31] More females than males reported "having been bullied" (66.9 per cent and 62.9 per cent respectively) as well as for having been "bullied this year" (71.4 per cent and 67.9 per cent respectively).[32] Those in the lowest grades reported the highest levels of bullying.[33]

A 2018 survey in Jamaica on the impact of social media on adolescent and youth mental health revealed that 47 per cent of 821 respondents, aged 13–29, believed that social media had a negative impact on their mental health.[34]

The internet has also become of one of the main sources of cyberbullying, which is variously described as

- an aggressive, intentional act carried out by a group or individual, using electronic forms of contact, repeatedly and over time against a victim who cannot easily defend him or herself (Smith et al. 2008, 376); and
- wilful and repeated harm inflicted through the use of computers, cell phones, and other electronic devices (Patchin and Hinduja 2006 cited in Hinduja and Patchin 2007, 3).

Cyberbullying can have a more adverse effect on victims than face-to-face bullying because of the anonymity factor that most cyberbullying entails—"you don't know who it is, so more scared" (Smith et al. 2008). It has the potential to be worse especially as it has the potential to be "all the time," so it can be "really hard to escape" (Smith et al. 2008). Cyberbullying has more of a devastating psychological effect on the victims, as, for example, victims may become more frightened if they are sent an "I will kill you" text message (Slonje and Smith 2008).

Victims of cyberbullying may not receive adequate support for the following reasons: (1) adults may lack awareness of cyberbullying; (2) friends might not perceive cyberbullying as such a serious issue, and most victims turn to their friends for support; or (3) victims often do not tell anyone of cyberbullying (Slonje and Smith 2008). Cyberbullying was significantly associated with increases in suicidal ideation (Hinduja and Patchin 2007). Cyberbullying victimization was a stronger predictor of suicidal thoughts and behaviours than cyberbullying offending (Hinduja and Patchin 2007). Cyberbullying victims were 1.9 times more likely to have attempted suicide than those who had not been cyberbullied (Hinduja and Patchin 2007). Students who experienced cyberbullying, either as a victim or a perpetrator, had significantly lower self-esteem than those having little or no experience of cyberbullying (Hinduja and Patchin 2007). Males were more likely to be cyberbullies than their female counterparts (Li 2006). Over a third of the cyber victims had been harassed more than three times and close to half of the cyberbullies had bullied others more than three times using electronic means (Li 2006).

Hinduja and Patchin (2007, 112) pointed to the provision of education, counselling, and pro-social outlets to help resolve strain experienced by cyberbullying victims. They note that this could be done through the provision of supplementary health-education programming to reduce the possibility of strain resulting from all forms of peer harassment, including cyberbullying.

In this chapter, we examined some of the main circumstances of violence affecting Caribbean SIDS which have both short-term and long-term impacts on hundreds of children living in these countries. The negative effects endanger childhood, compromise the quality of life that these children enjoy and reduce their chances of experiencing decent and productive lives.

Notes

1. http://www.who.int/violenceprevention/approach/definition/en/ (Accessed May 18, 2018).
2. http://www.who.int/violenceprevention/approach/definition/en/ (Accessed May 18, 2018).
3. http://www.ohchr.org/en/professionalinterest/pages/crc.aspx (Accessed November 28, 2018).

4. https://www.who.int/mediacentre/factsheets/violence-against-children/en/ (Accessed April 19, 2019).

5. http://jamaica-gleaner.com/article/news/20190108/jamaica-records-20-murders-first-seven-days-2019 (Accessed March 28, 2019).

6. http://jamaica-gleaner.com/article/news/20190108/jamaica-records-20-murders-first-seven-days-2019 (Accessed November 28, 2018).

7. http://jamaica-gleaner.com/article/commentary/20160921/editorial-normalising-high-crime-jamaican-neighbourhoods (Accessed July 14, 2019).

8. http://jamaica-gleaner.com/article/news/20160308/solving-jamaicas-problem-violence (Accessed November 28, 2018).

9. http://www.loopnewsbarbados.com/content/over-1000-cases-child-abuse-recorded-child-care-board.

10. http://www.ocr.gov.jm/index.php/statistics/2015-stats (Accessed April 9, 2019).

11. http://unicef.in/Story/197/All-You-Want-to-Know-About-Corporal-Punishment (Accessed November 29, 2016).

12. Source: http://www.corpun.com/15archive/bbs01501.htm (Accessed February 3, 2019).

13. http://www.newstalk93fm.com/news/jamaica-is-not-ready-for-anti-beating-laws-says-education-minister/ (Accessed November 28, 2018).

14. Source: Jamaica's *Youth Link* Newspaper, September 15–21, 2015.

15. Source: Violence against children in Haiti—Findings from a National Survey 2012. http://www.cdc.gov/violenceprevention/pdf/violence-haiti.pdf.

16. https://www.stlucianewsonline.com/st-lucia-to-abolish-corporal-punishment-in-schools/ (Accessed March 28, 2019).

17. http://stlucianationwide.com/2015/08/minister-says-corporal-punishment-too-rampant-in-st-lucia/ (Accessed June 3, 2018).

18. www.unicef.org/jamaica/parenting_corner_2904.htm (Accessed March 28, 2019).

19. http://www.nationnews.com/nationnews/news/82069/principal-teacher-attacked (Accessed July 14, 2019).

20. https://www.cdc.gov/violenceprevention/pdf/violence-haiti.pdf (Accessed December 9, 2016).

21. http://www.jamaicaobserver.com/news/School-violence-focus%2D%2D%2D%2DEducation-ministry-to-implement-measures-starting-summer (Accessed December 8, 2016).

22. http://www.jamaicaobserver.com/news/School-violence-focus%2D%2D%2D%2DEducation-ministry-to-implement-measures-starting-summer (Accessed December 8, 2016 and Accessed May 5, 2019).
23. https://www.google.com/url?client=internal-uds-cse&cx=partner-pub-4993191856924332:98b6e2-dgz1&q=http://jamaica-gleaner.com/article/news/20161031/photos-hundreds-protest-violence-against-children-outside-jamaica-college&sa=U&ved=2ahUKEwjEv6rCxbXjAhXMnuAKHQ9IByAQFjAAegQIARAC&usg=AOvVaw2kkpPqumXZ1_yfZShrle8J (Accessed July 14, 2019).
24. https://www.stlucianewsonline.com/student-arrested-after-knife-incident-at-george-charles-secondary/ (July 14, 2019).
25. https://www.theguardian.com/world/2018/jun/15/timeline-oxfam-sexual-exploitation-scandal-in-haiti (Accessed May 5, 2019).
26. http://www.emro.who.int/health-topics/suicide/index.html   (Accessed May 5, 2019).
27. http://www.emro.who.int/health-topics/suicide/index.html   (Accessed May 5, 2019).
28. http://www.emro.who.int/health-topics/suicide/index.html   (Accessed May 5, 2019).
29. https://www.who.int/news-room/fact-sheets/detail/suicide   (Accessed May 2019).
30. https://www.who.int/mental_health/suicide-prevention/exe_summary_english.pdf (Accessed May 5, 2019).
31. https://www.unicef.org/jamaica/bullying_FULL_REPORT_Anti_Bullying_Consultants_Report_Edited_2ac.pdf (Accessed April 19, 2019).
32. https://www.unicef.org/jamaica/bullying_FULL_REPORT_Anti_Bullying_Consultants_Report_Edited_2ac.pdf (Accessed April 19, 2019).
33. https://www.unicef.org/jamaica/bullying_FULL_REPORT_Anti_Bullying_Consultants_Report_Edited_2ac.pdf (Accessed April 19, 2019).
34. http://www.loopjamaica.com/content/suicides-30-2018 (Accessed April 19, 2019).

References

Bailey, C., Robinson, T., & Coore-Desai, C. (2014). Corporal punishment in the Caribbean: Attitudes and practices. *Social and Economic Studies, 63*(3), 207–233.

Baker-Henningham, H., Meeks-Gardner, J., Chang, S., & Walker, S. (2009). Experiences of violence and deficits in academic achievement among urban primary school children in Jamaica. *Child Abuse and Neglect, 33*(5), 296–306.

Barbados 2018 Human Rights Report. (2018). Retrieved May 4, 2019, from https://www.state.gov/documents/organization/289516.pdf.

Blosnich, J., & Bossarte, R. (2011). Low-level violence in schools: Is there an association between school safety measures and peer victimization? *Journal of School Health, 81*(2), 107–113.

CDB, Hornick, J. P., & Matheson, J. (2007). *Child development and children at risk in Saint Lucia. Volume 1: A review of the needs and services for children.* International Centre, University of Calgary.

Center for Disease Control and Prevention (CDC). (2014). Violence against children in Haiti—Findings from a National Survey, 2012. Interuniversity Institute for Research and Development, Comité de Coordination. Port-au-Prince, Haiti: Centers for Disease Control and Prevention. Retrieved June 3, 2016, from https://www.cdc.gov/violenceprevention/pdf/violence-haiti.pdf.

Daniels, J. A., Bradley, M. C., & Hays, M. (2007). The impact of school violence on school personnel: Implications for psychologists. *Professional Psychology: Research and Practice, 38*(6), 652.

Evans, H. L. (2001). *Inside Jamaican schools.* Kingston: University of the West Indies.

Flannery, D. J., Wester, K. L., & Singer, M. I. (2004). Impact of exposure to violence in school on child and adolescent mental health and behavior. *Journal of Community Psychology, 32*, 559–573.

Flouri, E. (2005). Post-traumatic stress disorder (PTSD): What we have learned and what we still have not found out. *Journal of Interpersonal Violence, 20*, 373–379.

Gilbert, L., Reza, A., Mercy, J., Lea, V., Lee, J., Xu, L., … Domercant, J. W. (2018). The experience of violence against children in domestic servitude in Haiti: Results from the Violence Against Children Survey, Haiti 2012. *Child Abuse and Neglect, 76*, 184–193.

Gittens, J. (2008). Violence and indiscipline in schools: Challenges. The experience of Barbadian Secondary Schools. Retrieved May 12, 2016, from http://www.butbarbados.com/wp-content/uploads/sites/22/2018/05/conference3.pdf.

Global Initiative to End All Corporal Punishment of Children. (2016b). Corporal punishment of children in Haiti. Retrieved December 9, 2016, from http://www.endcorporalpunishment.org/assets/pdfs/states-reports/Haiti.pdf.

Haiti Libre. (2015, July 3). School violence, 2 students stabbed. Retrieved December 9, 2018, from http://www.haitilibre.com/en/news-13326-haiti-security-school-violence-2-students-stabbed.html.

Hinduja, S., & Patchin, J. (2007). Offline consequences of online victimization: School violence and delinquency. *Journal of School Violence, 6*(3), 89–112.

Holder-Nevins, D., K. James, R. Bridgelal-Nagassar, A. Bailey, E. Thompson, H. Eldemire, …,W. D. Abel. (2012). Suicide among adolescents in Jamaica: What do we know? *West Indian Medical Journal,* 61(5), 516–520.

Holt, S., Buckley, H., & Whelan, S. (2008). The impact of exposure to domestic violence on children and young people: A review of the literature. *Child Abuse and Neglect, 32*(8), 797–810.

Humanium. (2013). Children of St Lucia: Realizing children's rights in St Lucia. Retrieved June 3, 2018, from http://www.humanium.org/en/americas/st-lucia/.

Jamaica Gleaner Online. (2015, May 11). Youth ministry not ready to ban corporal punishment. Retrieved April 3, 2018, from http://jamaica-gleaner.com/article/lead-stories/20150511/youth-ministry-not-ready-ban-corporal-punishment.

Jamaica Gleaner Online. (2016, October 31). PHOTOS: Hundreds protest violence against children outside Jamaica college gates. Retrieved November 30, 2018, from http://jamaica-gleaner.com/article/news/20161031/photos-hundreds-protest-violence-against-children-outside-jamaica-college.

Jamaica Observer. (2006, September 1). Crime the number one problem facing Jamaica. Retrieved January 31, 2018, from http://www.jamaicaobserver.com/news/112383_Crime-the-number-one-problem-facing-Jamaica.

Janosz, M., Archambault, I., Pagani, L. S., Pascal, S., Morin, A. J. S., & Bowen, F. (2008). Are there detrimental effects of witnessing school violence in early adolescence? *Journal of Adolescent Health, 43*(6), 600–608.

Jones, A., & E. Trotman Jemmott. (2009). Child sexual abuse in the Eastern Caribbean: The report of a study carried out across the Eastern Caribbean during the period October 2008 to June 2009. Retrieved April 9, 2019, from https://www.researchgate.net/publication/228827239_Child_Sexual_Abuse_in_the_Eastern_Caribbean.

Li, Q. (2006). Cyberbullying in schools: A research of gender differences. *School Psychology International, 27*(2), 157–170.

Matthies, B. K., Meeks-Gardner, J., Daley, A., & Crawford-Brown, C. (2008). Issues of violence in the Caribbean. *Perspectives in Caribbean Psychology,* 393–464.

Meeks Gardener, J., C. A. Powell, J. A. Thomas, & D. Millard. (2003). Perceptions and experiences of violence among secondary school students in urban Jamaica. *Pan American Journal of Public Health, 14*(2): 97–103. Retrieved June 3, 2018, from http://www.scielosp.org/pdf/rpsp/v14n2/a04v14n2.pdf.

Multiple Indicator Cluster Survey (MICS): UNICEF. (2012). Barbados Multiple Indicator Cluster Survey 2012. Retrieved January 9, 2018, from https://mics-surveys-prod.s3.amazonaws.com/MICS4/Latin%20America%20and%20Caribbean/Barbados/2012/Final/Barbados%202012%20MICS_English.pdf.

Miller, P. (2014). Children at risk: A review of sexual abuse incidents and child protection issues in Jamaica. *Open Review of Educational Research, 1*(1), 171–182.

Miller, T. (2008). *School violence and primary prevention.* New York: Springer.

National School Safety Center. (2007). The National School Safety Center serves as an advocate for safe, secure and peaceful schools worldwide and as a catalyst for the prevention of school crime and violence. Retrieved from http://www.schoolsafety.us/.

Office of the Children's registry (OCR). (2015). Statistics for Jamaica. Retrieved from http://www.ocr.gov.jm/index.php/statistics/2015-stats.

O'Keefe, M. (1997).Adolescents' exposure to community and school violence: Prevalence and behavioral correlates. *Journal of Adolescent Health, 20*(5): 368–376. Retrieved May 4, 2019, from https://www.sciencedirect.com/science/article/pii/S1054139X97801310.

Owen, S. (2015). Corporal punishment of children in St Lucia: Briefing for the Universal Periodic Review, 23rd session, 2015. Retrieved June 3, 2016, from http://www.upr-info.org/sites/default/files/document/saint_lucia/session_23_-_november_2015/gieacpc_upr23_lca_e_main.pdf.

Patchin, J. W., & Hinduja, S. (2006). Bullies move beyond the schoolyard: A preliminary look at cyberbullying. *Youth Violence and Juvenile Justice, 4*(2), 148–169.

Pinheiro, P. S. (Ed.). (2006). *World report on violence against children.* Geneva: United Nations. Retrieved January 21, 2019, from http://www.unviolencestudy.org/.

Planning Institute of Jamaica, Economic and Social Survey of Jamaica. (2017). Technical report.

Pottinger, A. M. (2012). Children's exposure to violence in Jamaica: Over a decade of research and interventions. *West Indian Medical Journal, 61*(4), 369–371.

Pottinger, A. M., & Stair, A. G. (2009). Bullying of students by teachers and peers and its effect on the psychological well-being of students in Jamaican schools. *Journal of School Violence, 8*(4), 312–327.

Shen, Y., & Sink, C. A. (2002). Helping elementary-age children cope with disasters. *Professional School Counselling, 5*, 322–330.

Slonje, R., & Smith, P. K. (2008). Cyberbullying: Another main type of bullying? *Scandinavian Journal of Psychology, 49*(2), 147–154.

Smith, P. K., Mahdavi, J., Carvalho, M., Fisher, S., Russell, S., & Tippett, N. (2008). Cyberbullying: Its nature and impact in secondary school pupils. *Journal of Child Psychology and Psychiatry, 49*(4), 376–385.

Soyibo, K., & Lee, M. (2000). Domestic and school violence among high school students in Jamaica. *West Indian Medical Journal, 49*(3), 232–236.

United Nations Children's Fund (UNICEF). (2006). Violence against children in the Caribbean region. Regional assessment. Retrieved January 13, 2019, from http://www.unicef.org/lac/Caribe_web(1).pdf.

United Nations Children's Fund (UNICEF). (2009b). Children in Barbados and the Eastern Caribbean: Child rights—The unfinished agenda. Retrieved January 9, 2018, from http://www.unicef.org/easterncaribbean/Child_Rights_-_The_Unfinished_Agenda.pdf.

United Nations Children's Fund (UNICEF). (2010). Child disciplinary practices at home evidence from a range of low- and middle-income countries. United Nations Children's Fund (UNICEF), Division of Policy and Practice. ISBN: 978-92-806-4547-7.

UNICEF. (2011). Jamaica Multiple Indicator Cluster Survey 2011. Retrieved January 9, 2018, from https://mics-surveys-prod.s3.amazonaws.com/MICS4/Latin%20America%20and%20Caribbean/Jamaica/2011/Final/Jamaica%202011%20MICS_English.pdf.

UNICEF. (2012a). Barbados Multiple Indicator Cluster Survey 2012. Retrieved January 9, 2018, from https://mics-surveys-prod.s3.amazonaws.com/MICS4/Latin%20America%20and%20Caribbean/Barbados/2012/Final/Barbados%202012%20MICS_English.pdf.

United Nations Children's Fund (UNICEF). (2013a). Corporal punishment of children in Jamaica. Retrieved June 3, 2018, from http://endcorporalpunishment.org/assets/pdfs/states-reports/Jamaica.pdf.

United Nations Children's Fund (UNICEF). (2013b). Corporal punishment of children in Haiti. Retrieved June 3, 2018, from http://www.endcorporalpunishment.org/assets/pdfs/states-reports/Haiti.pdf.

United Nations Children's Fund (UNICEF). (2014). Hidden in plain sight: A statistical analysis of violence against children. Retrieved November 29,

2018, from http://files.unicef.org/publications/files/Hidden_in_plain_ sight_statistical_analysis_EN_3_Sept_2014.pdf.

UNICEF. (2015a). Barbados child protection statistical digest. Retrieved May 24, 2017, from http://www.unicef.org/easterncaribbean/ECAO_BARBADOS_ Child_Protection_Statistical_Digest_2015.pdf.

UNICEF. (2015b). St Lucia child protection statistical digest. Retrieved May 24, 2017, from http://www.unicef.org/easterncaribbean/ECAO_St._Lucia__ Child_Protection_Statistical_Digest_2015.pdf.

United Nations Children's Fund (UNICEF). (2017). Situation analysis of children in St. Lucia. Retrieved April 18, 2019, from https://www.unicef.org/ easterncaribbean/ECA_St_Lucia_SitAn_2017_(002).pdf.

United Nations Convention on the Rights of the Child (UNCRC). (1989). Adopted and opened for signature, ratification and accession by General Assembly resolution 44/25 of 20 November 1989 entry into force 2 September 1990, in accordance with article 49. Retrieved November 28, 2018, from http://www.ohchr.org/en/professionalinterest/pages/crc.aspx.

United Nations Convention on the Rights of the Child (UNCRC) Haiti. (2015). Consideration of reports submitted by States parties under article 44 of the convention combined second and third periodic reports of states parties. Retrieved from https://documents-dds-ny.un.org/doc/UNDOC/ GEN/G15/046/17/PDF/G1504617.pdf?OpenElement.

United Nations Convention on the Rights of the Child (UNCRC) Jamaica. (2013). Consideration of reports submitted by States parties under article 44 of the convention. Third and fourth periodic reports of States parties due in 2008. Retrieved from http://tbinternet.ohchr.org/_layouts/treatybodyexternal/Download.aspx?symbolno=CRC%2fC%2fJAM%2f3-4&Lang=en.

Vince-Whitman, C. (2008). Preventing violence in schools: An international perspective and the role of Health and Family Life Education (HFLE) in the Caribbean. Retrieved May 4, 2019, from http://www.butbarbados.com/wp-content/uploads/sites/22/2018/05/conference11.pdf.

6

Voiceless Citizens

Learning to express oneself and participate in decision-making processes is essential for active citizenry in any society. When we do not empower our children to participate and express themselves from an early age, we "endanger" our children's citizenry and risk them becoming inactive and passive adult citizens. That is why child advocates call for age-appropriate child participation in the fulfilment of the rights of a child. The Articles listed below are commitments made by signatories to the Convention on the Rights of the Child (CRC) to implement effective child participation:

> States Parties shall assure to the child who is capable of forming his or her own views, the right to express those views freely in all matters affecting the child, the views of the child being given due weight in accordance with the age and maturity of the child.
> (CRC Article 12)
> The child shall have the right to freedom of expression; this right shall include freedom to seek, receive and impart information and ideas of all kinds, regardless of frontiers, either orally, in writing or in print, in the form of art, or through any other media of the child's choice.

© The Author(s) 2020
A. Henry-Lee, *Endangered and Transformative Childhood in Caribbean Small Island Developing States*, Studies in Childhood and Youth,
https://doi.org/10.1007/978-3-030-25568-8_6

(CRC Article 13)

States Parties shall respect the right of the child to freedom of thought, conscience and religion.

(CRC Article 14)

Articles 15 and 16 of the CRC also give the child the right to peaceful assembly and privacy. States have committed to these rights and they are duty-bound to institutionalize child participation in their respective societies.

However, there are several arguments against child participation. It is thought that children lack the competence or experience to participate and that children must learn to take responsibility before they can be granted rights (UNICEF 2001, 14), that giving children rights to be heard will take away their childhood and that child participation will lead to lack of respect for parents (UNICEF 2001, 14).

However, there are those who promote the importance of supporting and facilitating child participation. Children have different views from adults (UNICEF 2001, 11), and all children are capable of expressing a view (UNICEF 2001, 8). Child participation leads to better decisions since children have a body of experience and knowledge that is unique to their situation (UNICEF 2001, 10). Above all, learning to participate meaningfully in any discussion or process does not develop overnight. It has to be introduced and taught at an early age. When children are not allowed to participate, their interests are often disregarded in public policy (UNICEF 2001, 10). We need effective child participation as adults do not always act in children's best interests and may abuse their power over children (UNICEF 2001, 9), and denying children a voice, encourages impunity for abusers (UNICEF 2001, 10). Children who have not learnt to participate in the decision-making process will find it difficult to become active adult citizens and may be reluctant to involve themselves in the policy and political life of their societies. Fung (2004) states that participatory democratic governance can increase citizen involvement to facilitate innovative problem-solving and public action.

There are also published cases of effective child participation internationally. In Slovenia and Zimbabwe, there were successful child parliaments where the politicians listened to children and a report on the recommendations from the child parliamentarians was prepared (UNICEF 2001, 18–19). In Nigeria, effective youth participation was seen in the review of the constitution and a submission made by the youths (United Nations Youths 2013, 3); and in Malaysia, children submitted a children's report which supplemented the official Government report to the International Committee on the Rights of the Child (UNICEF 2012a).

In this chapter, we examine the levels and types of child participation in Barbados, Jamaica, Haiti and St. Lucia. Many models are analysed for their relevance in explaining the levels of participation that children in SIDS enjoy. This discussion on children's "voiceness" is interrogated through the secondary and primary data collected for this study on endangered childhood in Small Island Developing States. Secondary data include reports to the International Committee on the Rights of the Child and previous research. Primary data from a survey among high school students in Jamaica on perceptions of childhood are also examined. We begin with a critique of some models of participation.

Some Models of Participation

The word "participation" is easier to define than to measure. Effective participation must be accepted as having taken place by both the participant and others and cannot be confused with consultation. There is no universally accepted definition of participation. Hart (1992, 5) defines participation as a process of sharing in decisions which affect one's life and the life of the community in which one lives, and as a means by which a democracy is built, and a standard against which democracies should be measured. Chawla (2001, cited in Percy-Smith and Thomas 2009, 27) describes participation as "a process in which children and youth engage with other people around issues that concern their individual and collective life conditions." Upadhyay et al. (2008, 7) note that much of the practice of child participation is justified by children's right to expression in all matters affecting them (CRC Article 12). UNICEF, which provides many manuals and documents on child participation, notes that this involves encouraging and enabling children to make their views known on the issues that affect them.[1] UNICEF states that put into practice, child participation involves adults listening to children—to all their multiple and varied ways of communicating[2].

Child participation:

> includes a wide range of activities differing in form and style for children at different ages; seeking information, expressing the desire to learn even at a very young age, forming views, expressing ideas; taking part in activities and processes; being informed and consulted in decision-making; initiating ideas, processes, proposals and projects; analysing situations and making choices; respecting others and being treated with dignity. (UNICEF 2002, 14)

There are several models of participation and we focus here on only some of them. Arnstein (1969) presented an eight-rung ladder of citizen participation which ranges from manipulation at rung one to citizen control at rung eight.[3] She argues that power sharing is the real basis of participation as it enables one to make decisions. At the non-participation level, there is no power and citizens are voiceless.

In 2006, Tritter and McCallum proposed a model of their own and criticized Arnstein's model for its emphasis on power, stating that this emphasis limited the potential and importance of the involvement of all persons in shaping their own participation based on forms of knowledge and expertise.

Roger Hart enhances Arnstein's model to develop a ladder of young people's participation, which presents seven levels or rungs (Hart 1992). The lowest rungs represent the least amount of participation and the highest levels signify the highest amounts of participation.

For Malone and Hartung (2010, 25), Hart's ladder, having originated from Arnstein's community-participation model, draws on and adopts a variety of disciplines to describe children's participation (mostly adult or community-based theories) rather than drawing on intellectual works that should reflect successful and innovative developments in practice. One of the assumptions that Hart's ladder reflects is that children's individual agency in participating with each other to make decisions is a key factor in the achievement of good programmes, and programmes that are designed to fulfil their rights. Hart (2008, 26) noted the cultural limitation of the model, since the degree of emphasis on individual agency may not be appropriate to many cultures.

Phil Treseder (1997) presents a model which describes degrees of participation based on Hart's ladder of participation. Treseder's model rests on Hodgson's (1995) conditions for participation which are that: children must first have access to those in power; secondly, they must have access to relevant information; third, they must have real choices between different options; and fourth, support from trusted, independent persons. Finally, they must have a means of appeal or complaint if anything goes wrong. He calls for children's full empowerment in order to ensure effective child participation.

Shier's Pathways to Participation model (2001) describes a process for increasing child participation. He poses several questions that would enable facilitators to determine the "openings, opportunities and obligations" for child participation. Like Arnstein (1969), Shier suggests that power will determine the level of child participation that is taking place. Ultimately, the question that each country must answer in the positive is: *Is there a policy requirement that children and adults share power and responsibility for decisions?*

Tim Davies (2011) outlined six principles in relation to online participation based on the Convention on the Rights of the Child (CRC). Persons referring to the CRC, typically divide the child's rights into three main categories: provision, protection and participation. No one set of rights is more important than others. One side of the triangle of Child Rights will collapse if one set of rights is not taken into consideration.

The Organization for Economic Cooperation and Development (OECD) also developed a framework of participation with levels ranging from "information" to "consultation" to "active participation" (OECD 2001). Information was described as a one-way relationship in which governments produced and provided information for "passive" citizens. Examples of this information include public records, official gazettes and government websites. Consultation involved a two-way relationship in which citizens provided feedback to the government. The rules of engagement are set by the government and citizens are invited to contribute their views and opinions. Public opinion surveys and comments on draft legislation are examples of consultation. Active participation described a relationship based on partnership with government in which citizens actively set the agenda, proposed policy options and shaped the policy dialogue. Examples of active participation include consensus conferences and citizens' juries.

In assessing the framework presented by the OECD, Pedro Martin (2010) shows that the active participation level hardly goes beyond the levels of tokenism defined by Arnstein. Martin (2010) asserts that the OECD model ignores any kind of citizen control and rejects the transfer of power from the representative organs to citizens. He sees power and control as key to effective participation.

The Department for International Development's (DFID) youth working group put forward a three-lens approach to participation. The group asserts that it is essential that the practitioners consider all the three lenses which are not mutually exclusive. The ultimate aim is to ensure that youth become leaders or partners based on their level of agency—capacity to act, skills and capabilities, and their ability to change their own lives.[4]

Based on four case studies of children's and young people's successful political advocacy in Nicaragua, Shier et al. (2014) reviewed concepts and theories related to youth participation. They developed a conceptual framework, the foundation of which was based on the integration of two complementary approaches: human rights and human development. The researchers identified eight key concepts or areas which were essential to effective and responsive practice.

In the next section, we examine the relevance of these models to explaining child participation in Small Island Developing States (SIDS).

Child Participation in Selected Small Island Developing States (SIDS)

All models discussed earlier fail to portray the dynamism of child participation in the Small Island Developing States. With a history of slavery, colonialism and high levels of public and private poverty, the adult citizens are not always all actively participating in the political processes in the countries. Day-to-day survival, issues of poverty, political apathy and low trust in political leaders affect the adults' willingness to participate. It is highly unlikely that inactive adults will encourage and facilitate active child participation.

Caribbean citizens have struggled through the legacy of slavery to finally find their voice, especially post-independence. With a history of colonialism and still being regarded as "developing countries," "third world" and "under-privileged," SIDS have struggled to make themselves heard on the global stage. At the local level, a significant proportion of citizens have disengaged from the governance process. Citizens from SIDS are reluctant to participate to the electoral process. Barbados recorded the highest levels of voter turnout in recent times at 60 per cent with Haiti at a low of 17.8 per cent (Table 6.1). Jamaica and St. Lucia reported 48.4 per cent and 53.5 per cent, respectively in their last parliamentary elections (Table 6.1).

Lest citizens from SIDS be deemed totally passive, there have been occasions when they have even expressed themselves in violent ways. Haiti was the first country in the Caribbean to gain independence in 1804 and this was through a violent revolution. Since then, there have been several bouts of violence and rebellion as citizens have struggled to free themselves from persistent oppression. For example, McFadden (2015) informs us that "protesters burned tyres and threw rocks and glass bottles at riot police during another anti-government demonstration in Haiti's capital over long-delayed elections. A group of citizens made up mostly of young men demonstrated in Port-au-Prince to demand the departure of President Michel Martell (McFadden 2015).

Table 6.1 Voter turnout in selected SIDS for parliamentary elections

Country	Voter turnout (%)[a]	VAP (%)[b]
Barbados (2018)	60.3	67.1
Jamaica (2016)	48.4	46.2
Haiti (2015)	17.8	17.3
St. Lucia (2016)	53.5	70.0

Source: https://www.idea.int/data-tools/data/voter-turnout (Accessed April 12, 2019)
[a]The voter turnout defined as the percentage of registered voters who actually voted
[b]The voter turnout defined as the percentage of the voting age population that actually voted

In Jamaica, there was widespread rioting in April 1999, when former Prime Minister P. J. Patterson announced that a 31 per cent gas tax would be imposed (*Daily Gleaner* 2009). From Morant Point to Negril Point, tires went up in flames and businesses were forced to close as many Jamaicans joined in the infamous 1999 gas riots, the effect of which was the crippling of public transportation and the education system, while the police force, the military and the fire brigade, worked overtime to contain the protests. Many commuters were forced to walk long distances as bus drivers and taxi operators abandoned their routes and parked their vehicles (ibid.).

For both adults and children, levels of participation depend on some of the main following inputs: political will to facilitate effective participation, willingness to participate and quality of partnership among duty bearers to facilitate child participation and agency. These factors will determine the outcome and type of participation (Fig. 6.1). Important contextual factors in the implementation of child participation include the history of the society; the politics, culture and socio-economic conditions. If all the inputs are in place and the contexts are favourable, then effective child participation will occur. Although not included in the diagram, some of the confounding features that would affect the situation are sex, class, level of education and residential area. All these impact on

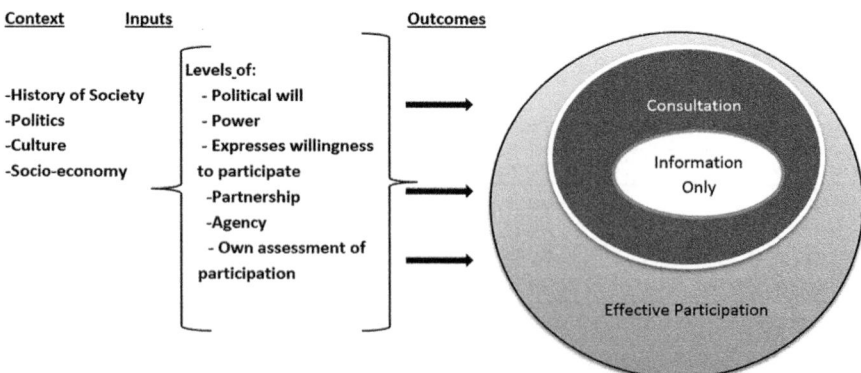

Fig. 6.1 Inputs and outcomes of participation in a contextual framework. (Source: Author's formulation)

the level and type of child participation. Ultimately, for participation to be described as "effective," the participants must determine that it is so.

Since the ratification of the Convention on the Rights of the Child in all four countries under review, there has been an effort to pay some attention to child participation, especially given the obligation to report on the implementation of the CRC to the international committee on child rights. Using secondary and primary data, we now assess child participation in these four SIDS.

Barbados

In Barbados, active participation of children in decisions affecting their personal lives is minimal (UNICEF 2009, 15). The use of Students' Councils and Activity Clubs in the school system has seen only limited participation from students and opportunities for participation of adolescents through Government Ministries/Departments of Youth have not had widespread success. This is primarily because of cultural norms which do not actively encourage participation in the early childhood years or during adolescence. Such norms are reflected in the inadequate administration of the school-level opportunities and a weak institutional and administrative base for coordinating youth work at the national level.

Measures that have been taken to ensure that children exercise their right to express their views include a mandatory establishment of student councils in all secondary schools by the ministry of education (Committee on the Rights of the Child 2014, 22). Through these Councils, students are given the opportunity to develop their leadership capacity and engage in self-representation while creating a cadre of young people who are highly motivated, disciplined, positive in outlook and willing to provide a "voice" for their peers. Also, the Division of Youth Affairs periodically conducts and publishes surveys on young people to ascertain their experiences and views in relation to a number of issues such as sex, HIV/AIDS, violence, and educational reform (Committee on the Rights of the Child 2014, 22). In addition, young people are also represented on the National Committee on Monitoring the Rights of the Child (Committee on the Rights of the Child 2014, 22).

Jamaica

In Jamaica, child participation has received the least attention of all the rights over the years. Primary data collected from 103 students in two secondary schools revealed that 72 per cent of them were not asked their opinions by their teachers about the teaching and learning process. Of all the students, 76 per cent said that their parents did not ask their opinions at all.

Gordon (2015, 71) found that the State's level of commitment to child participation was low and there was no budgetary allocation for child participation activities. There was also no specific policy that addressed child participation rights, except for what was stated in the Child Care and Protection Act (CCPA), 2004 (Gordon 2015, 71). The Child Development Agency (2004, 36) states that "the child has the right to be consulted, according to the child's abilities and to express his views about significant decisions affecting him/her." Gordon (2015) also found from her research that children were generally afraid to express themselves freely at home and at school.

Moncrieffe (2010) from her research in Jamaica noted that one of her respondents stated:

> Child participation is often on a token basis and, more often than not, pushed by international agencies. There is a real challenge to find appropriate modalities for Children's participation in policy deliberation and/or project/programme implementation on a meaningful basis. Identifying the gaps between commitments at the policy level and implementation should be straightforward. Filling the gaps will not take place until the institutional and cultural adjustments are made in the policy processes. (Written response, Moncrieffe 2010, 86)

In Jamaica, there have been some efforts to involve youth advocates in the discussion of policies affecting them, but there is no institutionalized mechanism to involve children and youth in the conceptualization, formulation, implementation, monitoring and evaluation of policies and programmes (Office of the Children's Advocate [OCA] and UNICEF 2009/2010, 13). There have also been some notable efforts to create safe spaces where youth can interact. With the assistance of UNICEF, the National Centre for Youth Development (NCYD) of the Ministry of Culture, Youth and Sports, currently operates Youth Information Centres (YICs) in Kingston & St. Andrew, St. Catherine, St. James, St. Mary and Portland. These are youth-friendly spaces where young people aged 10–24 years, and sometimes those as young as eight years, can discuss and access information on issues affecting them, including career development and HIV/AIDS prevention. These YICs also serve as training centres for youth and adolescents to build their knowledge base and life skills. The existing YICs have been used over 81,000 times in the last two years. The NCYD plans to establish a Youth Information Centre in each parish (OCA and UNICEF 2009/2010, 13).

At a more formal level, youth serve on National Secondary School Councils. They also participate in the seven-year-old Youth Parliament which allows sixty young parliamentarians to discuss issues concerning young Jamaicans (OCA and UNICEF 2009/2010, 13). A number of youth also serve as Youth Ambassadors. There are some agencies that seek to ensure child participation in the formulation of their policies. The Office of the Children's Advocate has involved children in the development of their corporate plan and sought the opinions of children on several issues affecting them. The Child Development Agency (CDA) has also sought the advice of children in their care and in the development of the agency's annual budget and corporate Strategic Plan 2009–2012. Children's views were also requested in the development of the National Youth Policy (Moncrieffe 2015, 36). UNICEF Jamaica has always strived to ensure that children are an integral part of their activities.

For the last fourteen years, the annual Caribbean Child Research Conference has provided an opportunity for young researchers from high schools to present their research on child-related matters. An outstanding researcher is selected each year from a group of top-ten child researchers.

The child researchers are very aware of the issues/challenges facing children in Jamaica. A survey of the topics presented by children between 2006 and 2017 revealed that the majority carried out research on the violent circumstances in which children live in Jamaica (Fig. 6.2). This is in keeping with the primary data findings from the survey carried among 103 children in this country. Of all the respondents, 80 per cent of them

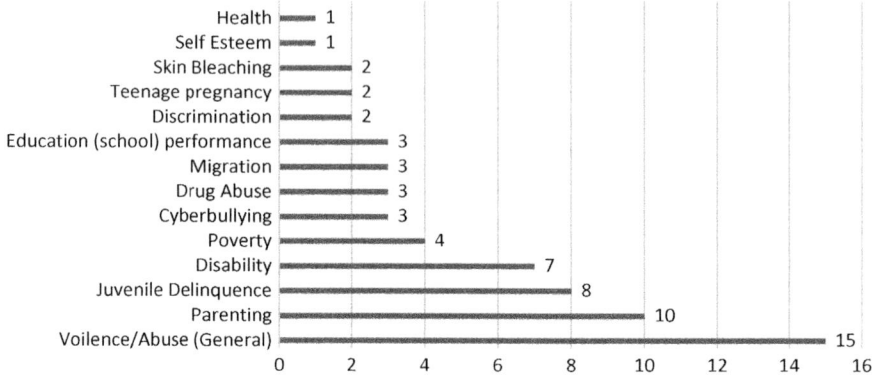

Fig. 6.2 Research topics presented by children at the Caribbean Child Research Conference 2006–2017. (Source: Author's analysis of topics presented by child researchers, Caribbean Child Research Conference 2006–2017)

reported that the levels of violence against children in Jamaica were either high or very high (see Table 5.1).

The second most popular topic for these child researchers was parenting (Fig. 6.2) and this was in keeping with the senior citizens' lamentation (discussed in Chap. 2) about the poor-quality parents that children endured in today's Jamaica. The third main top concern was juvenile delinquency followed by the issues facing children with disabilities. It is evident that children are able to effectively articulate the issues that concern them.

They were also able to put forward some valid recommendations for the reduction of violence in Jamaica. These child researchers proposed that interventions were needed from the government, community, individual and family.

UNICEF Jamaica also uses recommendations from youth on a social media platform called U-Report, available via SMS, Facebook and Twitter. Here young people express their opinions and share information on topics that affect them such as unemployment, dissemination and child marriage. Thus, they become positive agents of change as the views gathered are disseminated to community members and policy makers.[5] Jamaica and Haiti are two of the first Caribbean countries to launch U-Report. Jamaica launched their platform in 2018 with over 1300

U-Reporters. They noted that no conversations in Jamaica about youths should exclude youths and as such welcomed the UNICEF initiative.[6]

The International Committee on the Rights of the Child acknowledged that the views of the child were being promoted in homes and schools but noted that there was resistance on the part of some persons to adopt participatory approaches (Child Rights Connect Report 2015, 4). Additionally, efforts have been made over the period to ensure that the views of children are "given due consideration in courts, schools, family, relevant administrative processes and within families" (Committee on the Rights of the Child 2013, 39). One such effort involves the Office of the Children's Advocate (OCA) providing legal representation in court for all children and receiving and conducting investigations into reports made by or on behalf of children. Both the Child Development Agency (CDA) and the OCA host consultations with children. In 2007, the OCA held five such regional consultations (Committee on the Rights of the Child 2013, 40).

According to an OCA and UNICEF study of 2009/2010, even with these levels of child participation, many aspects of child and youth participation remain symbolic and tokenistic and the views of children do not generally influence the direction of policy in Jamaica. Although significant gains have been made in protecting and fulfilling the rights of the Jamaican child, the nation is currently at a very precarious point and the gains made to date face serious risk of reversal (OCA and UNICEF 2009/2010, 14). More urgent action is required to improve the welfare and well-being of Jamaican children, in keeping with Article 3 of the CRC, which maintains that "in all actions concerning children, whether undertaken by public or private social welfare institutions, courts of law, administrative authorities or legislative bodies, the best interests of the child shall be a primary consideration."

Haiti

In Haiti, youth participation is now on the reconstruction and recovery agenda. A National Youth Policy, a National Sport Policy and a National Civic Action Youth Policy were launched in 2011 by the Government, providing a foundation for the integration of youth and adolescent rights in national policies (UNICEF 2012b, 19). In addition to providing technical assistance for these efforts, UNICEF also helped to form the National Youth Council, representing over sixteen youth organizations and supported a workshop under the leadership of the youth ministry to produce national indicators to track progress on youth-related issues. On a larger scale than ever seen before, Haiti's youth made their voices heard, even beyond Haiti's borders. UNICEF used its strong convening power in 2011 to support a series of national youth forums that allowed hundreds of young people to exchange views and submit proposals on how to contribute to the reconstruction process (UNICEF 2012b, 19). It also facilitated opportunities for engaging local decision makers including candidates in local elections through town hall meetings, where youth expressed their views and made recommendations. Events involving the Scouts and the Red Cross were also held in the most remote areas to raise awareness on the contribution and impact young people can have on their environment. Youth voices also echoed beyond Haiti's borders that year, as UNICEF enabled young leaders to participate in global forums including the Climate Change Conference in December 2010, the High Level Meeting on Youth at the UN General Assembly in July 2011 and the UNESCO Youth Forum in October 2011 (UNICEF 2012b, 19).

According to the Report of the Committee on the Rights of the Child (2002, 14), the greatest obstacle in the way of respect for the views of the child remains the lack of any tradition of tolerance in general within Haitian society—a problem that becomes acute when children need to be allowed to express themselves and/or participate in decisions affecting them. Although the Constitution recognizes and guarantees every person's right to freedom of expression on any matter, by any means, domestic law does not recognize this right specifically for children. In spite of this, the Ministry for Social Affairs listens closely to their views as part of its "Assembly Points" project (Committee on the Rights of the Child 2002, 14). Additionally, Haiti also begun to support the U-Report platform with the view of enhancing youth participation in the social dialogue on key subject matters concerning them (UNICEF 2017).

St. Lucia

With respect to children's views in St. Lucia, the Ministry of Education closely coordinated with school principals and teachers, to receive feedback from students on issues that affect them (Child Rights Connect 2014, 3). The Child Rights Connect Report (2014, 3) indicated that children could, if they wished, participate in public decision-making in various ways. Some schools had a Youth Parliament, which participated in an annual general debate organized by the National Youth Council. Within these institutions, children could express their opinions on issues pertinent to them. Sometimes they were active through writing, music or the arts, or participated in direct discussions with ministries. Also, a number of NGOs were involved in promoting child participation.

According to the Report of the Committee on the Rights of the Child (2013, 14), the St. Lucia National Youth Policy provides for the full participation of youth in the political, economic, social and cultural life of the country. The annual Youth Parliament allows young men and women to debate issues of national, regional and international importance and articulate recommendations. The report also noted that although it was seasonal, the youth were also active in the National Youth Council and the National Student Councils (Committee on the Rights of the Child 2013, 40).

The examination of child participation is limited due to the paucity of data on these rights in Barbados, Jamaica, Haiti and St. Lucia. In all four countries, child participation has increased since the countries have ratified the CRC. However, there is no clear indication of the number of suggestions and inputs made by children get translated into policy. Using the conceptual framework presented earlier (Fig. 6.1) and on examination of the limited available data, it can be concluded that effective child participation has not been institutionalized or systematized. We note that there has been a change from "complete voicelessness" over the decades to "limited voiceness." However, the levels of input are low in many cases and thereby effective participation is elusive in all four countries (Table 6.2). The only inputs that are "medium" are in relation to the political will, expressed when States ratified the CRC but there is no

Table 6.2 Summary of inputs in the process of child participation in Caribbean SIDS

Level of input	Low	Medium	High
Political will (as seen in policy and legislative frameworks)		X: signatory of the CRC but child participation is not institutionalized	
Power of children to influence the policy process		X: some examples of child participation	
Access to relevant information	X		
Willingness to participate in the decision-making process	X		
State partnership with other agencies to ensure child participation	X		
Age appropriateness of child participation	X		
Agency: capacity to act, skills of the youth and capabilities, their ability to change their own lives	X		
Definition of participation by participants themselves	X		
Total assessment of level of input	X		

Source: Author's assessment

national supporting child participation policy. Effective child participation must be manifested by the involvement of children in the development of policy documents, strategic plans and programmes. In summary, with low levels of critical inputs, the outcome is ineffective child participation.

Much depends on political will and the efforts of individual ministries and agencies dealing with children. Though all the countries have noted the importance of that aspect of child development, efforts at child participation appear to be more progressive in Jamaica. Perhaps the biggest challenge to the implementation of full and effective child participation is the issue of age. The most appropriate age for children to be allowed to voice their opinions and to be taken seriously remains debatable. Among other barriers are the cultural norms and values, according to which children are still viewed as objects, personal property and unequal citizens. The issue of power dynamics becomes critical as adults fear the loss of control over their children. In many cases, children are not recognized as having valuable and legitimate contributions. While there were notable examples of child participation in all four countries, the dynamics of the participation and the clear evidence of the inclusion of the views of children in policies affecting them are not immediately apparent.

The quality of child participation is also determined by family background and class. Children living in poverty and in rural areas are particularly marginalized. There is also a lack of effort to create innovative ways to include children's views in the development of policies and programmes. Participation rights are marginalized in favour of legislation and policy intended to meet governments' other obligations under the CRC (namely provision and protection rights).

The difficulties in accessing data from the countries point to a significant institutional weakness which hampers efforts at coherent policy development and implementation. Priority has to be placed on developing the relevant data collection systems and building the capacity for collation, analysis and use of the data to inform decision-making. These data would allow for evidence-based programming in aligning legal and policy frameworks with the CRC and other commitments; improving survival, development, protection and participation rights; and in reducing vulnerability (UNICEF 2009, 15).

In summary, in the context of the conceptual framework presented in Fig. 6.1 and an examination of available primary and secondary data, we can conclude that in Barbados, Jamaica, Haiti and St. Lucia, effective child participation is low.

If we want active adult citizens, an enabling environment must be established for children to express their opinions on matters that concern them without fear of intimidation and victimization. To reduce the endangerment of our children's future active citizenry, we need to ensure that change is implemented at the macro, institutional and individual/household levels. The state/government has to institutionalize child participation in all aspects of the policy process. There should be deliberate establishment of procedures in the policy formulation, implementation, monitoring and evaluation phases that include children. This will necessitate the training of policy makers, parents and children.

Increasing Effective Child Participation

The debate continues as to the appropriate age for the initiation of child participation. While aspects of child participation can start as early as age two in areas such as allowing children to always express how they feel and their preference for clothing, it is necessary to determine when child participants must be included in a policy process. According to the Child Rights International Network (CRIN), children in Jamaica and St. Lucia are held criminally responsible at age twelve, in Barbados, at eleven and in Haiti, thirteen.[7] Consequently, children should be allowed to express their opinions on policy matters that concern them at the age of criminal responsibility. Gender-sensitive spaces to express their concerns and make recommendations should be made available to children in Caribbean SIDS.

Save the Children Sweden (2008) notes, participation is a virtue that must be cultivated. From an early age, the child must be encouraged to take part in age-appropriate activities. Norman Girvan (1993) presents some strategies to increase youth participation. He proposes that that for those aged less than twelve, the focus of participation should be in schools, organizations and clubs. For individuals aged 12–14, the interaction would be at youth centres and playing fields. Along with the intensification of the activities for this age group, he also includes activities for the school dropouts and unemployed. For those older than nineteen years, Girvan proposes community development activities at colleges and universities (Girvan 1993).

Moncrieffe (2015, 39) also provided some recommendations for improvement in child participation in Jamaica which are also applicable to the other Caribbean countries:

1. Include children's participation rights in the policies and protocols of organizations.
2. Educate parents on the importance of incorporating their children in decision-making.
3. Provide children with opportunities and spaces to participate, such as in community clubs, school boards and churches.
4. Institutionalize understanding of "meaningful" child participation and of the concept and implications of "evolving capacities."

5. Develop realistic, well-staged, processes for building recognition and support for meaningful child participation.
6. Ensure that child participation features more prominently and concretely in a revised Child Care and Protection Act.
7. Respond to "intersectionalities," such that groups who suffer overlapping forms of disadvantage can be included in ways that prompt their development.
8. Mainstream child participation.

Based on a study of thirty organizations which deal with youths in Jamaica, Dunn (2001) noted that the main areas for improvement in youth consultation were self-governance; membership on decision-making boards/committees; time, space and resources for adolescents; adolescents' input into the programme design; adolescents' input into programme evaluation and space to help adolescents develop their opinions.

UNICEF[8] cautions that to be meaningful, effective, ethical, systematic and sustainable, participation must be:

- transparent and informative
- voluntary
- respectful
- relevant to children's lives
- child-friendly
- inclusive
- supported by training for adults
- safe and sensitive to risk
- accountable

Effective child participation will not be institutionalized if there is not radical cultural change through advocacy and lobbying for children. The view of the child as an equal active citizen with opinions that are valid and useful needs to be promoted throughout the society in homes, schools, churches and in the streets. We must recognize, however, that effective child participation will not take place without providing relevant information to children so that they can make informed decisions on matters that affect them. The information must be presented in a child-friendly manner in the appropriate language and media that will facilitate increased knowledge. Unless children are encouraged to participate and an enabling environment fostered, future adult active citizenry will be "endangered."

Notes

1. http://www.unicef.org/sowc03/contents/childparticipation.html (Accessed November 2, 2015).
2. Ibid.
3. Source: Parr, J. (1999, 81). *In reviving democracy: Citizens at the heart of governance.*
4. DFID-CSO Youth Working Group. (2010). Youth participation in development: A tool for development. *Agencies and Policy Makers.*http://www.youthpolicy.org/library/documents/youth-participation-in-development-a-guide-for-development-agencies-and-policy-makers/ (Accessed July 14, 2019).
5. https://www.unicef.org/innovation/U-Report (Accessed April 21, 2019).
6. https://blogs.unicef.org/jamaica/youth-u-report-dont-talk-us-without-us/.
7. https://www.crin.org/en/home/ages.
8. http://www.unicef.org/eu/crtoolkit/downloads/Child-Rights-Toolkit-Module3-Web-Links.pdf.

References

Arnstein, S. (1969). A ladder of citizen participation. *Journal of American Planning, 35*(4), 216–224.

Chawla, L. (2001). Evaluating children's participation: Seeking areas of consensus. *PLA Notes, 42*(October), 9–13.

Child Development Agency. (2004). *Child Care and Protection Act, 2004: Implementation handbook for professionals*, p. 36.

Child Rights Connect. (2014). State party examination of Saint Lucia's second to fourth periodic report 66th session of the committee on the rights of the child 26 May–13 June 2014. Retrieved December 18, 2018, from http://

www.childrightsconnect.org/wp-content/uploads/2014/06/St.-Lucia_ Session-Report_St.-Lucia_FINAL.pdf.

Child Rights Connect. (2015). State party examination of Jamaica's third and fourth periodic report 68th session of the committee on the rights of the child 12 January–30 January 2015. Retrieved December 18, 2018, from http://www.childrightsconnect.org/wp-content/uploads/2013/10/Jamaica_ Session-Report_CRC.pdf.

Committee on the Rights of the Child. (2002). Consideration of reports submitted by States parties under article 44 of the Convention Initial reports of States parties due in 1997 Haiti. Retrieved December 18, 2018, from http:// tbinternet.ohchr.org/_layouts/treatybodyexternal/Download.aspx?symbolno =CRC%2fC%2f51%2fAdd.7&Lang=en.

Committee on the Rights of the Child. (2013). Consideration of reports submitted by States parties under article 44 of the convention third and fourth periodic reports of States parties due in 2008 Jamaica. Retrieved December 18, 2018, from http://tbinternet.ohchr.org/_layouts/TreatyBodyExternal/ Countries.aspx?CountryCode=JAM&Lang=EN.

Committee on the Rights of the Child. (2014). Consideration of reports submitted by states parties under article 44 of the convention second periodic reports of states parties due in 1997 Barbados. Retrieved December 18, 2018, from http://tbinternet.ohchr.org/_layouts/TreatyBodyExternal/Countries. aspx?CountryCode=BRB&Lang=EN.

Daily Gleaner. (2009, April 28). Gas riot in retrospect. Retrieved January 5, 2016, from http://jamaica-gleaner.com/power/8486.

Davies, T. (2011). Rethinking responses to children and young people's online lives. Retrieved December 15, 2018, from http://www.lse.ac.uk/media@lse/ research/EUKidsOnline/Conference%202011/Davies.pdf.

DFID-CSO Youth Working Group. (2010). Youth participation in development: A tool for development. Agencies and Policy Makers. Retrieved May2, 2019, from https://youtheconomicopportunities.org/sites/default/files/uploads/ resource/6962_Youth_Participation_in_Development.pdf.

Dunn, L. (2001). *Meeting the development and participation rights of in Jamaica: A joint UNFPA/UNICEF project.* Technical Report.

Fung, A. (2004). *Empowered participation: Reinventing urban democracy.* Princeton, NJ: Princeton University Press.

Girvan, N. (Ed.). (1993). *Working together for development: DTM Girvan on cooperatives and community development 1939–1968.* Kingston: Institute of Jamaica.

Gordon, L. (2015). Child participation in Jamaica: Cultural reality versus idealism. In special issues on children-reflections on adherence to child rights in the Caribbean. *Social and Economic Studies, 64*(1): 49–74.

Hart, R. (1992). Children's participation from tokenism to citizenship. Essay for UNICEF. Innocenti Essay No. 4.

Hart, R. (2008). *"Stepping back from 'The ladder'": Reflections on a model of participatory work with children* (pp. 19–31). Netherlands: Springer.

Hodgson, D. (1995). Participation of children and young people in social work. UNICEF.

Malone, K., & Hartung, C. (2010). Challenges of participatory practice with children. In *A handbook of children and young people's participation: Perspectives from theory and practice* (pp. 24–38). London: Routledge.

Martin, P. (2010). E-participation at the local level: The path to collaborative democracy. Retrieved May 5, 2019, from https://www.ippr.org/files/images/media/files/publication/2011/05/e_participation_in_local_government_1258.pdf.

McFadden, D. (2015, January 11). Haiti's anti-government's protests heat up. *Huffington Post.* Retrieved from http://www.huffingtonpost.com/2015/01/11/haiti-government protests_n_6451224.html.

Moncrieffe, J. (2010). *Situation of the promotion and protection of Rights of children and adolescents in Jamaica*. Report prepared for the organization of American States (Technical Report not available online).

Moncrieffe, J. (2015). *Caribbean child research conference: Summary of policy and strategy recommendations*. Kingston: Sir Arthur Lewis Institute of Social and Economic Studies.

Office of the Children's Advocate and UNICEF. (2009/2010). Jamaican children: Twenty years after the convention on the rights of the child. Retrieved November 25, 2015, from http://www.unicef.org/jamaica/CRC20_in_Jamaica.pdf.

Organization for Economic Cooperation and Development (OECD). (2001). Citizens as partners—Information, consultation and public participation in the policy making. Retrieved April 27, 2019, from https://www.internationalbudget.org/wp-content/uploads/Citizens-as-Partners-OECD-Handbook.pdf.

Parr, J. (1999). *In reviving democracy: Citizens at the heart of governance*. London: Earthscan.

Percy-Smith, B., & Thomas, N. (Eds.). (2009). *A handbook of children and young people's participation: Perspectives from theory and practice*. London and New York: Routledge.

Save the Children Sweden. (2008). Participation is a virtue that must be cultivated. An analysis of children's participation working methods and materials
within Save the Children Sweden. Retrieved January 4, 2016, from http://
www.hapinternational.org/pool/files/10121-participationisavirtue.pdf.

Shier, H. (2001). Pathways to participation: Openings, opportunities and obligations. *Children and Society, 15*(2), 107–117.

Shier, H., Méndez, M. H., Centeno, M., Arróliga, I., & González, M. (2014).
How children and young people influence policy-makers: Lessons from
Nicaragua. *Children and Society, 28*(1), 1–14.

Treseder, P. (1997). *Empowering children and young people: Promoting involvement in decision-making.* Retrieved from Amazon.co.uk.

Tritter, J. Q., & McCallum, A. (2006). The snakes and ladders of user involvement: Moving beyond Arnstein. *Health Policy, 76*(2): 156–168. E-Journals,
EBSCOhost.

UNICEF. (2001). Promoting children's participation in democratic decision-
making. Retrieved October 20, 2015, from https://www.unicef.org/
publications/files/pub_sowc03_en.pdf.

UNICEF. (2002). The state of the world's children 2003. New York: UNICEF.
Retrieved January 4, 2016, from https://www.unicef.org/sowc03/contents/
pdf/SOWCO3-eng.pdf.

UNICEF. (2009). Situation analysis of children and their families in the Eastern
Caribbean. Retrieved October 16, 2015, from http://www.unicef.org/
easterncaribbean/SITAN_Bdos.pdf.

UNICEF. (2012a). In Malaysia, celebrating every child's right to participation.
Retrieved November 25, 2015, from http://www.unicef.org/infobycountry/
malaysia_66403.html.

UNICEF. (2012b). Children of Haiti: Two years after. What is changing? Who
is making the change? Retrieved November 25, 2015, from http://www.
unicef.org/lac/Haiti_2yearsReport.pdf.

UNICEF. (2017). UNICEF Annual Report 2017—Haiti. Retrieved April 18,
2019, from https://www.unicef.org/about/annualreport/files/Haiti_2017_
COAR.pdf.

United Nations Youth. (2013). Youth, political participation and decision-
making. Retrieved October 20, 2015, from http://www.un.org/esa/socdev/
documents/youth/fact-sheets/youth-political-participation.pdf.

Upadhyay, J., Judith, E., Daniel, C., Henk, B., Joachim, T., Manuel, F., …
Laurence, G. (2008). *Children as active citizens: A policy programme guide.*
Bangkok: Inter-Agency Working Group on Children's Participation.

7

Children on the Periphery

Sometimes I think adults don' really care.
Female student, Jamaica, 2013

In the previous chapters, we focused on the endangerment of childhood in private and public spaces. So far, we have established, through the analysis of primary and secondary data, that children are exposed to many risks which may prevent them from becoming productive adults who realize their full potential. In this chapter, we concentrate on children who receive the least policy attention and whose endangerment is more intense because they "survive on the periphery" of the society. These children live in extremely difficult circumstances and include those living in poverty; those whose birth is not registered; children whose mothers are incarcerated; those with disabilities; children who are affected by and infected with HIV/AIDS; child labourers, teenage parents, missing children and those who are affected by migration. In Chap. 5, we considered the vulnerable group of children who live in violent circumstances, but in this chapter, we focus on those children who receive even less public attention.

© The Author(s) 2020
A. Henry-Lee, *Endangered and Transformative Childhood in Caribbean Small Island Developing States*, Studies in Childhood and Youth,
https://doi.org/10.1007/978-3-030-25568-8_7

Child Poverty as an *Endangering* Process

> Children remaining in monetary poverty are likely to stay in multi-dimensional poverty. However, children escaping from monetary poverty do not exist from multidimensional poverty. (Kim 2018, 1)

Child poverty is a violation of human rights. Children living below the poverty line are more likely to suffer intergenerational poverty; have less access to basic social services; are more likely to earn minimum wage as adults and have their own children born into the cycle of poverty.

> Children living in poverty are deprived of nutrition, water and sanitation facilities, access to basic health-care services, shelter, education, participation and protection, and that while a severe lack of goods and services hurts every human being, it is most threatening and harmful to children, leaving them unable to enjoy their rights, to reach their full potential and to participate as full members of the society. (UNICEF Press Centre 2007)

Sustainable Development Goal (SDG) 1 calls for the eradication of extreme poverty and hunger. However, in Latin America and the Caribbean, one in five children lives in extreme poverty; that is a total of 32 million children.[1] In Chap. 2, we reported the high levels of poverty and inequality in the Caribbean. Figure 7.1 provides data on child and poverty levels in selected Caribbean countries.

In Barbados, the most recent poverty assessment report stated that persons under fifteen years of age are overrepresented in poor households with 29.2 per cent of the indigent poor falling in that age category (SALISES 2012).

Gordon and Shailen (2007) indicate that more than four in ten children in Haiti live in absolute poverty. The same study indicates that seven out of ten children (2.66 million) experience at least one form of deprivation related to food, health, education, water, sanitation, shelter or information.[2] Approximately, 30 per cent of St. Lucian children live in poverty (Fig. 7.1).

We focus on Jamaica for further discussion on the characteristics of children living in poverty as the Jamaican data set was more easily available than those from the other countries. In 2015, the overall child poverty rate was 26.5 per cent; a 5.9 percentage point increase from 2004 (Table 7.1).

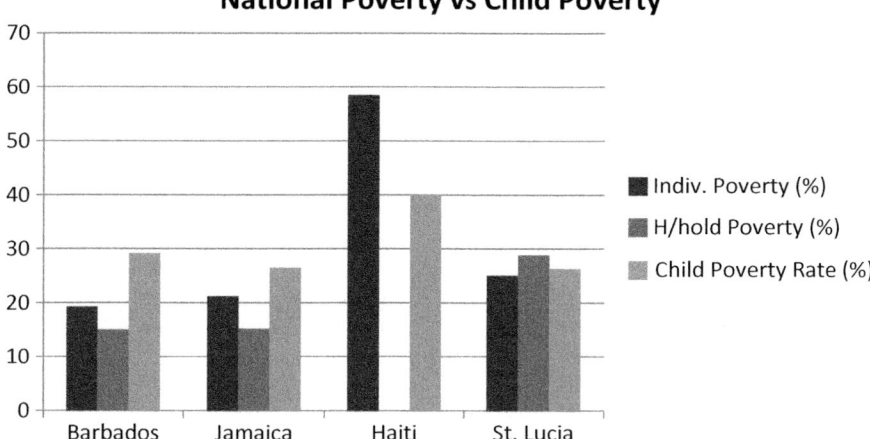

Fig. 7.1 Child and national poverty levels in selected Caribbean countries, latest years. (Sources: http://www.caribank.org/uploads/2012/12/Barbados-CALC-Volume-1-MainReport-FINAL-Dec-2012.pdf (Accessed March 3, 2019); Planning Institute of Jamaica 2015 Survey of Living Conditions (Kingston: Planning Institute of Jamaica); http://data.worldbank.org/country/haiti; http://www.caribank.org/uploads/2012/12/Barbados-CALC-Volume-1-MainReport-FINAL-Dec-2012.pdf; https://www.unicef.org/easterncaribbean/ECAO_St._Lucia__Child_Protection_Statistical_Digest_2015.pdf)

Table 7.1 Poverty prevalence by age group, 2004–2015 in Jamaica

Age group	2004 (%)	2007 (%)	2009 (%)	2010	2012	2014	2015
0–17 years	20.6	12.0	20.4	21.9	25.0	25.6	26.5
18–35 years	14.7	8.9	13.3	15.4	19.4	16.7*	18.8*
36–59 years	14.0	7.8	14.0	14.4	16.5	16.2**	16.3**
60 years and over	15.2	10.2	17.1	15.9	14.6	15.8	17.9
Total	16.9	9.9	16.5	17.6	19.9	20.0	21.2

Source: Planning Institute of Jamaica (2004, 2007, 2009, 2010, 2012, 2014, 2015)
  Jamaica Survey of Living Conditions (JSLC) data sets
Notes:*: 25–34 years and **: 35–59 years

Gender differentials were not significant (Table 7.2). The rural areas and the Kingston Metropolitan Area (KMA) recorded the highest proportion of children living in poverty (35.4 per cent) and poor households reported larger household sizes (Table 7.2).

Table 7.2 Characteristics of child poverty in Jamaica

		Percentage
Gender of child (N = 2836)	Male	26.2
	Female	26.9
Residential area (N = 2837)	KMA	18.7
	Other towns	17.7
	Rural areas	35.4
Mean household size (HH with children 0–17)	Poor households	5.5 person (N = 180)
	Non-poor households	4.1 person (N = 661)

Source: Planning Institute of Jamaica (2015) Jamaica Survey of Living Conditions (JSLC)
Data set calculated by Author

Huge disparities exist and the richest quintile (quintile 5) spends seventeen times more on education and almost six times more than the poorest quintile on health. On average, the poorest quintile spent J$1644 on education while the richest quintile spent J$28,691.[3] For health care, the poorest quintile spent 4177 and the richest quintile $J23,328.[4]

Table 7.3 examines the disparities between children living in poverty and those who are not. For the reference period of 20 days, nationally, on average children attended school on 19.2 of those days. Children in poor households attended school for 18.9 of those days, while those in non-poor households who attended school did so for 19.3 of those 20 days. The difference observed was not statistically significant (p = 0.04). The percentage of children in poor and non-poor households who had access to health insurance differed significantly, with approximately 16 per cent of children in non-poor households having access compared to only 3.7 per cent in poor households. The difference observed between the two groups was statistically significant (p = 0.00).

Investment in education was statistically different as non-poor households spent $155,103 while households with children below the poverty line spent $129,539 ($p$ = 0.001) (Table 7.4). A total of 65.8 per cent of the total population reported to have received benefits from Programme of Advancement Through Health and Education (PATH). Reports showed evidence of some leakage in social protection coverage with 59.4 per cent of non-poor households receiving PATH benefits. This amount increased to 80.4 per cent for poor households (p = 0.000) (Table 7.3).

Table 7.3 Some indicators on disparities between poor and non-poor children in Jamaica

	Poor	Non-poor	National
Mean age (years)* (N = 2837)	9.09	8.64	8.76
Mean number of children in household** (N = 1419)	2.6	1.9	2.0
Mean household size** (N = 1419)	5.5	4.1	4.4
Mean total annual consumption expenditure by household** (N = 1419)	J$512,955.38	J$1,146,429.86	J$1,017,313.09
Mean days of school attendance (20-day period)* (N = 2277)	18.9	19.3	19.2
Mean total education expenditure by household** (N = 1275)	J$129,538.90	J$155.103.49	J$149,904.56
% with health insurance** (N = 2837)	3.7	15.9	12.7
% of household receiving/have received benefit from PATH** (N = 767)	80.4	59.4	65.8

Source: JSLC 2015 data set (data for children under eighteen years old), analysis by authors using SPSS v.21
*p < 0.05 and **p < 0.01

Table 7.4 Share of persons with disability by broad age group (%) for selected Caribbean countries

Country	Total	0–4 years	5–19 years	20–39 years	40–59 years	60–79 years	80+ years
Barbados	4.0	0.7	1.7	2.2	4.0	11.3	34.4
Grenada	4.4	0.8	1.7	2.8	5.5	14.0	29.9
St. Lucia	4.9	1.4	2.4	3.9	6.2	16.6	26.0
Trinidad and Tobago	4.1	0.6	1.6	2.4	5.7	17.0	42.4

Source: ECLAC (2009, 25)

Analysis of these data reveals that children living in poverty are more disadvantaged than non-poor children; more females are in poverty; the household sizes of poor households are larger than those of non-poor houses; there is greater access to health insurance for non-poor children and more investment in education and health. Based on these disadvantages, children living in poverty are more likely to suffer from an endangered childhood.

In the countries under review, there are several programmes to support the needy and indigent. Due to inadequate financial and human resources, there is not 100 per cent coverage of all children living in poverty. For example, in Jamaica, the Programme of Advancement through Health and Education (PATH) is a conditional cash transfer (CCT) programme funded by the government through support from the World Bank has become the main social assistance program. As on December 2017, the number of registered PATH beneficiaries were 42,088 (0 to under 6 years) under health care and 198,502 (6–17 years) under education. The number of persons receiving benefits were 39,519 (0 to under 6 years) and 167,298 (6–17 years) (Planning Institute of Jamaica 2018)

In Haiti, an integrated social protection mechanism has been established. This delivers social services directly to families through household development agents (HDAs). They work with at least 100 households. The HDAs utilize a three-pronged strategy to: (1) raise awareness and increase knowledge of health, nutrition, hygiene, and sanitation practices; (2) provide a basic package of commodities and services; and (3) refer families to relevant social services. Regarding the protection of vulnerable people in Haiti, there is the National School Canteens Programme (PNCS) created in 1997 (ECLAC 2013). The PNCS's mission is primarily the management of canteens in public schools and the coordination of the regulating of all the interventions of donors and NGOs (ECLAC 2013). The programme provides a hot meal for students daily and a little over 150,000 students in 2007–2008 to just over 330,000 students in 2010–2011. In 2012, the PNCS and its partners (World Bank, PMA and USAID) achieved a nationwide coverage of 1.1 million of students from 3200 schools (ECLAC 2013).

Unregistered Children

The child shall be registered immediately after birth and shall have the right from birth to a name, the right to acquire a nationality and, as far as possible, the right to know and be cared for by his or her parents. (United Nations Convention on the Rights of the Child 1989, Article 7 (1))

The first proof of one's citizenship is birth registration. UNICEF estimates that one in four children globally is not registered.[5] Poverty is one of the main barriers to birth registration and children from the richest households are almost twice as likely to be registered as children from the poorest households.[6] One in every ten children in Latin America and the Caribbean is not registered at birth (UNICEF 2011, 4). One in seven registered children does not possess a birth certificate and there is a significant difference between those whose births are registered and those who actually have a birth certificate (UNICEF 2013a, 18). Without proof of citizenship, children lack legal identity, cannot access basic social services and will never be able to participate fully in their societies.

One data source revealed that in Jamaica, 10 per cent of births are not registered before the age of one;[7] 8 per cent of the children born in St. Lucia are unregistered and of all the children born in Haiti, 20 per cent of their births are not registered (source).[8] Although, in Haiti, birth registration is free until the age of two, the government does not register all births immediately (United States Department of State 2012). Once that two-year period has passed, birth registration becomes a very expensive procedure. After the 2010 earthquake, the problem of proof of birth registration became even more severe as several official documents were destroyed.

The countries have tried to increase birth registration. In 2012, Jamaica implemented a bedside registration programme and now birth registration is at 99.5 per cent (PIOJ 2012). In Haiti, the government adopted a presidential decree on February 1, 2002, allowing any person without a birth certificate to regularize his or her civil status by being registered. This decree granted a tax exemption for the related formalities and allowed late declarations without a judgement (Government of Haiti 2013). In St. Lucia, 8 per cent of all children are unregistered. In order to reduce the endangerment children face from non-registration, UNICEF (2011, 6) calls for universally free and timely registration immediately after birth.

Children with Disabilities

Fewer than 4 per cent of the persons with disabilities in the Caribbean are less than nineteen years old (Table 7.4). These children face many challenges and their citizenship is endangered every day. In each island, persons with disabilities represent approximately 5 per cent of the total population (Table 7.4). In its February 2014 report to the Committee on the Rights of the Child, the Barbados government reported that there were 2216 children living with disabilities in that country (Government of Barbados 2014, 35). UNICEF (2013a, 13) reported that 3.3 per cent of the population of children, nineteen years and younger were identified with a disability and this represented 1 per cent of the total population living with disabilities in Barbados.

All four countries under review have legislative support for the adherence to the rights of persons with disabilities (PWD). Jamaica, Haiti and St. Lucia ratified the Convention on the Rights of Persons with Disabilities in 2007, 2009 and 2013, respectively. Examples of legislations in support of persons with disabilities in these countries include:

Barbados	Constitution Article 23
Jamaica	The Disabilities Act 2014[9]
	Constitution Article 24
Haiti	Integration of Persons with Disabilities 2012
St. Lucia	*Draft National Policy for Persons with Disabilities*

https://treaties.un.org/Pages/ViewDetails.aspx?src=IND&mtdsg_ no=IV-15&chapter=4&lang=en (Accessed April 5, 2018)

In the report to the Committee on Children's Rights, the government of Barbados admitted that children with disabilities experienced some degree of discrimination and they still had to pay for standard secondary education or go to special schools (Government of Barbados 2014, 18). However, the government has begun to make the necessary physical and social changes in school to accommodate physically and visually impaired children.

UNICEF (2013a, 6) reported that in Haiti, 1.5 per cent of the total population is found to have disabilities. The prevalence of disabilities among children aged 0–4 is reported at 0.6 per cent and 1.1 per cent for children in the 13–19 age group (UNICEF 2013a, 6). There may be about 400,000 children and/or young adults with disabilities in Haiti.[10] Since the 2010 earthquake, there are over 4000 amputees to be added to this list. People with disabilities in Haiti include those with very limited mobility as a result of lack of ramps in schools, churches, shops, government buildings and foreign embassies.[11] Even where a ramp exists, it may be inaccessible, and very few children have wheelchairs, crutches or even simple white canes for the blind. Cultural practices are also sources of endangerment as those with disabilities are considered "burdens" and inferior.[12] Haitians often abandon babies with disabilities as they feel that these will bring harm to other children.[13]

According to the Jamaican 2011 census, there were 29,109 children aged 5–14 years old who reportedly had at least one disability. UNICEF reported on the State of the World's Children (2013a) some 93 million children, that is, 1 in 20 of those aged fourteen or younger live with a moderate or severe disability of some kind. Children with disabilities face many challenges. In a recent survey of eighty-four schools in Jamaica, it was revealed that only 23.3 per cent had ramps and 83.3 per cent had no bathroom facilities for those with disabilities. Reading and examination materials in an accessible format such as Braille was not available in over 80 per cent of the schools surveyed.[14] Gayle-Geddes (2010, 144) noted that available public disability assessment and diagnostic services are highly urbanized and are hampered by a paucity of specialists such as for speech and other rehabilitation, while private facilities are financially inaccessible to a significant number. She also highlighted their voicelessness. While adults can verbalize their complaints, children with disabilities need advocates to assist with the attitudinal, environmental and institutional challenges which they generally face (Gayle-Geddes 2010, 140).

A UNICEF (2013d) report listed the following priorities for children with disabilities in St. Lucia:

- Improving the attitudes and acceptance by the general public and family members and reducing/eliminating stigma and discrimination targeted at children with disabilities;
- improving the coordination of financial, social and educational efforts to better the lives of these children;
- increasing access to tools and resources for early detection, prevention and therapy;
- providing ongoing training of teachers, parents and other support personnel who care for them;

- improving basic health care and rehabilitation services and programmes;
- improving facilities and infrastructure to increase accessibility;
- providing transportation to move them around;
- increasing human, financial and physical resources, for example, touch-screen laptops, headsets, communication boards;
- creating greater regional collaboration opportunities;
- lobbying government to make them a priority;
- more timely development and adoption of legislation and policy; and
- improving parent counselling, financial and social service support (UNICEF 2013d, 19).

In all countries under discussion (although to varying degrees), children with disabilities lack access to good quality basic social services. Their endangerment is more intense because they are unable to realize their full potential. While the legal framework for the promotion of equal rights for children with disabilities is being established, cultural and social practices will delay the full adherence to their rights.

Children and Migration

There is another group whose childhood is not always enjoyable as migration has separated them from their parents. If the impact of migration on children is not handled with particular care, there can be long-term negative effects. We begin with a discussion on the issues of children whose parents have migrated.

Jokhan (2007, 1) has observed that Caribbean parents migrate in order to improve their standard of living and to economically support those left behind, mainly children. He noted that on the one hand, the experience fostered healthy growth and development and kinship relationships while on the other hand, it resulted in feelings of neglect, abandonment and loneliness. He further discerned that while the practice of remitting food, clothing and money back home was encouraged and appreciated, it was merely partial support at the expense of the psychological and emotional needs of the child. Jokhan (2007, 5–6) found that in an effort to minimize the disruption of their child's life after they had migrated, parents tried as best they could to put surrogate parenting systems in place. However, despite these measures, Caribbean children "left behind" received little or no physical and emotional nurturing from surrogate caregivers, and often felt a sense of abandonment by parents. These children were often exposed to harmful consequences or assumed adult-like responsibilities prematurely, and attendance and performance at school were adversely impacted.

"Children left behind" (Reis 2008) continue to form a very vulnerable group. Bakker et al. (2009, 2) noted that the negative impact of migration on children included reduced access to health and educational services; the experience by some of various psychosocial problems, and the risk of poor academic performance as well as interruption of schooling.

The term "barrel children" refers to children who are waiting for their parents to send for them, who receive material in the form of clothing and food shipped to them in barrels (Crawford-Brown 1999). These children, while materially better off than some of their peers, also do not experience the best possible childhood. Some would prefer to have their parents physically with them at home, or to go to meet them abroad. With the increase in migration worldwide and the growing number of barrel children, although the intentions of the parents are often good, the negative impact far outweighs the positive. Cappelloni (2011, 25–29) pointed to three broad categories of negatives that may be associated with parent(s) migrating leaving children behind. He looked at psychological issues, which included isolation, sadness and in extreme cases nervous breakdowns and suicides; educational concerns such as reduction in academic performance and school attendance; and social impact—juvenile crimes and susceptibility to teenage pregnancy, drug abuse and sexual/physical violence. Antman (2012) on the other hand, chose to zero in on the education and health implications for those children left behind. She found that although the practice of remittances generally relaxed the budget constraints and increased the possibilities for schooling and health, school attendance and performance were usually drastically affected. Child labour became an issue, as did proper dieting and attention to health care, since the keen monitoring was most times lacking with the absence of parent(s) through migration (Antman 2012, 7–8).

Children who themselves migrate can also be negatively impacted. They suffer from various psychosocial difficulties which include the feelings of alienation, experiences of xenophobia (racial intolerance), insecurity and depression. They are also faced with difficulties in the education system due to language barriers, stigmatization and ridicule by native children. These may also translate into disadvantages in the school system. Their health and access to healthcare can be compromised as out of fear of deportation, undocumented migrants may be reluctant to access health facilities(Bakker et al. 2009). The lack of birth registration of migrant children in the Caribbean can significantly hinder them from enjoying their full rights such as access to education and healthcare and they are vulnerable to child labour as they pursue economic survival strategies (Bakker et al. 2009).

Research has shown that Guyanese women and girls are trafficked for sexual exploitation to neighbouring countries such as Barbados, Trinidad and Tobago, Brazil, Suriname, or Venezuela, and that Guyanese men and boys are subject to labour exploitation in construction and agriculture in the same countries (Bakker et al. 2009, 12).

Children who have migrated suffer the indignity of being treated as "lesser citizens." Often, they lack access to good quality basic social services, suffer racism and social exclusion. Additionally, migrant children and children left behind are at a higher risk and more vulnerable to abuse and exploitation, including sexual abuse, child labour and trafficking.

Childhood is endangered for these groups of children.

Teenage Parents

The childhood experience of teenage parents is cut short, abruptly. They suddenly have to fend for themselves and for their own children. Most recent available adolescent fertility rates, births per 1000 women aged 15–19, range from 37 in Barbados and Haiti to 53 in Jamaica; St. Lucia recorded a rate of 41.[15] The adolescent fertility rate in St. Lucia recorded a rate of 41.[16]

There are several psychosocial problems associated with teenage pregnancy. It appears to have negative effects on educational attainment and the ability of the teenage parents to obtain well-paid employment. From as far back as 1978, Card and Wise in their study of teenage parents found that they were much more likely than their classmates who postponed childbearing to have their education truncated. Further, because of their relatively low educational attainment, adolescent parents were much more likely than their classmates to hold low-prestige jobs which reduced occupational attainment also meant lower incomes and greater job dissatisfaction, particularly for teenage mothers. Hoffman (1998) supported this view, stating that some of the effects of teenage pregnancy were lower family incomes and the likelihood that teenage mothers would likely to be poor and on welfare. Klein (2005) noted that other problems of teenage pregnancy included separation from the child's father, divorce and repeat pregnancy.

Teenage fathers are not immune to the negative effects of the phenomenon, as they too are more likely than their peers who are not fathers to have poor academic performance, higher school drop-out rates, limited financial resources, and decreased income potential (Klein 2005). The psychosocial effects also extend to the children of teenage parents, who tend to have lower Apgar scores (Chen et al. 2007). Klein (2005) reiterates the results of previous research which found that these children did not fare as well as those of adult mothers. They had increased risk of developmental delay, academic difficulties, behavioural disorders, substance abuse, early sexual activity, depression, and risked becoming adolescent parents themselves. Further, neonatal mortality increased with decreasing maternal age.

Children having children is another recipe for endangered childhood.

Children of Deadbeat Dads

Children who do not receive maintenance or support from their dads form another vulnerable group. In Jamaica, nearly 5000 fathers were brought before the courts for child maintenance; most fathers were under forty years old (Davis 2019). Davis noted that a major flaw in Jamaican Family Court is that there are no rigid monitoring mechanisms for identifying payment delinquency unless a mother makes new reports (2019).

The absent father creates the absent mother, who becomes the breadwinner, who often in desperation takes low-paying jobs which require her to work long, hard hours and force her to leave her children in vulnerable situations where they may be inadequately cared for (Leo-Rhynie 1993).

Children whose fathers do not support them or provide maintenance are also stigmatized and pained as a result of their fathers' irresponsibility and insensitivity.

Children Affected and Infected with HIV/AIDS

In Chap. 4, we examined some health outcomes for children. We noted that the Caribbean Region has the highest incidence rate of reported AIDS cases in the Americas. Overall there was an estimated 9900 children aged 0–14 living with HIV in the Caribbean.[17]

The HIV/AIDS epidemic is driven by numerous underlying factors. These include socio-cultural and religious taboos; lifestyle issues such as substance abuse; influences from external media; bio-medical deficiencies—lack of comprehensive management of people living with HIV/AIDS including antiretroviral (ARV) treatment; lack of individual skills such as negotiation, creation and maintenance of healthy human relationships, sex education and protective behaviours; and economic factors—disparities in income distribution within and between countries, and economic hardship within a consumption market.[18]

Children are negatively affected by HIV/AIDS as their childhood is diminished if they suffer its effects. Those whose parents die from the disease are robbed of parental care and are not always able to develop to their full potential. Some face stigma and discrimination which sometimes prohibit access to appropriate and timely basic social services such as health and education. Children infected with or affected by HIV/AIDS sometimes have to forgo schooling. There may be less food or clothing for them in the household. They may suffer from anxiety, depression and abuse.[19] Sometimes children whose parents have died from AIDS are often singled out for abuse in places where they seek support and care—harshly treated in foster homes, denied access to schooling and health care, stripped of their inheritances, and left to the streets.[20] All these negative effects endanger their childhood.

UNICEF-Jamaica reports that adolescents are a high-risk group for HIV infection as almost 10 per cent of all reported AIDS cases (1.5 per cent of Jamaica's population living with HIV) are among young people under age nineteen.[21] It notes that young girls are more at risk than young boys due to inter-generational and transactional sex and that the main mode of transmission of HIV is through heterosexual sexual intercourse.

The Planning Institute of Jamaica (PIOJ) (2012, 20) reports that individuals infected with and affected by HIV/AIDS have major problems with the supply, distribution and dispensing of ARV drugs. There is an inadequate number of pharmacies which stock them. Further, public pharmacies are completely overwhelmed, and patients have to wait long hours for prescriptions to be filled, often having to return on another day. Basic drugs for related conditions such as STIs are frequently not available in the public sector and in the private sector they are too expensive for most patients (PIOJ 2012, 20).

Though there is notable progress in the reduction and treatment of HIV/AIDS, there are still large numbers of children affected who do not realize their full potential. Given the fragile economies of the small island developing states (SIDS), their high levels of indebtedness and their inability to increase investment in children, the childhood of some children is endangered.

Children in Conflict with the Law and in Lock-Up

Much research focuses on children who have been victims of crime, but not so much on those who are in conflict with the law and whom the state seeks to punish. Those who end up in lock-up are extremely vulnerable, but they too have rights and need protection. The Convention on the Rights of the Child (CRC) states that children who are accused of breaking the law have the right to legal help and fair treatment in a justice system that respects their rights (CRC, Article 40). However, in SIDS, this group of children lacks equitable access to the basic social services and their rights are sometimes violated.

The age of criminal responsibility in Barbados is eleven. Children are tried in Juvenile Courts up to age sixteen (UNICEF 2015a, 11). In 2013, 207 children around 6–17 years old were admitted to the Juvenile Liaison Scheme, which was specially designed for children engaging in or at risk of involvement in criminal activities (UNICEF 2015a, 11–12). Of the numbers admitted, 51 per cent had been charged with criminal offences, the most common being assault, being armed with offensive weapons, causing a disturbance, theft and wandering. For the same period 386 juveniles (12–18 year olds) were arrested (UNICEF 2015a, 13).

In Haiti, there is no clearly developed policy relating to child protection. The number of children living on the street has doubled since the 2010 earthquake and now stands at no less than 4000.[22] With this number of unattended and uncared for children, child conflict with the law is almost inevitable and is prone to soar way above the national average. Approximately 4.5 per cent of prison detainees are female, while 3 per cent are children (United States Department of State 2013). Conditions having deteriorated since the earthquake, documentation is inadequate, and the authorities cannot always verify the age of the inmate. In towns outside of Port-au-Prince, minors and adults often occupy the same cells; juveniles are not segregated from adult prisoners nor convicted prisoners from pre-trial detainees as the law requires.

Criminal responsibility in Jamaica as set out in the State Party Report begins at age twelve.[23] The Child Care and Protection Act (2004) states that any child taken to a place of safety "shall not be detained there longer than 48 hours without having been brought before the Children's court." Clarke et al. (2010) noted that the majority of the children they surveyed did not appear before the court in the prescribed forty-eight hours. The rights of children in conflict with the law are not always upheld. The authors also found that 70 per cent of the children interviewed did not receive any counselling before appearing in court and were very afraid of the process.

Jamaica has approved a Child Diversion Policy. The aim of the policy and programme is to keep (or "divert") children who are accused of minor offences away from the criminal justice system.[24] This is an excellent initiative but an in-depth analysis to examine the status of the children who have been diverted.

According to UNICEF (2015b, 12), the age of criminal responsibility is set at twelve years in St. Lucia and young offenders may be sentenced to adult prisons from as early as age seventeen. The Boys Training Centre (BTC), which is the only residential care facility for troubled boys as at the end of 2013, housed a total of 140 boys under substandard conditions. Of these, 36.4 per cent or fifty-one were admitted as a result of having committed offences related mainly to stealing, assault, wounding, trespassing or drugs (UNICEF 2015b, 13–14). The Court Division Programme (Detention) accounted for 63 children of eighteen years and under who were probationers, dropouts or were habitually suspended from school (UNICEF 2015b, 15).

There was no separation of boys charged with crimes from those with social problems, and the facility was not designed to house children in conflict with the law. Girls under age sixteen charged with crimes had no residential facility and authorities generally released such girls on minimal bail (United States Department of State Report 2014). There were eight female inmates and sixty-three youth offenders aged 16–21 in St. Lucia. Female inmates were separated from male inmates and detainees were segregated from sentenced inmates.

As the data reveal, children in conflict with the law do not always enjoy their rights and in many instances, their childhood is endangered.

Children of Incarcerated Mothers

There is a group of children who suffer in silence and suffer great shame and stigma. This group comprises children whose mothers are incarcerated. Ten recently released women (who benefited from a church-run charitable organization) were interviewed in 2018. They provided written consent to be interviewed. Table 7.5 provides a profile of the respondents.

When asked about the impact of their imprisonment on their children, the mothers revealed that the impact was negative. The mothers

Table 7.5 Profile of recently released mothers who were interviewed

Length of time in prison	Offence	Age	Occupation	Highest level of education	Number of children
2 years	Bodily harm to a minor	37	Dressmaking	Secondary	1
2 years 6 months	Wounding	53	Counter clerk	Primary	2
2 years	Possession of stolen property	42	Sales representative	Secondary	1
1 year 8 months	Bank fraud	63	Bank clerk	Secondary	1
7 years	Drugs	39	Cook	Vocational	3
7 years 3 months	Manslaughter	50	Handcraft maker	Secondary	2
2 years	Drugs	45	Basic school teacher	Teachers' college	3
5 years 6 months	Embezzlement	46	Banker	Tertiary	2
5 years	Malicious wounding (acid)	39	Vending	Secondary school	1
3 years	Fraud	46	Accountant	Tertiary	2

Source: Primary data, 2018.

gave the following responses when they were asked how their children reacted to the news of their arrest:

- Father told them that I was overseas (shield)
- Confused
- Sad
- Hit him hard, stop talking at school and at home
- Lots of crying
- They did not understand
- Sad and angry; devastated; grades dropped
- (Source 2018 data)

When the children were told that their mothers were being tried in court, they

- felt emptiness,
- gave others the silent treatment,
- were cast down,
- were too young to understand and
- were not told anything (shielding the children).
- (Source: 2018 data)

When the children heard that their mothers were imprisoned, they

- were more angry and withdrawn,
- almost lost their minds,
- had hearts broken,
- never fully understood,
- withdrawn and very aggressive when spoken to and
- were angry with mothers.
- (Source: 2018 data)

The respondents also revealed that their children were ostracized by school staff, church members and community members. These findings are similar to an earlier study carried out by this author (Henry-Lee 2005). The 2005 and 2018 studies raised similar issues. This is a group of children who will be left behind. They are punished with their mothers and are scarred for life. They need great resilience to overcome these challenges and enjoy success. The actions of the mothers have "endangered" these children's childhoods and they need targeted attention to improve their situation.

Child Labourers

Child labour is defined as work that deprives children of their childhood, their potential and their dignity, and that is harmful to physical and mental development.[25] The ILO cautions that child labour is mentally, physically, socially or morally dangerous and harmful to children. It interferes with their schooling by depriving them of the opportunity to attend school, obliging them to leave prematurely or requiring them to attempt to combine school attendance with excessively long and heavy work.[26]

The organization estimates that globally, the number of children in child labour has declined by one-third since 2000, from 246 million to 168 million.[27] More than half of these, 85 million, are engaged in hazardous work that directly endangers their health, safety and moral development.[28]

Latin America and the Caribbean have experienced substantial declines in child labour. A significant number, 5.7 million working girls and boys, are under the minimum age for employment or are engaged in work that must be abolished, according to the ILO's Worst Forms of Child Labour Convention No. 182.[29] The majority of them work in agriculture, but there are also many thousands of girls and boys working in other high-risk sectors such as mining, domestic labour, fireworks manufacturing, fishing and on dumpsites.[30]

For the Caribbean countries under review, there are limited data on absolute numbers of child labourers. There has been no comprehensive study done in Jamaica, but in 2002, it was estimated that there were 6500 children working and living on the streets. This number is increasing, and these children are particularly vulnerable to being exposed to violence.[31]

It is estimated that there are 38,000 children involved in child labour in Jamaica.[32] Children are also found working as street vendors, shop assistants, baby sitters and domestic servants. According to the UNICEF report (2006, 73–74), the harsh economic situation in Jamaica often led children to engage in these activities to support themselves or to help supplement their families' income, and earlier studies have estimated that 22,000 children under age sixteen were active in the Jamaican labour market. Jamaica ratified the ILO Conventions 138 (Minimum Age of Employment) and 182 (Worst Forms of Child Labour) in 2003. The Jamaican government has started to implement strategies at the community level.[33]

Among the countries under discussion, Haiti has received a significant amount of international attention. In Haiti, there is social practice to use *restavèks* for domestic help. From the rural areas, some as young as five years old, they come to the urban areas to live with better-off families. In exchange for shelter, food and education, they perform household chores.

In a context of increasingly severe economic times the host families some-times find it very difficult to cope themselves. The *restavèks* become increasingly deprived of access to education, adequate nutrition, wages and health care. Although Chapter IX of the Haitian Labour Code which gave legitimacy to the practice of using *restavèks* was repealed by the Haitian parliament in 2003, the practice of hiring them remains. However, the new law does not contain penalties for such crimes, and legislation on trafficking has been pending in parliament for many years.

After the 2010 earthquake, the number of *restavèks* increased as many children were orphaned. In 2012 there were 659,864 children working, of whom 81.2 per cent were attending school, with 27.5 per cent com-bining work and school (United States Department of Labor 2013).

Missing Children

Then, there are those children who seem to disappear and are sometimes never found. One is never sure of the fate of these "missing children." This phenomenon causes pain and anguish for parents and their families and for the children themselves.

There is a paucity of data on missing children in the Caribbean. In 2015, in Barbados, The number of girls under the age of sixteen reported missing was six times as high as the number of boys.[34]

Name: Gabrella Nunes
Age: 16 years old
Date Last Seen: Sometime in December 2017
Place Last Seen: Pembroke Hall area
Description: Brown complexion, medium build and is around 163 centime-ters (5ft 4in). Last seen wearing a blue and white dress with black shoes.
Source: https://www.jamaicaobserver.com/news/missing-children_130012?profile=1373

As of June 2015, there were 1077 children missing in Jamaica.[35] Of those, 870 were found, 5 were deceased and 202 were stilling missing. The International Committee on the Rights of the Child expressed concern about the large number of missing children and the resultant abuse and neglect (United Nations Human Rights Office of the High Commissioner 2015). In Haiti, after the 2010 earthquake, there were reports of children leaving the country without any proper documentation.[36] On December 4, 2018, the St. Lucian police issued a public appeal help in locating a fifteen-year-old female who has been reported missing.[37]

Missing children are at risk of being exploited and abused. The quality of childhood for these children declines. The governments in all the four countries have expressed a desire to ensure that children are always protected and do not go missing.

Those Who Are Trafficked

Linked to child labour and exploitation is the phenomenon of human trafficking. Trafficking in persons (TIP) has become an international issue. Trafficking in Persons (TIP) is the recruitment, transportation, transfer, harbouring or receipt of persons, by means of the threat or use of force or other forms of coercion, of abduction, of fraud, of deception, of the abuse of power or of a position of vulnerability or of the giving or receiving of payments or benefits to achieve the consent of a person having control over another person, for the purpose of exploitation (Article 3, paragraph (a) of the Protocol to Prevent, Suppress and Punish Trafficking in Persons). Unfortunately, many children are victims of human trafficking.

For example, in Jamaica, it was reported that since the passing of the Trafficking in Persons Act in 2007, about 500 raids have been conducted, 3 prostitution rings have been disrupted and 86 victims were rescued from trafficking by the Trafficking in Persons Vice Squad of the Jamaica Constabulary Force (JCF).[38]

Gender inequalities and gender development issues contribute to the trafficking in persons.

Travel, migration and general exposure to global/Western cultures and lifestyles have raised economic expectations, changed values and behaviours that are more accommodating of activities related to human trafficking (Ricketts and Dunn 2007). The researchers found that the majority of victims (93.8 per cent) were from a lower socio-economic background (Ricketts and Dunn 2007).

Conclusion

Though all children in SIDS are exposed to endangerment from their very birth, there are some groups of children who are more susceptible to endangerment than others. They live on the periphery, and unless they are effectively targeted, will never realize their full potential.

In the next chapter, we discuss some cases of childhood transformation in selected Caribbean SIDS.

Notes

1. http://www.unicef.org/socialpolicy/index_46984.html (Accessed September 3, 2018).
2. Gordon, D., & Shailen, N. (2007). *Absolute child poverty in the 21st century in Haiti*. Bristol University/UNICEF Haiti. http://www.unicef.org/about/execboard/files/08-PL23-Haiti-English.pdf.
3. Source: Planning Institute of Jamaica (2015) Jamaica Survey of Living Conditions (JSLC).
4. Ibid.
5. http://data.unicef.org/child-protection/birth-registration.html.
6. Ibid.
7. http://www.humanium.org/en/jamaica (Accessed August 8, 2014).
8. Sources: http://data.unicef.org/child-protection/birth-registration.html (Accessed April 11, 2019).
    http://www.unicef.org/easterncaribbean/ECAO_BARBADOS_Child_Protection_Statistical_Digest_2015.pdf (Accessed April 11, 2019).
    http://www.unicef.org/easterncaribbean/ECAO_St._Lucia__Child_Protection_Statistical_Digest_2015.pdf (Accessed April 11, 2019).
9. Passed but not yet enforced into law.
10. https://academicpeds.org/specialInterestGroups/pdfs/oriol.pdf.
11. Ibid.

12. Ibid.
13. Words of Gail Buck of Healing Hands for Haiti (quoted by Kim Beeston: theguardian.com, Monday June 14, 2010. http://www.theguardian.com/journalismcompetition/haiti-disabled-children.
14. *Gleaner*, Newspaper, May 2, 2013.
15. http://data.worldbank.org/indicator/SP.ADO.TFRT (Accessed July 13, 2019).
16. Ibid.
17. UNAIDS Indicators. (2016). http://aidsinfo.unaids.org/ (Accessed May 24, 2018).
      Ibid.
18. http://www.unicef.org/aids/index_youngpeople.html (Accessed June 2, 2019).
19. Ibid.
20. http://www.unicef.org/jamaica/hiv_aids_1989.htm (Accessed June 2, 2019).
21. Ibid.
22. http://www.unicef-irc.org/portfolios/documents/399_jamaica.htm (Accessed September 15, 2015).
23. http://www.unicef.org/jamaica/violence.html (Accessed June 2, 2019).
24. https://www.moj.gov.jm/programmes/child-justice (Accessed June 2, 2019).
25. http://www.ilo.org/global/about-the-ilo/newsroom/news/WCMS_221568/lang%2D%2Den/index.htm (Accessed June 2, 2019).
26. Ibid.
27. Ibid.
28. Ibid.
29. http://www.ilo.org/ipec/Regionsandcountries/latin-america-and-caribbean/lang%2D%2Den/index.htm (Accessed June 2, 2019).
30. Ibid.
31. http://www.jamaicaobserver.com/news/40260_6-500-street%2D%2Dworking-children-in-Jamaica%2D%2D%2D%2Dsurvey (Accessed July 1, 2019).
32. https://www.mlss.gov.jm/?s=child+labour (Accessed July 1, 2019).
33. https://www.mlss.gov.jm/?s=child+labour (Accessed July 1, 2019).
34. http://barbadostoday.bb/2015/11/14/decline-in-the-number-of-missing-persons/ (Accessed June 2, 2019).
35. http://www.ocr.gov.jm/index.php/statistics/missing-children/missing-children-2015 (Accessed June 2, 2019).

36. https://www.youtube.com/watch?v=IX1TBoNdhbA (Accessed June 2, 2019).
37. https://stluciatimes.com/fifteen-year-old-reported-missing/   (Accessed July 1, 2019).
38. https://jis.gov.jm/jamaica-continues-to-make-progress-in-curbing-trafficking-in-persons (Accessed July 1, 2019).

References

Antman, F. M. (2012). The impact of migration on family left behind. Retrieved May 24, 2018, from http://www.iza.org/MigrationHandbook/16_Antman_The%20Impact%20of%20Migration%20on%20Family%20Left%20Behind.pdf.

Bakker, C., Elings-Pels, M., & Reis, M. (2009). The impact of migration on children in the Caribbean. UNICEF Office for Barbados and Eastern Caribbean. Retrieved May 4, 2019, from http://www.unicef.org/easterncaribbean/Impact_of_Migration_Paper.pdf.

Cappelloni, C. (2011). Going beyond material well-being: Looking at the hidden costs of migration on children left behind. Retrieved June 24, 2018, from http://fletcher.tufts.edu/~/media/Fletcher/Microsites/praxis/xxvi/CoreyCappelloni.pdf.

Card, J. J., & Wise, L. L. (1978). Teenage mothers and teenage fathers: Theimpact of early childbearing on the parents' personal and professional lives. *Family Planning Perspective, 10*(4): 199–205. Retrieved May 4, 2019, from https://www.socio.com/digitized-publications/Paper-1978-FAMPP-Teenage-mothers-and-teenage-fathers-CaWi.pdf.

Chen, X.-K., Chen, S. W., Kitaw, N. F., George, D., Rhoads, G., & Walker, M. (2007). Teenage pregnancy and adverse birth outcomes: A large population based retrospective cohort study. *International Journal of Epidemiology, 36*, 368–373. https://doi.org/10.1093/ije/dyl284

Clarke, M., Cargill, D., & Fraser-Binns, S. (2010). The justice system and children in Jamaica. In A. Henry-Lee & J. M. Gardner (Eds.), *Promoting child rights through research volume 2; Selected papers from the Caribbean Child Research Conference 2007–2008*. Kingston: Sir Arthur Lewis Institute of Social and Economic Studies, University of the West Indies.

Crawford-Brown, C. (1999). *Who will save our children: The plight of the Jamaican child in the nineties*. Kingston: University of the West Indies Canoe Press.

Davis, C. (2019). Courting deadbeats—Thousands face law annually for child maintenance. Retrieved May 13, 2019, from http://jamaica-gleaner.com/article/lead-stories/20190317/courting-deadbeats-thousands-face-law-annually-child-maintenance.

Economic Commission for Latin America and the Caribbean (ECLAC). (2009). A further study on disability in the Caribbean: Rights, commitment, statistical analysis and monitoring. Retrieved May 4, 2018, from http://repositorio.cepal.org/bitstream/handle/11362/27727/S2009003_en.pdf;jsessionid=8CBC8B01E0F1DBD0999FD5F6B070ED97?sequence=1.

Economic Commission for Latin America and the Caribbean (ECLAC). (2013). Social protection systems in Latin America and the Caribbean: Haiti. Retrieved May 25, 2018, from http://archivo.cepal.org/pdfs/2013/S2013068.pdf.

Gayle-Geddes, A. (2010). Parenting children with disabilities in Jamaica: Identifying the main challenges and policy implications. In A. Henry-Lee & J. M. Gardner (Eds.), *Promoting child rights through research volume 2: Selected papers from the Caribbean child research conference 2007–2008.* Kingston: Sir Arthur Lewis Institute of Social and Economic Studies, University of the West Indies.

Gordon, D., & Shailen, N. (2007). *Absolute child poverty in the 21st century in Haiti.* Bristol University/UNICEF Haiti. Retrieved May 4, 2019, from http://www.unicef.org/about/execboard/files/08-PL23-Haiti-English.pdf.

Government of Barbados. (2014). Report to the committee on the rights of the child. Retrieved June 14, 2018, from http://tbinternet.ohchr.org/_layouts/treatybodyexternal/Download.aspx?symbolno=CRC%2fC%2fBAR%2f2-5&Lang=en.

Government of Haiti. (2013). Report to the committee on the rights of the child. Retrieved January 31, 2018, from https://daccess-ods.un.org/TMP/3051310.77766418.html.

Henry-Lee, A. (2005). *Women in prison: The impact of incarceration on women, their children and families.* Kingston: Planning Institute of Jamaica.

Hoffman, S. D. (1998). Teenage childbearing is not so bad after all...or is it? A review of the new literature. *Family Planning Perspectives, 30*(5): 236–239, 243. Retrieved May 1, 2018, from http://www.jstor.org/stable/2991610?seq=4#page_scan_tab_contents.

Jokhan, M. (2007). *Parental absence as a consequence of migration: Exploring its origins and perpetuation with special reference to Trinidad.* MPhil dissertation, University of the West Indies, St. Augustine.

Kim, H. (2018). Beyond monetary poverty analysis: The dynamics of multidimensional child poverty in developing countries. *Social Indicators Research, 141*(3), 1107–1136.

Klein, J. D. (2005). Adolescent pregnancy: Current trends and issues. *Pediatrics, 116*(1), 281–286. Retrieved from http://pediatrics.aappublications.org/content/pediatrics/116/1/281.full.pdf

Leo-Rhynie, E. (1993). *The Jamaican family: Continuity and change. The annual Grace Kennedy Foundation Lecture.* Kingston, Jamaica: Grace Kennedy.

Planning Institute of Jamaica (PIOJ). (2004).

Planning Institute of Jamaica. (2007).

Planning Institute of Jamaica. (2009).

Planning Institute of Jamaica. (2010).

Planning Institute of Jamaica. (2012). Jamaica country assessment. Preliminary draft. Retrieved May 4, 2018, from http://www.vpaj.org/sites/default/files/ja_country_assessment_pioj_apr12_preliminary_draft.pdf.

Planning Institute of Jamaica. (2012). *Jamaica survey of living conditions.* Kingston, Jamaica: Planning Institute of Jamaica (PIOJ).

Planning Institute of Jamaica. (2014).

Planning Institute of Jamaica. (2015).

Planning Institute of Jamaica. (2018). Economic and social survey Jamaica 2017. Planning Institute of Jamaica.

Reis, M. (2008). Country assessment report: Dominica. UNICEF internal document.

Ricketts, S., & Dunn, L. (2007). Human trafficking for sexual exploitation and forced labour in Jamaica. Searchcon Resource Consultants.

Sir Arthur Lewis Institute of Social and Economic Studies (SALISES). (2012). *Barbados country assessment of living conditions 2010. Volume 1: Human development challenges in a global crisis: Addressing growth and social inclusion.* Caribbean Development Bank Country Poverty Assessment Report. Retrieved May 26, 2014, from http://www.caribank.org/uploads/2012/12/Barbados-CALC-Volume-1-MainReport-FINAL-Dec-2012.pdf.

UNICEF. (2006). Violence against children in the Caribbean region. Regional assessment: UN Secretary General's study on violence against children. Retrieved May 24, 2017, from http://www.uwi.edu/ccdc/downloads/violence_against_children.pdfandhttp://www.unicef.org/lac/Caribe_web(1).pdf.

UNICEF. (2011). Challenges. The right to an identity: Birth registration in Latin America and the Caribbean. Newsletter on progress towards the

Millennium Development Goals from a child rights perspective Number 13, November. Retrieved January 31, 2017, from http://www.unicef.org/lac/challenges-13-ECLAC-UNICEF.pdf.

UNICEF. (2013a). Every child's birth right. Inequities and trends in birth registration. Retrieved May 24, 2017, from http://www.unicef.org/gambia/Every_childs_birth_right_-inequities_and_trends_in_birth_registration-2013_report.pdf.

UNICEF. (2013d). Challenges: Rights of children and adolescents with disabilities. Newsletter on progress towards the millennium development goals from a child rights perspective Number 15, April. Retrieved May 24, 2018, from http://www.unicef.org/lac/Challenges-15-web.pdf.

UNICEF. (2015a). Barbados child protection statistical digest. Retrieved May 24, 2017, from http://www.unicef.org/easterncaribbean/ECAO_BARBADOS_Child_Protection_Statistical_Digest_2015.pdf.

UNICEF. (2015b). St Lucia child protection statistical digest. Retrieved May 24, 2017, from http://www.unicef.org/easterncaribbean/ECAO_St._Lucia__Child_Protection_Statistical_Digest_2015.pdf.

UNICEF Press Centre. (2007, January 10). UN General Assembly adopts powerful definition of child poverty. *News Note*. Retrieved October 4, 2014, from http://www.unicef.org/media/media_38003.html.

United Nations Human Rights Office of the High Commissioner (2015). Concluding Observations. https://tbinternet.ohchr.org/_layouts/15/treatybodyexternal/Download.aspx?symbolno=CRC%2fC%2fJAM%2fCO%2f3-4&Lang=en. Retrieved October 27, 2019.

United States Department of Labor. (2013). Bureau of International Labor Affairs, Haiti. Retrieved November 10, 2018, from http://www.dol.gov/ilab/reports/child-labor/findings/2013TDA/haiti.pdf.

United States Department of State. (2012). Human Rights Reports: Haiti. Retrieved November 10, 2018, from http://www.state.gov/j/drl/rls/hrrpt/2012/wha/204458.htm.

United States Department of State. (2013). Human Rights Reports: Haiti. Retrieved from http://www.state.gov/documents/organization/220661.pdf.

United States Department of State. (2014). Human Rights Report: St Lucia. Retrieved from http://www.state.gov/documents/organization/236926.pdf.

8

Transformative Childhood

These politicians are not serious. It is words and more words. No real change
and they are not interested.
Child advocate in St. Lucia, April 2019
It not easy to be a child today
Senior citizen in Jamaica, April 2013

Introduction

In the last seven chapters we have discussed "endangered childhood" in the Caribbean. However, at the macro level, children do appear to function, and the majority of children perform reasonably well in school, literacy rates are high and most transition successfully into the workplace. Micro analysis of indicators of educational outcomes revealed that passes in the core subjects, English and Mathematics, were less than desirable at the secondary school-leaving examinations and human capital investment in children remains inadequate.

There are significant proportions of children whose childhood is "endangered" and who do not have adequate access to the basic social services

© The Author(s) 2020
A. Henry-Lee, *Endangered and Transformative Childhood in Caribbean Small Island Developing States*, Studies in Childhood and Youth,
https://doi.org/10.1007/978-3-030-25568-8_8

considered valuable in their societies. They are at risk of not fulfilling their full potential and enjoying productive adulthood. Too many children face violence and exploitation every day in public and private places. If we do not reduce the number of children who experience "endangered childhood," sustainable development will remain elusive in Caribbean SIDS.

All is not lost. There are children who are coping and demonstrating resilience. There are success cases of children who have escaped endangerment and are experiencing a "transformative childhood" with care, love and protection. Many of them are succeeding by their society's established standards.

Coping, Resilience and Transformation?

In anticipation of the future critiques of the theory of transformation discussed in this book, we spend some time dissecting the terms "coping," "resilience" and "transformation" before the case studies are presented. There are many definitions of the terms "coping" and "resilience." Lazarus and Folkman (1984, 282–325) reveal that in the medical field, extensive work has been completed by those who defined coping as "the constantly changing cognitive and behavioural efforts to manage specific external and/or internal demands that are appraised as taxing or exceeding the resources of the person." There are several coping strategies that individuals employ: confrontative, coping, distancing, self-controlling, seeking social support, accepting responsibility, escape, avoidance, problem-solving and positive reappraisal (Lazarus 1991).

Some 103 children in the Jamaican study were asked how they dealt with violent circumstances and conflict with their parents and with other children. The following are some of the strategies they described:

> I pray;
> I close my eyes;
> I do not listen to the news;
> I just curse my parents in my mind;
> I think of my teacher as a vicious bull-dog in my mind.
> (Primary data: 2013)

Most of them depended on their individual actions and not the support from others.

Resilience Theory states that all children have each of these four common attributes: social competence, problem-solving skills, autonomy, sense of purpose and future (Benard 1991). Whether these attributes are strong enough to help individuals to cope with adversity in their lives depends on protective factors in families, school and communities (Benard 1991).

There are three types of resilient children:

1. Children who do not succumb to adversities, despite their high-risk status (e.g. babies of low birth weight);
2. Children who develop coping strategies in situations of chronic stress (e.g. the children of drug-using or alcoholic parents); and
3. Children who have suffered extreme trauma (e.g. through disasters, sudden loss of a close relative, or abuse, and who have recovered and prospered) (Masten et al. 1990).

O'Dougherty Wright and Masten (2006, 21) state that "children judged to show resilience have typically negotiated these developmental tasks with reasonable success, despite risks and adversities they have endured."

Violence against children is a major problem in Jamaica, yet they can exhibit resilience despite the high levels. Analysis of primary data collected from 103 secondary school students supports this conclusion. When asked about their perception of violence in the home, 62 per cent of them stated that the violence faced at home was high or very high, while 32 per cent revealed that the violence in communities that children experienced was high or very high, and 80 per cent perceived that the violence against children in Jamaica was high or very high.

However, despite their high ratings of violence against children, 72 per cent rated the quality of life in Jamaica as fair to very good (see Table 2.5). Of those who rated the quality of life as bad or very bad, 70 per cent revealed that that was due to financial problems; 12 per cent said it was because of violence and another 16 per cent blamed their uncertain future.

The group of children discussed in this study may fall into the second category of resilient children who develop coping strategies in situations of chronic stress—in this case, high levels of violence (Masten et al. 1990). Of course, we may want to add another characteristic—they cope by ascending into an imaginary world where life in Jamaica is good. However, we argue that resilience evidenced sometimes by denial of the "real world" is not sustainable and children should experience transformative childhood to ensure self-realization and productive adulthood.

An examination of the literature shows that theories of transformation have been developed in many fields—science, education, economics, psychology and crime. For example, Davies (2012) outlines a global theory of social transformation based on religious communication. Hatzigianni (2018) speaks of transforming early childhood experiences with digital technologies.

We want to go beyond what is detailed in the literature about coping, resilience and transformation. One may be resilient—that is not succumbing to adverse childhood experiences—but the quality of life may not have changed. For example, many children living in the violent inner cities exist every day without exhibiting symptoms of the trauma expected from the persons who have to face daily doses of violence. A child who experiences transformation would be one who performs beyond expectation and excels; even doing better than those who do not face these adverse childhood experiences.

Consequently in our context, transformation involves demonstrating coping, resilience, improving the quality of life, and putting in place strategies that would ensure sustainable child development. This transformation can be possible through partnership of agencies—agency by parents and agency by the children themselves. The following case studies demonstrate that children can break the cycle of "endangerment" if duty bearers and the children themselves implement strategies to place the children's needs at the centre of their concern and action.

In this book, transformation demonstrated by transformative childhood is realized by child agency and the support of duty bearers. A transformative childhood sets the individual on a path of self-realization and productive adulthood.

Transformative Childhood in Practice

We present eight cases in which children have not only coped but have excelled and gained recognition for their outstanding achievements. A transformative childhood is one in which the child overcomes adverse circumstances, excels and is on the path of sustainable development. For transformation to take place, the child must exhibit both resilience and coping strategies in the face of adversity.

Much has been said about child agency (see Huijsmans 2011). In all the cases presented below, the child demonstrated agency—a willingness to act for him or herself and make transformative choices. There was evidence of the use of positive coping strategies, strong motivation and resilience even at a very young age. A twelve-year-old from Haiti survived a cracked skull, was uprooted from her home in Haiti to live with foster parents in the USA and yet overcame loneliness and language barriers to begin to fulfil her dream of becoming a neurologist. The cases reveal that children can conquer the negative effects of natural disaster, violence in the home, poverty, death and disability to enjoy transformation and success. Transformation is not gender-sensitive and can be experienced by both boys and girls. Assistance from the state, a relative, foster parent, or non-government organization also proved critical in supporting the efforts of the children. The cases indicate that child agency and support from duty bearers are critical to the attainment of a transformative childhood.

Case 1: Two Girls and a Blind Mother

Kelly and Niomi are sisters. Their mother is blind and poor. They are the youngest of six children. Both girls attended public primary and secondary schools and could not afford extra lessons. They received support from Jamaica's main public assistance system, the Programme for Advancement Through Health and Education (PATH). The mother also received assistance from the Jamaica Society for the Blind and the Council for Persons with Disabilities. The support was not enough, and Niomi had to sell sweets at school so that she could pay for her graduation expenses. Many times, the girls came to school without any money. Both girls studied hard and performed well at school. In Grade Seven, Niomi won a scholarship from M&M Company to cover her expenses for Grade Eight. Both girls were not discouraged and at the secondary regional exit examinations for Caribbean children, Niomi passed six subjects and Kelly, seven.[1]

Case 2: Child of Teenage Mom Overcomes the Odds

Michael Maragh is now the Principal Finance Officer in a government ministry in Jamaica. He is also a motivational speaker and pastor. He was the child of a teenage mom. His father was murdered when he was three years old. He lived with his mom in a volatile urban inner-city area. Life was hard and he could recall taking his shoes for repair and the shoemaker telling him not to bring them back. He sat one exam at a time until he matriculated for university. He was successful in his exams and is now a role model for young men.[2]

Case 3: Law Student Overcomes Rural Poverty

Jermaine Haughton was born in Clarendon, a rural community in Jamaica. The family was very poor and usually ate on only four days a week. In a good week, they ate five times. He had to share a school bag with his uncles and when they arrived at school, they would then share the books and go to class. As a child, he worked hard and always topped his class.

He stated that "I always knew that I would be the one to make a change. Many times I would be eating, and I would just stop and start daydreaming, thinking of how I would lift my family out of poverty, even at the tender age of eight. It was then I knew that education was the only way out."

He migrated to the USA and continued to excel at school until he graduated from the University of Baltimore School of Law.[3]

Case 4: Ward of the State Graduates from University

Dwayne Haynes is currently pursuing a master's in international public development management studies after having graduated with a degree in management studies. He is the Public Relations Officer for the Caribbean Tertiary Level Personnel Association, Jamaica Chapter. He also served as Resident Adviser for students on one of his University's halls of residence.

Dwayne was born to a Mom who suffered from schizophrenia and he was placed in one of the state's homes for children in need of care and protection. His father was always absent and did not take care of him. His grandfather found out and came to take him to live with him when he was nine years old. Living with his grandfather who did not have the resources to give him all that he needed was tough.

The state continued to support his basic needs, but life was still difficult. He kept this status as a ward of the state a secret until he became head boy at his secondary school. It was during an interview with the principal of the school that she discovered his true status.

"When I was doing the interviews for the position of head boy at St. Jago High School, that's when the principal found out. And she thought that I came from a family with mother, father, everything. And I said to her, 'It's my grandfather that grew me and taught me how to carry myself.' Not that I'm deceiving anyone, but just always putting my best foot forward."

Dwayne credits his success to the steadfast support from his grandfather and he wants to be a role model for others. "I've always wanted to impact someone else's life because persons have impacted mine. I know that other persons are suffering, and they want to know that somebody else made it through their struggles, despite the fact that I never had any family, apart from my grandfather."[4]

Case 5: From a Dysfunctional Family to Stardom

Robyn Rihanna Fenty, born in Barbados, is worth US$260 million.[5] Her awards include eight Grammys, twelve American Music Awards, and twelve Billboard music awards. She has several charitable foundations and helps several needy and chronically ill children.[6]

Rihanna was born to Ronal Fenty, who owned a garment warehouse, and Monica Braithwaite, an accountant. She and her brother grew up in a troubled home with a father who was an alcoholic and who beat her mother and hit her once.

Her domestic situation took a toll on her health and she suffered from intense headaches. The doctors thought that she might have had a tumour. When her parents divorced, the headaches stopped. Her mother continued to work full-time and Rihanna had to take care of her little brother:

"I grew up fast, kind of like the second Mom."[7]

Case 6: I Want to Be an Engineer

Joseph Gerchon Jean won the 2018 Haiti Academic Achievement Award as well as a scholarship to help pay for his 2018–2019 school tuition. Jean wants to become an engineer. He works very hard and was ranked best in his class on the Haiti National Exam.

Jean is in Grade Nine and very focussed. Daily, he spends one hour studying before school and two hours after school. Life is not easy. He has a two-hour walk to school and recently moved from his grandmother's house to his mother's house to help with the daily chores.

Jean excels in English, Spanish, Creole and History. In spite of his excellent performance in these areas, Jean has his eyes set on being an engineer and is hoping that he receives scholarship to cover his university costs.[8]

Case 7: Recovering from a Natural Disaster

Adlene is college bound and has dreams of becoming a neurologist and joining Doctors Without Borders to go and help Third World countries. Adlene, who was twelve years old at the time, survived the 2010 earthquake in Haiti that killed her younger sister. In a coma, with a cracked skull and numerous broken bones, she was airlifted to the Jackson Memorial Hospital in Florida, where she spent four months.

She was taken in foster care by a family in South Florida. With no family, she cried every day and found life difficult. She was however determined to learn English and succeed. Amelia Diaz, the counsellor at the school she attended, told her, "You've been severely injured, you're unable to speak English. You now have to learn English." Diaz says, "I mean she had everything stacked against her and she could've just sunk into the cracks and said, 'Oh well,' but she chose not to do that."

Adlene does not know the meaning of the word "quit." She said, "I feel like I can overcome anything. I mean, look what I have gone through. No one should ever give up on their dream."[9]

Case 8: Self-Motivation in the Midst of Violence

After an extremely difficult childhood growing up in Castries, St. Lucia, Arnold Henry became the first St. Lucian to receive a Division 1 Men's College Basketball scholarship in the United States as a freshman at the University of Vermont. Henry grew up in a very domestically violent home and had to contend with the absence of his father. Since finishing college in 2009, Henry has worked to inspire others to overcome the kinds of challenges he faced as a youth and intends to publish his autobiography *Hanging on to My Dreams* soon.[10]

Conclusion

In the last seven chapters, we examined the types and processes of endangerment that children face in SIDS. In this chapter, we began to examine transformative childhoods. We argue that transformation involves the use of positive/developmental coping strategies, exhibiting resilience and experiencing transformation. Eight cases have been presented that reveal evidence of transformative childhood in the face of endangered conditions. These conditions have been discussed in the previous chapters and include: the negative impact of natural disasters, violence in the home, poverty and disabilities. There are several other cases of coping, resilience and transformation; we chose to present only eight. However, what is noteworthy is that each child emerged from endangered childhood and experienced a transformative childhood. In the next chapter, we will examine strategies to ensure that each child living in a SIDS experience a transformative childhood. We purport that it is possible that from birth, all children can enjoy a childhood which will transform them into decent productive human beings.

Notes

1. The *Jamaica Gleaner*. (2013). A story of grit: Two girls and blind mother. http://jamaica-gleaner.com/gleaner/20131013/news/news9.html (Accessed September 17, 2018).
2. The *Gleaner*. (2018). Beating the odds—Some children of teenage mothers achieve success despite struggles. http://jamaica-gleaner.com/article/news/20180603/beating-odds-some-children-teenage-mothers-achieve-success-despite-struggles (Accessed September 17, 2018).
3. The *Gleaner*. (2018). Raised in poverty, Jamaican rises to top at Baltimore Law School. http://jamaica-gleaner.com/article/lead-stories/20151207/raised-poverty-jamaican-rises-top-baltimore-law-school (Accessed September 18, 2018).
4. Small, S. (2019, March 19). Former ward of the state credits grandfather for his achievements. *The Star*. http://jamaica-star.com/article/news/20190319/former-ward-state-credits-grandfather-his-achievements http://jamaica-star.com/article/news/20190319/former-ward-state-credits-grandfather-his-achievements (Accessed March 19, 2019).

5. Rihanna Net Worth. https://www.celebritynetworth.com/richest-celebrities/singers/rihanna-net-worth/ (Accessed March 22, 2019).
6. Rihanna Net Worth. https://www.celebritynetworth.com/richest-celebrities/singers/rihanna-net-worth/ (Accessed March 22, 2019).
7. Medeiros, J. (2018). https://www.goalcast.com/2018/01/30/rihannas-life-story/ (Accessed May 4, 2019).
8. https://www.nbcmiami.com/news/local/Haiti-Earthquake-Survivor-Excels-at-Cutler-Bay-High-School-369420291.html (Accessed March 1, 2019).
9. Odzer, A. (2016). Haiti earthquake survivor excels at Cutler Bay High School. *NBC*, p. 6, February 19. https://www.nbcmiami.com/news/local/Haiti-Earthquake-Survivor-Excels-at-Cutler-l (Accessed April 4, 2019).
10. Britell, A. (2019). https://www.caribjournal.com/2011/12/01/st-lucias-arnold-henry-on-life-basketball-and-his-new-book/ (Accessed May 4, 2019).

References

Benard, B. (1991). *Fostering resiliency in kids: Protective factors in the family, school, and community*. Portland, OR: Western Center for Drug-Free Schools and Communities.

Davies, O. (2012). Religion, politics and ethics: Towards a global theory of social transformation. *Frontiers of Philosophy in China, 7*(4), 572–597.

Hatzigianni, M. (2018). Transforming early childhood experiences with digital technologies. *Global Studies of Childhood, 8*(2), 173–183.

Huijsmans, R. (2011). Child migration and questions of agency. *Development and Change, 42*(5), 1307–1321.

Lazarus, R. S. (1991). *Emotion and adaptation*. New York: Oxford University Press.

Lazarus, R. S., & Folkman, S. (1984). *Stress, appraisal, and coping*. New York: Springer.

Masten, A. S., Best, K. M., & Garmezy, N. (1990). Resilience and development: Contributions from the study of children who overcome adversity. *Development and Psychopathology, 2*(4), 425–444.

O'Dougherty, M. W., & Masten, A. (2006). Resilience processes—Development, fostering positive adaptation in the context of adversity. In S. Goldstein & R. Brooks (Eds.), *Handbook of resilience in children* (pp. 17–37). New York: Springer.

9

Re-engineering Childhood in Caribbean SIDS

Introduction

In 2019, we celebrate the 30th anniversary of the adoption of the Convention on the Rights of the Child (CRC). This book aimed to accomplish two main tasks:

1. Examine the progress for children in Caribbean SIDS since the ratification of the Convention on the Rights of the Child.
2. Discuss which theory best explains childhood in the SIDS.

Many researchers have underscored the importance of valuing and investing in children:

> Children represent the link between the past, the present and the future as such they should be tremendously valued by all societies. (Elsa Leo-Rhynie 2010, 8)

It would not have been possible to focus on all SIDS, consequently, the book focused on four Caribbean countries (Barbados, Jamaica, Haiti and St. Lucia)

© The Author(s) 2020
A. Henry-Lee, *Endangered and Transformative Childhood in Caribbean Small Island Developing States*, Studies in Childhood and Youth,
https://doi.org/10.1007/978-3-030-25568-8_9

that have different levels of human development but share similar histories of exploitation and colonialism. The specific research questions were as follows:

1. What are the definitions, perceptions and experiences of "children" and "childhood" in Caribbean SIDS?
2. Which theories best explain the nature of childhood in the Caribbean SIDS?
3. How can we transform childhood in Caribbean SIDS?

Using primary and secondary data, the book examined childhood in four Caribbean SIDS—Barbados, Haiti, Jamaica and St. Lucia. Primary data were collected in Jamaica from

- 103 high school children,
- 10 senior citizens,
- 10 recently released mothers and
- elite interviews with children's advocates in St. Lucia and Jamaica

Although the samples are unrepresentative, they present informative indications of the issues that the children experience in Caribbean SIDS. Data from the 2016 national Jamaica Survey of Living Conditions (JSLC) were also analysed to examine the disparities among children living in poverty and those who do not. The research topics presented by child researchers at the annual Caribbean Child Research Conference held in 2006–2017 were examined to determine the main issues that concerned children in Jamaica. Similar studies were not completed for the other countries under discussion due to cost constraints and the discussion on childhood in Barbados and Haiti depends heavily on secondary data.

Macro-level data showed a reasonable quality of life for children in Caribbean SIDS. However, analysis of primary and secondary data reveals that there is a process of endangerment of childhood and thousands of children are experiencing this "endangered childhood" in private and public spaces. The author argues that the intrinsic characteristics of SIDS impede wholesome investment in children. Further, the failure of the adult citizens to fully recognize the value of children to sustainable development has retarded progress for children and ultimately, for the SIDS themselves.

Definitions, Perceptions and Experiences of Childhood

All four Caribbean SIDS under review adhere to the CRC's definition of a child as any individual aged under eighteen. It is therefore generally accepted that the period in one's life when one is in need of special care and protection ends at the age of eighteen. But the experience of childhood can be defined by other age markers. For example, in Jamaica, a child can be held criminally responsible by age twelve; may legally work at fourteen and give sexual consent at sixteen. Yet, the CRC obliges us to provide and protect this group of persons up to the age of eighteen. These age markers continue to pose difficulty in defining and determining the expectations, responsibilities and behaviour of children.

Both the primary and secondary data reveal that there are changing perceptions of childhood. As a senior citizen interviewed in the exploratory study in Jamaica asserted, "In our time, children had to be seen and not heard. Now, they are heard and sometimes, are rude." Children themselves express confidence that they have more agency than their parents did but note that "we cannot ever contradict adults" as "they think they are God and nobody can talk to them" (Jamaican high school student 2013).

There is an increasing number of opportunities for children to be heard, such as through children's advisory boards, social media programmes and youth organizations in schools and communities. However, there is not enough evidence to support the view that in Caribbean SIDS there is effective child participation and that their views are systematically sought and implemented in the home, school and community. Children, senior citizens in Jamaica and elite respondents in the Caribbean SIDS under discussion, reveal that cultural barriers exist that impede the effective participation of children. They are viewed as "lesser citizens" as they do not vote and are considered peripheral to the governance structure. Until we "value" children and childhood, effective child participation will remain elusive.

Childhood experiences in SIDS are determined by what happens in the natural environment, the home, school, community and by the action of state and non-state bodies. SIDS, by their nature, are very susceptible to natural disasters. Findings discussed in Chap. 3 reveal that children in SIDS are very vulnerable to climate change when a disaster occurs, they are more at risk than adults as they are physically less able to protect themselves. As we saw in Haiti, there was much exploitation of children in shelters, and in all four countries, children lost many school days and suffered food insecurity during natural disasters. Further, natural disasters retard economic growth and ultimately result in reduction in investment in child health and education.

Examination of the secondary data reveals that since the adoption of the CRC in these Caribbean SIDS, there has been much improvement for children. This improvement has been manifested by the increased pieces of legislation, programmes and policies that have been implemented that directly target children. On the macro level, health and education outcomes measured by literacy, enrolment, attendance seem fairly reasonable in all four countries except, Haiti. The countries with more stable economies and more investment in health and education record better indicators for childhood experiences. Barbados' figures for investment and outcomes in health and education are the best while Haiti records the worst.

However, micro data analysis reveals that the high level of enrolment at the primary level in all countries does not translate into high levels of performance in the secondary school exit examinations. Transition rates from primary to secondary schools are high, yet in three of these SIDS, St. Lucia, Jamaica and Barbados, overall passes in the Caribbean Secondary Examination Council (CSEC) exit examinations are only 73.3, 68.4 and 68 per cent respectively (see Chap. 4 for further discussion). It is surprising that although Barbados invests so much in education, the overall passes in these exit examinations are not higher. Girls outperform boys at most levels of the education sector. It should be noted that only 20 per cent of the eligible Caribbean population are allowed to write the CSEC exam and of this cohort some

13 per cent pass no subjects.[1] There seem to be issues of teacher quality, irrelevant curricula, classroom mismanagement and disengagement of students at the secondary school level. The children surveyed in Jamaica revealed some disenchantment in their teachers. Several persons are leaving their secondary schools ill-equipped to obtain non-minimum wage employment.

Health indicators at the macro level also mask serious health issues. While indicators for immunization, malnutrition, and infant mortality appear reasonable (except for Haiti), these mask some grave health matters. Increasing obesity, high levels of marijuana and alcohol; teenage pregnancy; large numbers of children with no close friends and suicidal ideation demonstrate that all is not well with the physical and health of our children.

In addition to the health issues that our children face, many of them face abuse daily. The abuse comes in several forms—physical, sexual, psychological, corporal punishment, neglect and negligence. Both the secondary and primary data reveal high levels of violence against children, especially in Jamaica and Haiti. Nearly eighty of the students interviewed in Jamaica revealed that levels of violence against children were high or very high. One student summed it up for the rest of her peers, "You cannot walk in Jamaica without worrying about an attack" (Jamaican student 2013).

Although the data were collected five years ago, daily accounts of violence against children still dominate electronic and print media in Jamaica and confirm childhood endangerment. Haiti reports high levels of violence against children, especially *restavèks*—child labourers—who are often beaten and neglected. In all countries, corporal punishment is culturally entrenched and although St. Lucia and Jamaica have made determined steps to abolish it, elite respondents revealed the adage "spare the rod and spoil the child" remains a popular view among the majority of citizens in these four countries. Sexual abuse of children continues as well, and elite interviewees claim that this has its roots in the legacy of slavery and exploitation.

There are some groups of children who exist on the periphery of the society and receive inadequate policy attention. Child poverty is high, with one in five children living in poverty in Jamaica and Barbados, four in ten in Haiti, and one in three in St. Lucia. Some do not have many of their basic needs met. As revealed by a student in Jamaica, "I am a teenager now and I do not get any of the needs for myself" (Jamaican student 2013).

These children have limited access to basic social services. Their guardians make inadequate investments in health and education and consequently these children are well-placed to continue the inter-generational cycle of poverty.

Other children living on the periphery include children whose birth is not registered; those whose parents are incarcerated; those who are teenage parents; children with disabilities; those infected and affected by HIV/AIDS, children whose parents have migrated and missing children. These children lack the resources to reduce the impact of their current situation and will unlikely achieve their full potential.

There appears to be an element of *genderized* endangerment. For example, more girls than boys suffer from sexual abuse and suicide ideation. More boys than girls are victims and perpetrators of crime. In Jamaica and St. Lucia, girls and boys are equally at risk of bullying although in Barbados, the incidence was lower for girls. However, girls outperform boys at school and are more likely to complete tertiary education; boys are more at risk of not completing their education. Generally, however, both boys and girls are at risk of childhood endangerment.

There are cases of children who have broken out of their adverse situations and excelled. In Chap. 8, several cases of transformation were presented. Their own agency, and assistance from duty bearers, helped these children overcome adverse conditions and transform their childhoods.

Explaining Children in SIDS

SIDS are characterized by significant susceptibility to economic and environmental shocks; small labour markets compounded by limited skilled labour and high unemployment; limited productive sectors and heavy reliance on imports; tourism as a driving force of the economy; an impending large increase in the size of the elderly population and high levels of poverty and inequality (Williams et al. 2013, 9). These intrinsic characteristics make SIDS susceptible to economic and social endangerment. This endangerment is transmitted to the children in SIDS with thousands of them experiencing an endangered childhood. None of the current theories of childhood can adequately explain childhood in SIDS.

The most relevant features of the current theories are their emphasis on the importance of the nurturing of children and their insistence that the actions of adults influence the quality of lives that children experience in Caribbean SIDS. A comprehensive critique of the current main childhood theories is provided in Chap. 2. As concluded, what is missing from these theories is an explanation of the impact of the peculiarities of the natural, economic and social environments that children experience in the SIDS. As much of the research informing the theories is carried out in the developed countries, the realities of SIDS are not accounted for and given any relevance. The cultural nuances that exist and the voices of these children are absent in many current sociological discourses on childhood. The vulnerabilities of SIDS are not accounted for and the impact of these vulnerabilities is not discussed. Another theory is needed to explain childhood in the SIDS.

This book put forward the theory of endangerment to explain the general features of childhood in SIDS in the Caribbean. This Endangerment Theory draws on Bronfenbrenner's theory (discussed in Chap. 2) which examines different levels of influence on childhood. In the consideration of risks that children face at an early age, we also draw from the Social Risk Management Model proposed by the World Bank (Holzmann et al. 2003). In the Endangerment Theory, the influences are discussed at the macro, meso and micro levels.

Drawing on the *Oxford Online Dictionary*, "endangerment" is defined as the action of putting someone or something at risk or in danger. Children of the SIDS in the Caribbean are an endangered species, at risk in private and public spaces. Child endangerment is the process of exposing the younger generation to risks such as inadequate provision of basic necessities; insufficient protection, and insufficient facilitation of opportunities for child participation. Endangerment takes place by both primary and secondary agents of socialization and at the macro, meso and micro levels in SIDS. Some children have done well in spite of this endangerment and they have displayed a "resilience" that needs to be explored. They have managed to transform their childhoods. However, radical transformation is needed to ensure that more children fulfil their potential.

Using the conceptual framework discussed at length in Chap. 2 (see Fig. 2.1 and Table 2.1), endangered childhood is discussed in Caribbean SIDS. Analysis of primary and secondary data shows the risks of endangerment that children face in Caribbean SIDS. Chapters 3, 4, 5, 6 and 7 presented data on these risks. The data supported the view that childhood is endangered in Caribbean SIDS. The section above on perception and quality of childhood provides a summary of the risks that children face at home, at school and in the community.

In the eight preceding chapters we have examined child endangerment in the home, school and community. We conclude that the process of child endangerment begins with the natural environment in which the children in SIDS are born—vulnerable societies which are globally themselves on the periphery. The actors in the process of endangerment include the developed countries (through facilitators such as the World Trade Organization) which perpetuate child endangerment in SIDS. The developed countries, the global organizations that remain unresponsive to the needs of SIDS, the local governments in the pursuit of neo-liberal policies do not value children enough and therefore invest inadequately in child health and education, and do not provide effective social protection for children. Other actors include families, parents, teachers and other community members who by their actions promote the view that children should be seen and not heard.

All children face endangerment as they are members of the most vulnerable group in the society. However, some are more endangered than others—such as children with disabilities, those whose birth is not registered and those whose mothers are incarcerated. These children suffer more social exclusion than their peers. Children themselves may entrench their own endangerment as demonstrated by the fact that even as they complain about high levels of violence they face, the majority of children claimed that the quality of life in Jamaica was good or very good. They have adapted to their environment and become passive and increasingly insensitive. This passivity inhibits advocacy for improvement of the treatment of children. This retreatism is evident in the low voter turnout by adults who prefer to disengage than challenge the status quo. These destructive actions that endanger childhood are rooted in a legacy of slavery, oppression, colonialism and globalization as discussed in Chap. 2.

A critical question is who is responsible for ending the endangerment? The answer is *everyone*, even the children, themselves. As discussed in Chap. 8, there are many children who have experienced transformative childhood through the use of resilience and positive coping strategies. An insufficient number of children exert their child agency and often, cannot do so, as they are inhibited by physical, social and cultural constraints. It is evident that much more child agency is needed to radically change childhood in Caribbean SIDS. An examination of the literature shows that theories of transformation have been developed in many fields—science, education, economics, psychology and crime. For example, Davies (2012) outlines a global theory of social transformation based on religious communication and Hatzigianni (2018) speaks of transforming early childhood experiences with digital technologies.

Childhood transformation is needed in Caribbean SIDS. This book goes beyond the research on coping and resilience. One may be resilient; that is, not succumbing to adverse childhood experiences though the quality of life has not changed. For example, many children living in the violent inner cities exist every day without exhibiting symptoms of the trauma expected from the persons who face daily doses of violence. A child who experiences transformation would be one who performs beyond expectation and excels; even doing better than those who do not face these adverse childhood experiences. Transformative childhood can be defined as that which prepares children from birth to eighteen years, for a decent and productive adult citizenry.

How Do We Begin the Process of Transformation?

First we need to immediately recognize that childhood is in crisis in Caribbean SIDS. This "crisis perspective" has to be embraced by all citizens. The reactions to this crisis must be similar to those that we implement when we are informed that a category five hurricane is headed our way. We need to mobilize all sectors of the society to implement strategies that will safeguard children, childhood and the future of Caribbean SIDS.

Childhood transformation begins with the children themselves. In Chap. 8, we saw how child agency can transform childhood and overcome adverse conditions. This child agency must be escalated to the national level. The children must start this social revolution. They are aware of the high levels of violence against them and the issues they face everywhere they go. The CRC can be used as the catalyst for change. There are several children's advisory boards and youth clubs in these countries. They must use their status to call attention to the plight of children by going to the media and discussing their situation in youth parliaments and school councils. As leaders of the social group of children, they must begin the call for transformation in the education system that is failing them and ill-preparing them for adulthood.

The recent discussion in the Jamaican Gleaner[2] about the skin bleaching of students in high schools reminds us that our black children in Caribbean SIDS still struggle with self-identity and consider that "whiteness" is better than "blackness." The older children must, by their example, help the younger children to embrace their blackness and increase their self-worth not by bleaching their skin but by education and a productive adult life:

> Families, parents and caregivers play a central role in child well-being and development. (Mary Daly et al. 2015, 1)

Parents as primary caregivers must accept their duties with diligence and protect their children from exploitation and oppression. Too many parents neglect their duties and endanger their children. Teachers must respond to the call for change and examine the curriculum, pedagogy and relevance to an ever-changing labour market, and the classroom must be a place where all children with different learning styles can excel. The same is true for all duty bearers; they must examine their role in the endangerment of childhood and take corrective actions. Some specific actions at the macro, meso and micro levels are proposed in Table 9.1.

At the macro level, there must be genuine and sustained efforts at reducing the vulnerabilities that SIDS face and ensure that actions at the global level do not retard progress for SIDS and ultimately for their children. There are several laws, policies and programmes that have been implemented since the ratification of the CRC in the Caribbean. There is, however, an implementation deficit. The electorate needs to hold the government accountable and demand improved implementation of all these commitments.

Table 9.1 Re-engineering childhood to deal with risks faced by children in Caribbean SIDS

	Factors	Risks	Re-engineering childhood (some main interventions)
Macro	Natural	Loss of life, shelter, food, education and health.	Policies and programmes to deal with Climate Action: Caribbean Climate Action Fund for Children. Local comprehensive Child-centred Disaster Management Plans.
	International	Global economic crisis, unfavourable international trading terms and markets; nations' inability to influence global governance systems.	Implement favourable policies and programmes that reduce vulnerability of Caribbean SIDS.
	Regional	History of the region leaves citizens scarred by remnants of slavery, colonialism and neo-liberalism.	Reparation and Universities in the UK and France implement targeted programmes that provide opportunities for the education for Caribbean children.
	National	High levels of indebtedness, slow economic growth, high levels of public and private poverty, business failure and high levels of unemployment.	Debt-forgiveness for all countries. Child-centred policies.

(*continued*)

Table 9.1 (continued)

	Factors	Risks	Re-engineering childhood (some main interventions)
Meso	School	Access to poor quality education reduces opportunity to realize full potential.	Teacher training for class management and gender-specific pedagogy. Curriculum which caters for children with different learning styles.
	Health services	Access to poor quality health services reduces ability to realize full potential. Illness, injury, concerns all social groups.	Interventions to deal with impact of HIV/AIDS, obesity; mental health; drug abuse and negative impact of violence.
	Social protection	Inadequate social protection for the poor and vulnerable.	Reduce leakage of Social Protection Programmes. Increased targeting of children in rural areas and urban poor areas.
Micro	Individual traits	Individual traits (genes, disability, etc.) can influence the quality of childhood.	Increased access to basic social services for children with disabilities. Curriculum changes that are more relevant to Caribbean realities.
	Characteristics of the family	Large household size, poverty, low investment in education and health etc.	Cultural changes to recognize the value of children.

Source: Author's outline

All this transformation would require a change at the micro level. This must begin with a change in individual mindset. Child representatives must lobby for the legacies of slavery that value children as property and vassals of labour be rejected. They must press for cultural change through public forums and via electronic and print media. Children must use the technology to their advantage. In the same way they use social media to socialize, they must use it to de-socialize and re-socialize with their peers to stand up for change. The message must be consistent: *We need to be treated better. You ratified the CRC: live it.* Cultural change is very slow but with education of younger children as soon as they can understand these matters, the pace of transformation will be increased. The family has not fulfilled its role as the primary agent of socialization and many children do not feel safe at homes. For all children to experience transformative childhood, parents must be held accountable for the quality of care they provide for their children. For those parents who cannot provide materially for their children, the State should ensure that the basic needs of all children are met and no child is left behind in the fulfillment of the CRC.

Children are the most valuable asset a nation possesses and until everybody shares this view, child endangerment will continue for centuries to come. Radical transformation must be now. It will be a tumultuous road, politically, economically and culturally, but as we are reminded:

The journey of a thousand miles begins with one single step. (Lao Tzu)

Notes

1. https://newsday.co.tt/2018/08/12/cxc-11000-pupils-got-zero-passes/ (Accessed November 26, 2018).
2. http://jamaica-gleaner.com/article/letters/20190626/skin-bleaching-not-black-and-white (Accessed July 13, 2019).

References

Daly, M., Bruckhauf, Z., Byrne, J., Pecnik, N., Samms-Vaughan, M., Bray, R., …, UNICEF Office of Research—Innocenti. (2015). *Family and parenting support: Policy and provision in a global context.* Papers innins770, Innocenti Insights.

Davies, O. (2012). Religion, politics and ethics: Towards a global theory of social transformation front. *Frontiers of Philosophy in China, 7*(4), 572–597. Retrieved May 4, 2019, from https://www.researchgate.net/profile/Oliver_Davies3/publication/292513252_Religion_politics_and_ethics_Towards_a_global_theory_of_social_transformation/links/57d293eb08ae6399a38d7376/Religion-politics-and-ethics-Towards-a-global-theory-of-social-transformation.pdf.

Hatzigianni, M., Gregoriadis, A., Karagiorgou, I., & Chatzigeorgiadou, S. (2018). Using tablets in free play: The implementation of the digital play framework in Greece. *British Journal of Educational Technology, 49*, 928–942. https://doi.org/10.1111/bjet.12620

Holzmann, R., Sherboune-Benz, L., & Tesliuc, E. (2003). The World Bank's approach to social protection in a globalizing world. Retrieved November 21, 2018, from http://siteresources.worldbank.org/SOCIALPROTECTION/Publications/20847129/SRMWBApproachtoSP.pdf.

Leo-Rhynie, E. (2010). Rights, wrongs and research on children. In A. Henry-Lee & J. M. Gardner (Eds.), *Promoting child rights through research* (Vol. 2). Kingston, Jamaica: Sir Arthur Lewis Institute of Social and Economic Studies.

Williams, A., Cheston, T., Coudouel, A., & Subran, L. (2013). *Tailoring social protection to small island developing states—Lessons from the Caribbean.* Social Protection and Labor Discussion Paper, No. SP 1306.World Bank, Washington, DC. Retrieved May 26, 2014, from http://documents.worldbank.org/curated/en/2013/08/18086868/tailoring-social-protection-small-island-developing-states-lessons-learned-caribbean.

Index

© The Author(s) 2020
A. Henry-Lee, *Endangered and Transformative Childhood in Caribbean Small Island Developing States*, Studies in Childhood and Youth, https://doi.org/10.1007/978-3-030-25568-8

Printed by Printforce, the Netherlands